Palgrave Studies in European Union Politics

Series Editors
Michelle Egan, American University, Washington, USA
William E. Paterson, Aston University, Birmingham, UK
Kolja Raube, KU Leuven, Leuven, Belgium

Following on the sustained success of the acclaimed European Union Series, which essentially publishes research-based textbooks, Palgrave Studies in European Union Politics publishes cutting edge research-driven monographs. The remit of the series is broadly defined, both in terms of subject and academic discipline. All topics of significance concerning the nature and operation of the European Union potentially fall within the scope of the series. The series is multidisciplinary to reflect the growing importance of the EU as a political, economic and social phenomenon. To submit a proposal, please contact Senior Editor Ambra Finotello ambra.finotello@palgrave.com. This series is indexed by Scopus.

Martin Heipertz

Merkelism and the Fine Art of Flat Politics

An Insider's Account of the Early Euro Crisis

palgrave
macmillan

Martin Heipertz
Max Planck Institute for the Study
of Societies
Berlin, Germany

Cologne, Germany

ISSN 2662-5873 ISSN 2662-5881 (electronic)
Palgrave Studies in European Union Politics
ISBN 978-3-031-87591-5 ISBN 978-3-031-87592-2 (eBook)
https://doi.org/10.1007/978-3-031-87592-2

Disclaimer: The views represented in this book are solely my own and do not represent official positions of any institution with which I was or remain affiliated.

Cover illustration: Magic Lens/Shutterstock

This Palgrave Macmillan imprint is published by the registered company Springer Nature Switzerland AG
The registered company address is: Gewerbestrasse 11, 6330 Cham, Switzerland

For Romina

Preface

The Property of Power

Power is the ability to pursue one's interests even against the countervailing forces of other actors. In moral terms, at least those expressed by Blaise Pascal according to Christian belief, power is granted by divine Providence to a political actor with the duty to protect the powerless. This is what Pascal calls the 'property of power': to protect.

A state has interests—not morals, at least according to Machiavelli, for whom the separation of morals and politics is a precondition for the functioning and stability of the state. But when historians or political scientists speak of national interests as informing and guiding the pursuit of power, a moral appraisal of these interests is nevertheless possible. Such a moral appraisal would ask: Whose interests are being served? According to Pascal and other Christian thinkers such as Augustine or Thomas Aquinas, but also according to Jewish and Islamic schools of thought, every bearer of power is responsible for a clearly defined group of people.

In pre-modern times, these people were the subjects of kings or kalifs and the like or, say, the *demos* of an Attic *polis*. In a modern nation-state, the people are the citizens of said nation-state. In the European Union (EU), a political entity *sui generis*, there is arguably no *demos*. Political power is shared and pooled among national governments and European institutions. They are all to serve the common good—but what is the common good in financial terms if Europeans divide into debtors and creditors, into net contributors and net recipients?

From a moral point of view of traditional Christian persuasion, the German government has the duty to serve the citizens of Germany. It can and indeed must use the power at its disposal to protect their interests. It cannot employ moral arguments to justify doing otherwise, at least not in conjunction with classical ethics. While this seems obvious and even on the brink of the trivial, it is worth remembering for what follows—not least because the ruling political party of Germany during the events described in this book habitually refers to itself as 'Christian Democratic'.

Matters become more complicated if, among several nations, a hegemon emerges, thanks to superior power. It can be argued that the hegemonic state, because of its power, has a moral duty—and possibly even an interest—to also protect the citizens of other states. Up to a point, this can even amount to significant cost to its own citizens. This is often referred to as the 'hegemon's burden' and usually gives rise to protracted debates on burden-sharing. But still, the government of a hegemonic state has the duty to assess whether, on balance, its citizens are being served by the existing arrangements and the use of its power.

If Christian political thought is of any relevance to 'Christian Democrats', there should be a notion of what Saint Augustine called *ordo armoris*, a ranking in the order of love: It is not only permissible but in fact required to love members of one's family over strangers and to care for one's own people over foreign peoples. What counts for the state is true even among individuals: Charity, *Nächstenliebe* in German, is, quite literally, the love and compassion for a person physically close to me and for whom I have the concrete power and therefore duty to help and protect—quite in contrast to physically distant persons.

The United States of America (USA) serves as the prime example of a hegemonic state, primarily in military matters. Germany, a military dwarf but an economic giant, can be seen as a semi-hegemon within the EU, given her economic and financial resources of power. Because of her lack of 'hard power' and, even more so, because of her lack of political will to use power at all, post-war Germany has often been described as a 'reluctant hegemon'.

During the initial phase of the euro crisis, covered in this book, the self-awareness of having to carry something like an economic hegemon's burden was very much present in the mind of German political actors and senior administrators. Charles P. Kindleberger's (1973) 'Hegemonic Stability Theory' was, in fact, a popular idea in 2010 and good for many quotes in official speeches—especially when applied not to Germany alone but to a fictitious Franco-German tandem.[1]

In a variant of the old 'German question', Germany under Angela Merkel was too powerful not to be seen as the fiscal backstop to the euro crisis. This was true for as long as the crisis was being addressed mainly by fiscal rather than monetary means, i.e. roughly from 2010 to 2012, and for as long as the monetary stabilisation of the euro area by the European Central Bank (ECB) still seemed to require at least tacit German consent. But even at the height of her power, Merkel lacked the force and political will to fully impose creditor interests upon debtor states or to pursue a radically different strategy for Europe altogether. This, in a nutshell, is the story of this book.

Whatever It Takes

The famous words 'whatever it takes' are usually associated with a speech delivered by ECB President Mario Draghi in London on 26 July 2012: 'Within our mandate, the ECB is ready to do whatever it takes to preserve the euro. And believe me, it will be enough'.[2]

But Draghi was simply reiterating a common theme. The slogan 'whatever it takes' had been used many times before by policymakers in the euro crisis, for example, by Commission President José Manuel Barroso already in May 2010: 'We will defend the euro, whatever it takes' (The Telegraph, 08.05.2010).

Speaking about the crisis at my alma mater, Oxford University, on 5 October 2012, I used different words but tried to convey a similar message: 'Do not underestimate our determination.'[3]

Chancellor Angela Merkel most prominently stated in the Bundestag, Germany's Federal Parliament, on 19 May 2010: 'If the euro fails, Europe fails'.[4] Previously, on 5 May 2010, she had declared her policy to be 'without alternative'.[5]

[1] E.g. https://internationalepolitik.de/de/was-fuer-ein-hegemon.

[2] https://www.ecb.europa.eu/press/key/date/2012/html/sp120726.en.html.

[3] https://podcasts.ox.ac.uk/after-crash-restoring-economic-growth.

[4] https://dserver.bundestag.de/btp/17/17042.pdf#P.4125.

[5] https://dserver.bundestag.de/btp/17/17039.pdf.

Examples of this type of political language on the euro crisis are legion. This is because the crisis of the euro, in essence, is a crisis of political credibility.

The Nature of Political Crises

A political crisis occurs when policy abruptly adjusts to reality. This can happen for two reasons:

First, it might occur that reality changes in a manner which is both rapid and profound. In such cases, policy adjusts to change. It does so in a similar fashion and through events which are equally rapid and profound—and this is commonly perceived as a crisis.

Second, by contrast, the underlying reality might be stable—but policy has departed from it too far and for too long. This is typically the case when policy is driven by ideology or beliefs which defy reality. The euro crisis is of this type. Much of this book is about substantiating this claim.

Both types of crisis and the corresponding policy adjustment are characterised by extreme uncertainty and time pressure. Decisions must be taken swiftly and often by trial and error. Consequences are typically unknown and, in the words of former US Secretary of Defence Donald Rumsfeld:

> We also know there are known unknowns; that is to say we know there are some things we do not know. But there are also unknown unknowns—the ones we don't know we don't know.[6]

This book argues that actors matter in politics. One important way in which they matter is their willingness to take risk.

Risk is often described as a mathematical probability attached to a cost. But this is entirely hypothetical in the midst of a political crisis. Given the prevalence of uncertainty, both the probability and the cost are 'known unknowns' according to Rumsfeld's terminology. And risk is further exacerbated by the gut feeling that there may be 'unknown unknowns' as well with even higher cost and probability. It takes many things to become and remain a political actor, and the ability to tolerate extreme levels of risk in the above sense is not the least important one.

[6] https://archive.vn/20180320091111/http://archive.defense.gov/Transcripts/Transcript.aspx?TranscriptID=2636.

Besides risk, the next important element is time. An immediate risk is more relevant than a distant risk of the same magnitude. And not unlike financial cost and return, there is also a discount and a transformation of terms of risk over time: Even a more elevated risk can be less relevant than a small risk if the former is expected in the distant future.

The personality of political actors as well as their individual situation come into play: Many politicians will accept substantial long-term risks in exchange for alleviating even small short-term risks—guided by the proverbial fact that the future is unknown anyway. This attitude can occur because of personality as much as culture and simple circumstances, for example, electoral cycles in democratic political systems which arguably tend to create short-termism. In fact, it can make the difference between politics and statecraft.

Finally, the perception of tail-risk matters. Even at small probability, most individuals and many policymakers focus on the worst-case scenario. They often accept a long-term risk, despite high probabilities attached to it, in exchange for alleviating a short-term tail risk. By contrast, those to become historical figures do quite the opposite and take extreme bets under a short time horizon. Posterity considers these figures 'great' if and because their bets in fact stand the test of time. This is true especially in military affairs but, often enough, also in matters economic and financial.

The Merkel Legacy

This text is one of the early book-length academic accounts of Angela Merkel's political legacy in one specific policy field: European Economic and Monetary Union (EMU). It is driven by the understanding that, without Merkel, the development of EMU might very well have taken different turns at several points of contemporary history.

Having ruled the EU's most populous and economically powerful country for 16 years, her influence is monumental in many other fields of European and German politics, such as migration, energy, and foreign security or even Brexit. But the course of EMU under Merkel's reign is an issue for which the author can claim a certain amount of insight, and which remains relevant until today and beyond. Two examples substantiate this claim:

First, debt mutualisation has become a well-known fact in the EU since the Covid-pandemic and the Ukraine war. Before that, the only commonly denominated EU debt was issued by the European Investment Bank (EIB) and, in very small quantity, by the Commission. Since Covid and the Ukraine war, however, there is a sea change towards ever closer debt union in the EU.

Second, the monetisation of state finance has become another pervasive feature of the euro area. The ECB holds enormous quantities of EU governments' debt and provides liquidity to the European banking sector, which, at times, also ends up buying significant amounts of EU governments' debt.

Where lie the origins of both phenomena? After all, the Maastricht Treaty on EMU contains a no-bailout provision. Nevertheless, Greece, and, successively, Ireland, Portugal, Spain, and Cyprus have received substantial loans, guarantees and transfers. The Maastricht Treaty also prohibits monetary financing of states. Nevertheless, the ECB and the European System of Central Banks (ESCB) have purchased EU Member States' debt at hitherto unthinkable levels and have provided liquidity to the banking system in the EU for doing likewise.

This book argues that there was one overarching critical juncture for the road towards debt mutualisation and monetisation: 7–9 May 2010 and the high politics surrounding the first Greek bailout. Most of what followed was path-dependent.

The Merkel government played a crucial role in this decision and in the subsequent path-dependent ones. These decisions have been and continue to be massively controversial and subject to intense legal, public, political, and academic debate. To the extent that the German government under Angel Merkel mattered in their coming about, these traits are part and parcel of her legacy.

There is no doubt that both of these traits, fiscal bailouts and monetisation, have been fundamental in stabilising the euro area for the time being—albeit at the cost of higher inflation and the undermining of the rules-based system of EMU governance. Furthermore, Germany's power to shape events has evaporated in the process.

This is a case at hand of the above-mentioned transformation of the terms of risk over time under huge uncertainty. This book argues that the Merkel government traded the immediate and very concrete risk of financial breakdown for a vague long-term cost in terms of inflation, impairment to governance and the weakening of Germany's power.

The Scope of This Book

This study provides a detailed, comprehensive, and chronological reconstruction of those events and elements of politico-administrative positioning by the Federal Ministry of Finance within Angela Merkel's government which have contained or contributed to crucial policy decisions for EMU during the year 2010. It covers the first and formative year of the euro crisis.

By covering events in 2010, this book contains two case studies of fiscal bailouts: Greece and Ireland. Interestingly, these two cases describe the polar opposites of possible positions held by euro area Member States within the socio-economic fabric of EMU: Greece being archetypical of a Southern, demand-oriented, import-led economic model of low growth, high inflation and high public debt—Ireland by contrast being archetypical of a Northern, export-oriented, supply-sided economic model of high growth, low inflation and low public debt.

This book is written from the author's perspective during that time: a civil servant in the political staff of the German Federal Ministry of Finance. It is hence not a historical account drawing on a variety of different sources of different relevant actors. Instead, it is the personal and reflective report of an eyewitness trained in political thought. The perspective is neither comprehensive nor authoritative—at best a source for future historians and, maybe, food for the thoughts of contemporary observers of European affairs.

The book discusses the first, multilateral euro area bailout package mustered for Greece in early summer 2010 as well as the subsequent case of Ireland in November of that year, dealt with by an intergovernmental bailout fund newly instated for that purpose. Subsequent developments are alluded to in this text; including bank rescue measures, debt buyback operations, private sector bail-in decisions and haircuts plus roll over operations, renegotiations, and follow-up programmes for specific countries.

By limiting the scope of this book to events in 2010, I will ascertain those developments which occurred at the critical juncture of the first sovereign default in the history of the euro—Greece in May 2010—and which thereby created path-dependency for subsequent events. I will establish how and why decisions were taken to bail out Greece and to subsequently set up a bailout fund with its first case of application being Ireland in November 2010.

In terms of institutions and agencies, I pay particular attention to the formation and application of the intergovernmental bailout funds, the temporary European Financial Stabilisation Facility (EFSF) and the permanent European Stability Mechanism (ESM), as well as the use of the communal European Financial Stabilisation Mechanism (EFSM). I allude to the subsequent setting up of both the Single Supervisory Mechanism (SSM) and the Single Resolution Fund (SRF) to avert banking crises as well as to other agencies in the field of financial market policy.

Running by the chronological order of events, my appraisal will also look at the nature and evolution of domestic stabilisation programmes and their effects in recipient countries—as perceived and interpreted in Berlin. The successive rescue packages were conditional on such programmes with the intention to protect creditor interests by reducing moral hazard and ensuring credit service and redemption. In the case of Greece, the opposite was achieved. Such programmes typically pertained to the areas of social policy, financial market policy, taxation policy, and labour market policy, inter alia—often linked to serious hardship, substantial domestic political turmoil and changes of government in the countries concerned.

Furthermore, my appraisal covers the evolution of monetary policy, again as perceived from Berlin. Developments in Frankfurt started with the involvement of the ECB in the so-called Troika, jointly managing recipient countries' programmes alongside the European Commission (EC) and the International Monetary Fund (IMF). We discuss the important decision of the ECB to buy Greek and other peripheral debt in May 2010 under the Securities Markets Programme (SMP), later-on leading up to the strategic decision by ECB President Mario Draghi to commit his institution to unlimited central bank purchasing of EU government bonds, reached in the summer of 2012, and unfolding into subsequent asset purchasing programmes by the ESCB.

In this book, I will also pay attention to Berlin's take on institutional and strategic policy debates about European integration, such as the inconclusive discussion on a debt resolution mechanism in the so-called Van Rompuy Task Force in 2010. I will also look at domestic policy developments in Germany during 2010, exemplifying the political dynamics within a creditor state. This includes legal and constitutional challenges faced by the government as well as the emergence of party-political competition with a eurosceptic take.

The study is based on publicly available information about relevant events as perceived through the author's academic and professional worldview. Most of the events and many details about the political decision-making have been made public by former Minister of Finance Wolfgang Schäuble himself in his memoirs (2024). In this book, I go into more detail and provide my best take at rationalisation and scholarly analysis of these events. Personal views and assessments can change over time as new information and insight become available. I try to be as transparent as possible about the evolution of my own thinking on the matters under consideration.

The Aim of This Book

This book aims to contribute to our understanding of what undoubtedly has been a watershed in the history of European integration. The literature has shown considerable interest in comprehensive and objective, non-normative, factual inside-accounts of the political and administrative events which have occurred during the euro crisis. In Chapter 2, I engage with those academic books and articles that have had the most profound impact on my understanding of the euro crisis—and I believe that their treatment offers a good, albeit not entirely comprehensive, account of the academic discussion of the matter at hand. It also offer my personal receipt of these academic contributions in light of the narrative that follows in the subsequent chapters.

To this academic debate, I contribute a German insider's perspective of facts and developments that are still—and sometimes increasingly—relevant to researchers and students of political economy. As a historical, narrative reconstruction, this book intends to facilitate actor-centred institutional analysis in the field of ongoing research in European integration and the functioning and evolution of EMU. It does not presuppose expert knowledge in integration theory or economic and financial policy. The author hopes that the book will appeal to scholars of European integration as well as to readers with a general interest in the euro crisis.

Beyond EMU matters, this work intends to provide a case study of political decision-making in crisis reaction mode under German Chancellor Angela Merkel. The reader should better understand how and why certain decisions have been made, how actors perceived themselves and their situation, how they related to other actors and to the public at large. The reader should ultimately get a feeling of why and how tactical considerations weighed more heavily than subsequent strategic problems.

In essence, this is also a case study in 'incrementalism' as proposed by decision-making theory. In conceptual terms, this book aims to elucidate the evolution of political rule in the EU under the stress of crisis. Its core aim is to propose that our understanding of the preceding period of EU policy-making as 'governance' should be complemented by conceptualising the subsequent period of crisis reaction as one of 'muddling through' by flat politics.

Berlin and Cologne, Germany

Martin Heipertz

Acknowledgements

A book is like a pilgrimage. As you walk along, sometimes cheerful and sometimes completely exhausted, you encounter many good people who inspire you, give valuable advice, improve your understanding and help you take decisions. I will not be able to list all of them. But the ones most important for this work include, at the final stage of the journey, my anonymous reviewers and the wonderful team at Palgrave Macmillan around Ambra Finotello and Geetha Chockalingam and the series' editors.

At the early stage of the journey, there were my academic teachers, friends and colleagues in Cologne. First of all, Martin Höpner encouraged me to seek shelter and return to the Max Planck Institute for the Study of Societies 20 years after my dissertation. He also pointed me to Charles Lindblom and his theory of 'muddling through' as a way to think and write about Merkel's political style. Wolfgang Streeck proved to be the most reliable, free-minded and engaging teacher and friend that anyone could aspire to. For all of my academic work, I am most deeply indebted to Fritz Scharpf, and it is my greatest honour to have learned from him over a quarter of a century now. My conversations with Renate Mayntz were immensely valuable—she gave me confidence that a good, relevant narrative and the reconstruction of important facts for the benefit of research is already a scholarly achievement. She also indicated to me that 'muddling through' might be the appropriate way to speak about the new European political reality in crisis, following the 'governance turn'.

When I had nowhere to go, Lucio Baccaro and Jens Beckert were so brave to take me under their wings as directors of the Institute, enabling me to write this book in the first place. There would not be a single line without their trust and support and their stand for the freedom of science. Among the great, new generation of social scientists in Cologne, I felt incredibly close to Donato di Carlo, Rex Panneman, Maximilian Kieker, Leon Wansleben and Björn Bremer and benefited greatly from my exchanges and friendship with them. And always present in my thinking and writing are my teacher Wolfgang Wessels and, above all, my friend and co-author Amy Verdun, despite being physically so distant in Canada.

I owe a great deal of gratitude to the HR team in the German Federal Ministry of Finance at the time who allowed me to retreat to Cologne for two years and who gave me advice on the publication of this work. I would like to name in particular Robert Oswald, Oliver Lamprecht, Vera Weyand and Robert Bartz.

Many of my friends and colleagues have given me the honour to engage with this work at various stages. I received numerous and incredibly valuable advice from them—especially from Andrea Capussela, Adam Lerrick, Ludger Schuknecht, José Marín Arcas, Anton Comanescu, Erik Jones, Carlos Egea, Quentin Peel and Ingo Wagner. And my academic fraternity in Cologne provided not only accommodation to me, but also a good deal of distraction after a day of writing—special thanks go to Victor Minich in that respect. Father Jürgen Knobel is my spiritual friend and was the very first person to point me towards this endeavour when I knew no more what to do.

I am a weak man, and there was a moment of desperation before I set out to write this book. But closest to me are a few women who make my life worth living. My family members Frances and Maria, Christel and Katrin Sophie are these—and then came Romina who simply believed in me and who helped me to believe in myself again. Her love enabled me to carry on. I lay this book at her feet.

Praise for "*Merkelism and the Fine Art of Flat Politics*"

"The language is clear, the style engaging, the rhythm sustained, the narration enlightening, the analysis cogent."

—Andrea Capussela, *London School of Economics, UK*

"This book is essential reading for anyone interested in crisis policy-making or the future of European integration."

—Erik Jones, *European University Institute, Italy*

"Offering behind-the-scenes domestic political debates taking place with far-reaching consequences for European integration, Heipertz contributes to our knowledge of the euro crisis and sheds new light on how the euro was saved, but in a way that sowed the roots for later instability. A timely must-read book for understanding the euro crisis and its legacy."

—Michele Chang, *Director of the College of Europe, Belgium*

"A major contribution to the state of comparative political economy."

—Fritz W. Scharpf, *Max Planck Institute for the Study of Societies, Germany*

"A fascinating analysis of one of the most important moments in recent European integration – a must read for anyone with an interest in the past, present and future of European integration."

—Amy Verdun, *University of Victoria BC, Canada, and Leiden University, The Netherlands*

The property of power is to protect. (Blaise Pascal, Pensées)

Contents

About the Author

Martin Heipertz studied PPE in Oxford and Economics at the College of Europe, Bruges. He wrote his dissertation at the Max Planck Institute for the Study of Societies in Cologne and at Sciences-Po Paris. He published on the Euro and served at the ECB, in Kosovo and at the EIB before joining the Federal Ministry of Finance in Berlin in 2010. As Deputy Head of Office to Wolfgang Schäuble, Personal Advisor to the Finance State Secretary, and Head of the European Policy Division, he witnessed the German decision-making process during the euro crisis firsthand. He also advised Jean-Claude Juncker and worked extensively on Brexit affairs.

Abbreviations

AfD	Alternative für Deutschland
BaFin	Bundesanstalt für Finanzdienstleistungsaufsicht
BIS	Bank for International Settlements
CAC	Collective Action Clauses
CCSF	Common Currency Stabilisation Fund
CDS	Credit Default Swap
CEO	Chief Executive Officer
CFO	Chief Financial Officer
DG-ECFIN	Directorate General for Economic and Financial Affairs
DSA	Debt Sustainability Analysis
EBA	European Banking Authority
EC	European Commission
ECB	European Central Bank
ECOFIN	Economic and Financial Affairs Council of Ministers
ECU	European Currency Unit
EDP	Excessive deficit procedure
EFC	Economic and Financial Committee
EFSF	European Financial Stabilisation Facility
EFSI	European Fund for Strategic Investments
EFSM	European Financial Stabilisation Mechanism
EIB	European Investment Bank
EIOPA	European Insurance and Occupational Pensions Authority
ELA	Emergency Liquidity Assistance
EMF	European Monetary Fund
EMS	European Monetary System
EMU	Economic and Monetary Union

EPC	Economic Policy Committee
ERM	Exchange Rate Mechanism
ESCB	European System of Central Banks
ESM	European Stability Mechanism
ESMA	European Securities and Markets Authority
ESRB	European Systemic Risk Board
EU	European Union
EUR	Euro
EUSF	European Union Solidarity Fund
Eurostat	European Statistical Office
EWG	Eurogroup Working Group
FSB	Financial Stability Board
FTT	Financial Transaction Tax
GDP	Gross domestic product
IGC	Intergovernmental Conference
IMF	International Monetary Fund
KfW	Kreditanstalt für Wiederaufbau
NGO	Non-governmental organisation
NRW	Nordrhein-Westphalen
OMO	Open Market Operation
PSI	Private Sector Involvement
SBRM	Sovereign Bond Restructuring Mechanism
SDR	Special Drawing Rights
SDRM	Sovereign Debt Restructuring Mechanism
SGP	Stability and Growth Pact
SMP	Securities Markets Programme
SoFFin	Sonderfonds Finanzmarktstabilisierung
SPV	Special Purpose Vehicle
SRB	Single Resolution Board
SRF	Single Resolution Fund
SSM	Single Supervisory Mechanism
TFEU	Treaty on the Functioning of the European Union
TINA	There is no alternative
USA	United States of America
USD	United States Dollar

CHAPTER 1

Introduction

A Very Short History of EMU

EMU has a long pedigree. The political aim of introducing a single currency dates back to monetary policy challenges arising from the demise of the Bretton-Woods system of fixed exchange rates. It gained speed with the ups and downs of the European Monetary System (EMS), a system designed to manage the foreign exchange policies of Member States to the then European Community.

The EMS, in essence, pegged participating Member States' currencies to the Deutschmark. By 'shadowing' the monetary policy of the Bundesbank, Germany's once powerful central bank, the other Member States were able to import low levels of inflation while foregoing monetary sovereignty. Until its de facto demise[1] in the wake of exchange rate crises of the early 1990s, the EMS allowed Germany to slow down the rise of the Deutschmark's external value and thereby supported her export-led economic growth model.

[1] Initially, under the original Exchange Rate Mechanism (ERM) of the EMS, participating currencies were required to maintain exchange rates within a narrow band of ±2.25% around their central parity against the European Currency Unit (ECU). To restore stability and reduce pressure from speculative attacks, on August 2, 1993, the EMS authorities decided to widen the fluctuation bands to ±15% around central parities, thereby practically relinquishing the nature of a fixed exchange rate system.

M. Heipertz, *Merkelism and the Fine Art of Flat Politics*, Palgrave Studies in European Union Politics,
https://doi.org/10.1007/978-3-031-87592-2_1

Monetary union is, in economic terms, identical to replacing a permanently fixed exchange rate with a joint currency. The difference lies in the realm of monetary policy and is a difference of political power: While a fixed exchange rate with a dominant player represents an asymmetric set-up of power, a common currency with pooled sovereignty over monetary policy transfers that power to the jointly run, common central bank. In the absence of Political Union, the political independence of that pooled monetary sovereignty reaches a higher degree than the hitherto national central bank even of the dominant currency.

The Bundesbank used to see the bedrock of its political independence in Germany's stability culture or *Stabilitätskultur*. One of the strongest arguments of Northern EMU critics is the absence of stability culture in Southern Europe, alike to moving sands not anchoring the independence of the European Central Bank (ECB) well.

In December 1989, German Chancellor Helmut Kohl accepted monetary union against resistance by the Bundesbank in a deal with French President François Mitterrand who in turn acquiesced in German reunification. This Franco-German deal opened the way to negotiating the Maastricht Treaty and the introduction of the euro by 1999.

Rules-Based Fiscal Policy

The architects of EMU, at least on the German side, expected it to comprise the previous Deutschmark zone of hard currency countries plus France and Benelux. They were hopeful to compensate for the lack of Political and Fiscal Union by a rules-based system for fiscal policy, centred on so-called reference values for public debt and deficits at 60 and 3% of gross domestic product (GDP), respectively.

In 1995, the entry date to EMU was approaching and many more governments than expected were making efforts for their countries to join. Germany under Helmut Kohl then thought it wise to put the fiscal policy focus entirely on the 3% of GDP deficit reference value. It sought and obtained the Stability and Growth Pact (SGP) with the declared aim to 'operationalise' the deficit reference value towards a balanced-budget rule plus financial sanctions if the upper limit of 3% were breached (Heipertz and Verdun 2010).

In the event, all willing Member States were able to join the euro at the start, except for Greece. Besides tangible but short-lived fiscal adjustments towards the deficit reference value, a good deal of cosmetical public accounting had helped. Greece joined two years later amidst extensive political controversy in Germany under Chancellor Gerhard Schröder.

Shortly thereafter, economies deteriorated in the wake of the internet bubble bursting, most notably in Germany. In 2003, Germany and France forced the Council to overrule Commission recommendations made under the SGP for stricter consolidation and thereby called the bluff of the rules-based system. Despite several attempts at reform and resuscitation, the SGP never recovered from that blow.

The single monetary policy of EMU forces countries with immensely different economic growth models into 'one size fits all'. Adjustments to economic deviations and shocks can no longer occur through changes in the exchange rate. The full onus falls onto the real economy and tends to drive up deficit and debt levels to the extent that public investment and consumption come into play.

This is particularly the case in the absence of transfers. Such transfers would have to occur either transnationally between surplus and deficit countries or supranationally through a fiscal equalisation scheme and a central 'federal' budget—in fact like Germany's national public finance arrangements. It goes without saying that the latter presupposes a fully-fledged Political Union with a proper democratic government at the federal level.

These institutional shortcomings of EMU were well known and established in academic circles and among the wider public before the euro crisis struck. Therefore, we have previously labelled the euro crisis as one of politics adjusting to reality after having been based too long on false beliefs. An illustration of this point is given by the following discussion on macroeconomic imbalances in the euro area:

The Eurogroup of Finance Ministers of EU Member States participating in the single currency had agreed in 2009 to include an in-depth analysis of competitiveness in their macroeconomic surveillance routine, entailing country reports that, in the course of 2010, were to be translated into country-specific recommendations.[2]

Germany had insisted on discussing the rather stark divergences in competitiveness which had become noticeable over the previous couple of years. From the German point of view, Greece, Portugal, Spain, and Ireland had experienced persistently high rates of inflation undermining

[2] https://ec.europa.eu/economy_finance/publications/european_economy/2010/pdf/ee-2010-1_en.pdf.

the ECB's monetary policy and contributing to current account deficits. The Commission report was seen to confirm the German position that countries with weak competitiveness and current account deficits had to undertake significant efforts at fiscal and structural reform—as Germany had previously also undertaken under great strains.

However, the discussion in the Eurogroup on 18 January 2010 took a different turn: The Commission as well as Southern European countries, in particular Spain and Greece, criticised Germany for its excessive export-orientation at the expense of others. Imbalances were argued to have been caused principally by Germany herself and should be addressed by reducing the German focus on export-driven growth.

In the end, that debate did nothing to change policy or even perception within Germany. European governance, when relying on 'soft coordination' as in this case, achieved little to no effect. The ultimate ineffectiveness of 'governance' is the reason why it was superseded by a period of crisis and 'muddling through'.

The Road to Crisis

The ground for the developments of 2010 was primarily laid by preceding decades of rising public debt in all advanced industrialised democracies during the second half of the twentieth century. Excess debt was much more frequently discussed by various European governance fora than macroeconomic imbalances and it was potentially subject to 'hard' forms of policy coordination such as the SGP—but also to no avail.

Greece was by no means alone in being over-indebted—it was simply the most advanced case and suffered from the weakest domestic institutional environment, compared to other European countries. A chain is only as strong as its weakest link. But Germany fared no better, presenting a façade of fiscal prudence not through improved efficiency and effectiveness in her public finances, but by neglecting her infrastructure, her military, and indeed the entire range of services provided by the state. This, also, is Merkel's legacy.

Domestic democratic governance has proven no more apt at preserving the sustainability of public finances than authoritarian regimes. Theoretical explanations point to a so-called 'deficit bias' of public finances in democracies, implying that voting constituencies of parliamentary forms of democracy routinely fall prey to 'fiscal illusion', inducing them to tolerate levels of government spending that systematically lie above public revenues. Twentieth-century voting systems and the reliance on political representation through Parliaments are seen to have caused a systematic underestimation of the public cost of state borrowing. At the same time, the financing of this debt through the financial markets is facilitated by the abundance of monetary liquidity and the effects of banking regulation favouring the accumulation of public debt by the respective financial sectors of those nation-states.

As mentioned above, the monetary unification of segregated nation-states with separate fiscal policies provided an average interest rate that did not fit to any specific economy. Peripheral countries were able to borrow at relatively low real interest rates by historical standards, while Germany as the core had to undergo painful adjustment in real terms (mainly real wage depression) to make ends meet at relatively high real interest rates by historical standards.

Further still, the money raised through the continued build-up of debt was often put to little use. Over decades, the governments of highly indebted countries were notoriously bad at investing their resources in an economically intelligent way. Their highly inefficient welfare systems sought to capture voting support by redistributing vast sums to poorer parts of the population in a large array of spending programmes with limited rationality, while the very substantial and mobile capital gains and non-labour incomes of society's richest segments by and large remained spared from being put to that use. Even worse, corruption is pervasive, and states are often captured by particular interest groups behind the mask of democracy, exploiting public resources for their own purposes (Crouch 2004).

In sum, by the turn of the millennium, indebtedness had become a pervasive feature of democratic economic existence across the entire Western hemisphere, concerning the public sectors of nation-states as well as their private households and business sectors. In most cases, the aggregate sums of debt in each national economy stood at or above 200% of the respective national incomes. This problem was not at all limited to Member States of the EU; in many respects the entire trend, in fact, originated in the USA. However, the institutional and financial fabric of the euro area proved particularly conducive to the build-up of the problem and, subsequently, particularly vulnerable to the ensuing crisis: The US had a fiscal back-stop—the EU did not.

The calamity naturally took its beginning with the de facto insolvency of the most highly indebted Member State—Greece. The Euro area's vulnerability and inability to cope with the fast-evolving events of that crisis was intricately linked to the non-political nature of this purely monetary and economic commonwealth. This, in turn, had been caused by the fundamental design flaws of EMU already alluded to.

Elemental economic aspects of monetary unification had been subordinated to the political priorities of the project, which in essence amounted to containing the strategic readjustment imposed by the end of the Cold War. With the implosion of Soviet power, Germany, thanks to American support, was able to reunite and looked set to regain a position of economic superiority from which it could have claimed more than just hegemonic dominance over Europe.

Instead of doing so and in a remarkable show of self-restraint, Germany sought to reinforce European integration jointly with France, its traditional competitor on the continent. From a French national perspective, monetary integration held the key to suppress German economic dominance. From a German, post-war and post-national perspective, monetary integration was the stepping stone for the political integration of Western Europe. These could have been the ingredients for something great. But consensus between France and Germany tragically pertained only to monetary integration, and German ambitions for political integration were lastingly frustrated and then vanished in the Treaties of Maastricht and Amsterdam.

This, as discussed, proved economically fatal, but it took the crisis to demonstrate that Monetary Union would have required Political Union to function properly. Instead of an effective institutional setting, the euro area had received an unfitting suit of full-scale monetary integration with continued segregation in the domains of fiscal and economic policy. The dysfunctional nature of this design, not least due to pervasive, in-built moral hazard, was obvious to most economists since its inception and had initially contributed to vocal opposition in Germany.

In fact, a sizable majority of the German people were against the introduction of the single currency. But, given the functioning of Germany's political system, this democratic policy preference did not translate into government policy.

Hence, the euro took shape but was ill equipped already for the global banking crisis that broke out in 2007. The bursting of a bubble in the American real estate market, caused by global excess liquidity and regulatory failure, triggered a process of uncontrolled deleveraging across the financial market and exposed several systemically important institutions to bankruptcy. The banking crisis was only brought under control by shifting large amounts of financial risk onto public balance sheets.

By consequence, the situation of public debt—already unsustainable in some euro area countries—quickly became no longer manageable for the most exposed European countries when investors withdrew their funds. As the first of several actor-victims, the Hellenic Republic entered liquidity shortages in late 2009 that very rapidly evolved into full-blown state insolvency. Although most European governments had ample pre-war experience with state bankruptcy, there was massive uncertainty and fear about its possible consequences within the context of EMU and under the enormous degree of financial leverage obtained since the loosening of the monetary reigns at the turn of the millennium.

The fragility of the euro area's institutional edifice was painfully brought home to national and European leaders when they realised that a possible default of Greece could have similar systemic consequences to those experienced in the preceding banking crisis. Exposure of the German and French domestic banking systems to Greek government debt was significant, and, amidst an overall lack of information, there was concrete but unclear risk of contagion throughout the financial system—a 'known unknown' in Rumsfeld's terms mentioned above.

Additionally, feedback loops between national banking and public sectors implied that the solvency crisis could rapidly spread geographically, so that the situation could potentially spiral out of control very rapidly. Given the prevalent uncertainty and sheer fear, political leaders initially shied away from the inevitable restructuring of Greek national debt. Instead, they decided to buy time by overstepping the so-called 'no-bailout' principle (which had been one of the founding, misguided self-deceits of EMU) and extended an emergency credit line to Athens.

This, however, failed to slow down the continued withdrawal of funds from peripheral European state debt, implying that, soon enough, Germany was pressed to agree on a massive bailout fund for the entire euro area, big enough to cover the refinancing needs of all peripheral countries—except Italy's—for about two years. The moral hazard attached to this state of affairs was as obvious as immense, and Germany's attempts at submerging debtor countries to so-called 'conditionality', i.e. incentivising them to regain solvency on their own, were repeatedly frustrated. Germany and the other creditor states now had to deal with sovereign nations rather than domestic banking sectors in distress and realised that they were in fact in a very weak position to exert influence and control over the use that their funds were being put to. Popular resistance to the perceived expropriation of national wealth for the refinancing of foreign debt grew rapidly.

Still, debtor countries underwent painstaking attempts at reform and consolidation, extracting a high social and economic price from their respective polities and encountering an even more intense political backlash against the austerity imposed on them. The system was stretched to the limit and clearly at pains to deal with a potential further aggravation in the summer of 2012. Against this backdrop, the ECB committed to stabilise the euro area through, if necessary, unlimited monetisation. Except for the Greek saga, which erupted until 2015, the ECB thereby enabled the crisis to transform from a fiscal to a monetary phenomenon and from the spectre of state insolvency to that of inflation.

What Is the Question?

In this book, I introduce the concept of 'flat politics' to describe a governance style characterised by horizontal decision-making, consensus-driven incremental adjustments, and a reliance on media and network dynamics rather than top-down hierarchical directives. 'Flat politics' reflects a milieu where actors operate through iterative, decentralised negotiations, often without a clear hierarchical lead, embodying Angela Merkel's approach of pragmatic, step-by-step crisis management in the euro crisis. 'Flat politics' is both the process and outcome of 'muddling through'—as this style of governance falls short of fundamental political reform and leadership.

The initial question this book aims to answer is: How did the Merkel government react to the outbreak of the euro crisis?

This initial question subdivides into several sub-questions: What options did decision-makers perceive? What information was available to them, and how did they make sense of the situation? What were their political constraints and influences, foreign and domestic, and which interests did they pursue? How was decision-making in the Federal Ministry of Finance at times superseded by the Chancellery?

Can we also learn from the case studies on Greece and Ireland, during the early stage of that crisis, how later stages were being handled?

We will also aim to infer, from the narrative of this book, three general conclusions about issues that reach far beyond the two cases at hand:

First, what can be said about EMU, the euro, and the EU, based on this narrative? Do the case studies enhance our understanding of European integration in monetary and economic affairs? Do we gain better insight into the institutional situation of the EU and the euro area—and can we make suggestions for certain improvements of deficiencies that have become clear?

Second, can we gain insights about the way in which other crises were handled, under Merkel and in general? In other words: What can maybe be said quite generally about the government of a contemporary Western country in crisis reaction mode, even pertaining to recent phenomena such as migration, the Covid pandemic or the Ukraine war?

Third and final, what was the nature of government prevalent in Germany and in the EU at the time? After 'steering' in the 1980s (Mayntz 1987; Mayntz and Scharpf 1995) and the 'governance turn' in the 1990s (Kohler-Koch and Rittberger 2006), did the age of 'polycrisis' (Morin 1999) give rise to a different type of political rule? After 'problem-solving capacity', 'modes of governance' and the 'regulatory state'—do we need a new conceptual approach to understand policy-making in Germany and Europe?

In short, this book proposes 'muddling through' as a fitting description of the nature of government for the period following those characterised as 'steering' and 'governance' and applicable to the crisis years as of 2007. The lasting product of 'muddling through' is, alas, 'flat politics' as alluded to by the title of this book.

CHAPTER 2

Engaging the Literature

Academic Accounts of the Euro Crisis

The academic literature on the euro crisis is vast. Without aiming to cover the entire field, I will, in the following, take recourse to those works which relate directly to the topic of this book, aiming to show how the different accounts and perspectives inform each other. In doing so, I shall highlight important propositions and hypotheses entertained by other scholars and commentators that can be confirmed or maybe challenged by the empirical material offered in this book.

In "Europe's Orphan: The Future of the Euro and the Politics of Debt", Martin Sandbu (2017) argues that the euro itself is not to blame for the euro crisis of the earlys 2010. Instead, he posits that the crisis was largely the result of misguided economic policies, particularly those focused on so-called austerity and the insistence on internal devaluations (i.e. lowering wages and prices within countries rather than adjusting currency exchange rates). Sandbu defends the euro, contending that the shared currency has provided many benefits to Europe, such as fostering economic integration and preventing currency wars, but that poor policy choices magnified its vulnerabilities.

I disagree with Sandbu (and many others) on the notion of austerity. Not all forms of fiscal consolidation are detrimental to growth, and the sustainability of state finance is, in fact, a prerequisite for growth. Austerity

M. Heipertz, *Merkelism and the Fine Art of Flat Politics*, Palgrave Studies in European Union Politics,
https://doi.org/10.1007/978-3-031-87592-2_2

can become inevitable if states have lived beyond their means too much for too long. At the same time, I realise that austerity, when it has become inevitable, is of course detrimental to growth and prosperity. However, it is a consequence of previous policy mistakes and should not be confounded with these.

Sandbu critiques what he sees as a dominant narrative, i.e. that the euro crisis was inevitable due to the structural flaws of the single currency. Sandbu emphasises that these crises were policy failures, not inherent faults of the euro itself. By focusing on fiscal retrenchment (austerity measures) as the main tool to solve the crisis, European policymakers caused prolonged economic stagnation and social suffering. He argues that they should have pursued fiscal stimulus and promoted stronger aggregate demand to counter the effects of the crisis.

By contrast, this book argues that there are indeed structural flaws in the institutional architecture of EMU. With an effectively functioning Fiscal and Political Union to support EMU, I argue, the crisis could have been prevented or at least handled much more swiftly. Accounting for the events of 2010, I aim to show how efforts at improving EMU governance have been made, albeit in a too limited and piecemeal fashion and therefore to no avail.

Sandbu also discusses alternatives that could have been adopted, such as fiscal transfers between countries and more flexible fiscal rules. He asserts that, had policymakers followed more Keynesian approaches such as higher public investment and less draconian fiscal cuts, the crisis would have been much shorter and less painful. Ultimately, Sandbu is optimistic about the future of the euro, but stresses that the policy framework needs significant reform.

In this book, I argue that fiscal transfers, as well as common debt, would require Political Union and a democratic polity with proportional representation if they were not to increase the EU's legitimacy crisis and democratic deficit even further. I go at great length to demonstrate the implications that the imposition of other countries' liabilities on the German taxpayer meant for German domestic politics. I agree with Sandbu on the general need for reform—but I disagree on the type of reform required. Rather than fostering the continued building up of national and European debt, I side with those who advocate fixing the institutional and democratic shortfalls of EMU and bolstering its institutional credibility.

Very much in line with Sandbu, Yanis Varoufakis offers a detailed, first-person account of his time as Greece's finance minister in 2015, i.e. five years after the events described in this work. His book "Adults in the Room" (2017) is both a memoir and a political analysis of his battle with the 'deep establishment' of the EU, IMF and ECB, i.e. the 'Troika' which, according to Varoufakis, imposed excessively harsh austerity measures on Greece in exchange for bailout funds. Varoufakis presents himself as a reformer who entered the Greek government under the radical left-wing Syriza party with the goal of renegotiating Greece's unsustainable debt burden. He argues that the austerity programmes imposed by the Troika were economically destructive, worsening Greece's economic crisis and deepening social suffering. Varoufakis claims to have proposed alternative solutions that involved debt restructuring and growth-oriented reforms.

Based on clandestine audio recording (Schäuble 2024), Varoufakis details his interactions with key figures in European politics, including German finance minister Wolfgang Schäuble, IMF chief Christine Lagarde, and ECB president Mario Draghi. His book provides an insider's perspective on the intense negotiations, backroom discussions, and power plays that characterised Greece's debt crisis in a later stage compared to the 2010 perspective offered by this book. Varoufakis describes how he was often isolated and frustrated in his efforts to reach a fair deal for Greece, feeling that European leaders prioritised protecting the interests of powerful banks and creditors over the welfare of the Greek people. Throughout the book, Varoufakis critiques the EU's democratic deficit, its opaque decision-making processes, and the power dynamics that favour large countries like Germany. He recounts how Greece's calls for debt relief and a more growth-oriented economic policy were ignored or dismissed, and how his government was pressured into accepting further austerity measures that Varoufakis believed would only prolong the country's suffering.

Varoufakis ultimately resigned from his post as finance minister in 2015 when the Greek government, led by Prime Minister Alexis Tsipras, capitulated to the demands of the Troika, accepting another bailout package that Varoufakis opposed. The book ends with a reflection on the broader implications of the Greek crisis for the future of the EU, arguing that the undemocratic nature of its institutions and their policies could lead to the erosion of democracy across Europe.

This book to some degree concurs with Varoufakis. It provides additional evidence on the democratic deficiencies of EMU governance and confirms the rationale for debt restructuring, while also pointing out that this insight was politically unattainable during the period under consideration. It also acknowledges Sandbu's and Varoufakis' claim that harsh fiscal consolidation, while being unavoidable in the event of state bankruptcy, is inevitably massively detrimental in the short term to economic growth and to the material welfare of society at large and hurts primarily the weakest members of the social spectrum. As regards power imbalances in the Euro area, this book describes the self-perception prevalent among German policymakers about their role as representing a would-be hegemon *malgré soi*, i.e. without having wished to be one. It exposes the historic responsibility that the Merkel government enjoyed for a brief moment in time when it could have shoved European integration into a quantum leap by engaging in serious governance reform and institutional innovation as a precondition for bailouts. This book also lends support to Varoufakis' claim that the interests and needs of European banks have been highly influential in the formulation of bailout policies. Varoufakis, very much in contrast to Sandbu, advocates European reform in terms of institutions and governance—a claim that is obviously backed by my narrative.

In "Tangled Governance: International Regime Complexity, the Troika, and the Euro Crisis", Randall Henning (2017) analyses the intricate administrative complex that emerged during the euro crisis, particularly focusing on the interactions between different institutions involved in the financial rescue efforts. The book explores how the Troika coordinated its efforts to stabilise euro area countries. Henning introduces the concept of 'international regime complexity', referring to how overlapping international organisations and governance structures influence decision-making in times of crisis. He examines the difficulties and political tensions that arise when multiple institutions, each with its own interests, mandates, priorities, and sources of authority, must work together. The book delves into the ways the Troika's actions were shaped by these overlapping responsibilities and conflicting goals, leading to challenges in accountability, coordination, and legitimacy. Henning critically assesses the effectiveness of the Troika, analysing how it managed to resolve immediate financial crises but at the cost of public trust, democratic legitimacy, and long-term economic stability. He highlights how the power imbalances and institutional conflicts within the Troika hindered more comprehensive solutions, particularly in terms of balancing austerity and growth, as well as respecting national sovereignty.

This book concurs with Henning's appraisal of the suboptimal institutional architecture that arose during the crisis years in a haphazard way—compared to a strategic, state-like sort of Political Union with fully-fledged problem-solving capacity and democratic legitimacy. Henning's concept of 'regime complexity' describes the institutional outcome of a process which, in this book, is portrayed as 'incrementalism' or 'muddling through'. While Henning focuses on the output and result as well as on the features of the newly arisen complexity, this book looks at the process that led there as well as at the underlying reasons. Also, while Henning analyses the decision-making dynamics among the Troika, this book adds primarily the German perspective for the early stages of the interaction—and in that sense, this book is complementary to Henning's work. Besides the Troika, it will be important to attain studies of the political decision-making in relevant capitals (not only Berlin). As regards the Troika itself, I disagree to some extent with Henning's judgement that sees a systematic dominance of IMF and ECB positions over those of the Commission—precisely for the reason that the Commission positions were often aligned with powerful national interests, particularly those of France.

Similar to Sandbu and Varoufakis, Henning is explicitly critical of 'austerity' while I stick to the notion that fiscal rectitude has to be observed over the medium-to-long term if episodes of radical consolidation and/or inflation are to be avoided. However, I share Henning's critical appraisal of the Troika's shortcomings in terms of legitimacy and accountability, leading to a sense of disenfranchisement and fuelling political backlash in many euro area countries (including donor states). I concur with Henning's scepticism as regards the severe limits of the prevalent form of crisis management and its qualitative shortfall in terms of economic policy outcomes—including high and protracted inflation as well as subdued growth and persistent lack of competitiveness. I echo his call for EMU governance reforms, without endorsing all of the concrete elements suggested by him.

In a similar vein compared to Henning, Paul Blustein in "Laid Low" (2016) provides a detailed, behind-the-scenes account of how the euro crisis unfolded, with a particular focus on the role of international financial institutions, especially the IMF. Blustein's book offers yet another narrative of how Europe was "laid low" by the 2008 global financial crisis and the subsequent sovereign debt crises. Blustein draws on interviews with key players, internal documents, and his extensive expertise in international economic affairs to provide an insider's view of the crisis management efforts from mainly a Washington perspective. He examines how national and European leaders, the ECB, and the IMF struggled to contain the crisis and prevent the euro area from disintegrating. The book highlights the deep divisions within the IMF regarding the best course of action, as well as tensions between the IMF and European institutions over the handling of the crisis. These disagreements often resulted in inconsistent and sometimes contradictory policies, according to Blustein. The IMF faced significant pressure from European authorities, who were reluctant to follow IMF-standard recommendations, such as debt restructuring and austerity programmes. Blustein describes how the IMF made several controversial decisions, including supporting massive bailouts that many viewed as overly favourable to European interests, especially Germany, while imposing harsh austerity on countries like Greece. Blustein also covers the political and economic dynamics within the euro area, highlighting how national interests clashed with collective action. The book provides a deep dive into the economic policies imposed during the crisis and the broader institutional failures that exacerbated the situation.

One of the central themes of "Laid Low" is the failure of European institutions and the IMF to adequately manage the euro crisis. Blustein argues that internal divisions, political pressures, and a lack of coordination between the IMF and European authorities led to policy responses that were often too late or insufficient to fully address the crisis. His argument is backed up by the narrative of this book to quite some extent. Beyond the scope of this book, however, Blustein highlights how the IMF, normally an independent arbiter in international financial crises, was constrained by European political dynamics. Blustein argues that the IMF, under pressure from powerful European nations like Germany and France, compromised its usual policy approach, including delaying debt restructuring in Greece and supporting harsh austerity measures. This hurt the IMF's credibility and contributed to long-term economic pain in crisis-hit countries, according to Blustein. Similar to the previously mentioned authors, Blustein critically examines the policy of austerity and argues that the severe cuts in public spending exacerbated economic contraction, worsened unemployment, and led to a vicious cycle of debt and stagnation. The social costs of austerity—widespread unemployment, poverty, and social unrest—are highlighted as major failures of crisis management, different from the more orthodox views portrayed in this book, from a German perspective.

Blustein emphasises how the euro crisis revealed deep divisions between different EU Member States, particularly between Northern creditor nations (like Germany) and Southern debtor nations (like Greece). National interests frequently clashed with the need for collective action, leading to half-measures and policies that prolonged the crisis. In stark contrast to Sandbu, for example, Blustein underscores how the euro area's fundamental structural flaws—such as the lack of a Fiscal Union in the light of a one-size-fits-all monetary policy—made the crisis inevitable. This book echoes Blustein's core argument that the crisis exposed the inherent weaknesses in the euro area's design, where countries shared a currency but lacked the necessary institutional mechanisms to coordinate fiscal policy effectively. I also concur with Blustein in his critical appraisal of political leadership in specific cases, in particular that of Merkel, and in his concern that the euro crisis shook confidence in the European project more generally. The crisis revealed not only the economic challenges facing the EU but also the political divisions that threatened European integration. The rise of populism and anti-EU sentiment in countries like Greece and Italy—but, according to this book, also in Germany—is to be seen as a direct consequence of the crisis and the mishandling of it, including by Merkel.

The narrative and verdict of this book are close to Ashoka Mody's account "EuroTragedy: A Drama in Nine Acts" (2018). Mody offers a critical history of the euro, tracing its development from its inception to the euro crisis and beyond. Mody, a former IMF official, argues that the creation of the euro was a fundamentally flawed political project, driven by a vision of European unity that ignored the economic realities and diversity among the euro area's Member States. The 'drama' of his book unfolds in nine acts, with each chapter chronicling a different phase in the euro's troubled history. Mody takes readers through the origins of the euro, examining the political motivations behind its creation, particularly the role of French and German leaders in pushing the project forward despite widespread scepticism among economists and the wider public. The Maastricht Treaty is portrayed as a political compromise that overlooked key economic issues such as the need for fiscal coordination and the economic divergence between Northern and Southern European countries. Mody delves into the structural problems of the euro area, similar compared to previously mentioned works and including the lack of a Fiscal Union as well as the one-size-fits-all monetary policy. According to Mody, these issues came to the forefront during the 2007/8 global financial crisis, which exposed the euro area's vulnerabilities and triggered the sovereign debt crisis.

Mody provides a detailed account of the euro crisis, criticising the responses of European leaders and institutions, including the ECB, the EC, and the IMF. In a similar vein to the other authors, also Mody argues that the imposition of harsh austerity measures and the focus on preserving the euro at all costs exacerbated the crisis, deepening economic pain in Southern Europe and leading to a prolonged period of stagnation and political instability. He is deeply critical of the ideological commitment to the euro, which he argues was based more on a desire for political unity than on sound economic principles. He contends that the euro has done more harm than good, particularly for countries in Southern Europe, which have been trapped in a cycle of low growth, high debt, and rising populism. Mody also questions whether the euro area can ever function effectively without significant reforms, such as the creation of a Fiscal Union or mechanisms for debt restructuring.

This book concurs with Mody's argument that the creation and also the stabilisation of the euro were primarily driven by political motivations, particularly the desire for European unity. This political project ignored critical economic realities, such as the divergence in productivity and economic structures between Northern and Southern Europe. As mentioned previously, the developments described in this book refer to that type of crisis which occurs when policy adjusts to reality. The euro lacks sound economic and institutional foundations, particularly those associated with the Fiscal and Political Union. I also side with Mody with regard to the negative impact on democratic legitimacy and sovereignty entailed by the status quo of euro area governance. In terms of deficient crisis management, this book explains why sovereign debt restructuring was out of political reach at first. I share Mody's pessimism about the long-term future of the euro area without real institutional reform towards fiscal and political integration as well as provisions on debt restructuring.

In "Crashed: How a Decade of Financial Crises Changed the World" (2018), historian Adam Tooze provides a comprehensive, global account of the 2007/8 financial crisis and its far-reaching consequences, first and foremost the euro debt crisis. His book traces how the initial banking crisis, which began in the U.S. subprime mortgage market, quickly spread to global financial systems, triggering economic turmoil across Europe and beyond. Tooze argues that the financial crisis was not an isolated event but rather the culmination of deep-seated imbalances and vulnerabilities in the global economy. He explores how the responses to the crisis reshaped the world's political and economic landscape over the following decade. His narrative weaves together the key events of the financial meltdown, including the collapse of Lehman Brothers, the bailout of global banks, and the sovereign debt crises that emerged in the euro area. He places special emphasis on the interconnectedness of financial markets and institutions, showing how the crisis exposed the risks of globalisation and the fragility of financial systems.

The book also covers the political implications of the crisis, particularly the rise of populism and nationalist movements in Europe and the United States. Tooze highlights how so-called austerity measures and the unequal distribution of the economic recovery fuelled social discontent and political polarisation. He argues that the crisis and its aftermath marked a turning point, with the geopolitical order shifting in unpredictable ways—most notably with the rise of China and the weakening of transatlantic relations. "Crashed" also delves into the roles of key players, such as the U.S. Federal Reserve, the ECB, the IMF and other international financial institutions. Tooze critically examines the policy responses, both successful and failed, and their implications for the future of global capitalism and governance.

I endorse Tooze's emphasis that the 2007/8 financial crisis was not just an American problem but a global event that reverberated across Europe, Asia, and beyond. The interconnectedness of the global financial system meant that the collapse of U.S. housing markets triggered a domino effect, exposing vulnerabilities across the world, leading ultimately also to the European debt crisis. This book hence confirms Tooze's claim that the financial crisis highlighted the risks inherent in globalisation, particularly the interdependence of financial institutions. Tooze demonstrates how the highly integrated global financial system, which allowed for the rapid flow of information, capital and financial products across borders, also magnified the scale and speed of the crisis, and I show concrete examples of how that happened.

In the present work, I explain, along lines similar to "Crashed", how the sovereign debt crises in Europe, particularly in Greece, were not separate from the preceding financial crisis but were a direct consequence of it. Like Tooze, also this book argues that Europe's crisis was exacerbated by its own structural weaknesses, including a flawed monetary union and conflicting economic ideologies between Northern and Southern Europe. I also concur with Tooze's argument that the crisis marked a shift in global power dynamics. The rise of China as an economic power, the weakening of Europe, and the challenges facing U.S. leadership all pointed to a transformation in the global order. The crisis accelerated the decline of Western dominance and increased the prominence of emerging economies. Unlike Tooze, however, the core message of this book is to point out that the German government—for the period under consideration—would have had the power but lacked the political will and vision to fundamentally address the institutional flaws of European integration.

According to Tooze, but also according to this book, one of the key political consequences of the financial crisis was the rise of populist and nationalist movements, particularly in Europe and the United States. Tooze argues that the social dislocation and inequality exacerbated by the crisis fuelled political polarisation, leading to movements such as Brexit and Donald Trump. I concur and add a specific German perspective to this picture, i.e. the emergence of the AfD political party as a direct result of Merkel's way of handling the euro crisis.

Tooze offers a critical evaluation of the policy responses to the crisis, particularly the actions taken by central banks such as the Federal Reserve and the ECB. While central banks played a key role in stabilising financial markets, the reliance on monetary policy and austerity measures, according to Tooze, failed to address the deeper social and political consequences of the crisis. This book agrees largely with this interpretation and would offer, as an additional consideration, that the EU's handling of the euro crisis initially combined both fiscal and monetary instruments—particularly during the time under consideration in this book. However, over the course of the crisis, the fiscal measures became increasingly controversial politically—which is why, by 2012, monetary measures took over and have meanwhile become the only way of stabilising the common currency. This has occurred at the cost of risking price stability.

As a standard theme, also compared with the other authors here under discussion, Tooze argues that the implementation of austerity measures exacerbated economic inequality and social discontent. He reiterates that austerity policies led to prolonged economic stagnation, especially in Southern European countries, and contributed to the political backlash against elites and traditional institutions. More broadly, Tooze argues that the financial crisis exposed the fundamental weaknesses of global capitalism, including the overreliance on financial markets, unsustainable levels of debt, and the failure to regulate financial institutions. The book suggests that, without substantial reforms, the global economy remains vulnerable to future crises. Tooze underscores how the crisis reshaped global governance, with institutions such as the IMF and the EU facing legitimacy crises. He also highlights the rise of new financial and political alliances, such as China's growing influence in global finance, and how these shifts are changing the international order. His perspective is much broader than the one of this book, but I add colour to his account by focusing on Germany's role in this global development. In that sense, I concur with Tooze that the decade following the 2007/8 crisis was one of profound transformation, with long-term effects on politics, economics, and international relations. The crisis marked the high time and possibly the beginning of the end of globalisation and the emergence of a much more fragmented and unstable global order.

Integration Theory

Integration theory was a central interest of mine during my years in academia. Wolfgang Wessels was one of my teachers then and has later-on made significant contributions to the study of the Euro crisis, particularly regarding the role of the European Council and its implications for European integration. His analysis primarily revolves around the European Council's growing authority and its impact on his 'fusion theory' of European integration (Wessels 2016, 2017 and 2018, Wessels and Lang 2015, Wessels and Rummel 2016).

Wessel's fusion theory posits that, over time, national and EU-level governance structures blend as European policies demand increasing cooperation and coordination between Member States and EU institutions. Wessels argues that the euro crisis was a decisive moment, accelerating this fusion due to the European Council's central role in crisis management. In this book, I concur with Wessel's analysis of the European Council's emergence as the primary decision-making body during the Euro crisis. However, I disagree in part with Wessels' notion that the Heads of State or Government increasingly took the lead in crisis response, sidelining traditional EU institutions. On the one hand, I share Wessels' notion of a centralisation of power, where the European Council acts as a quasi-executive body, coordinating national policies while maintaining sovereignty concerns. On the other hand, this book points to the alignment of French national interest with the ECB and the Commission, and I would strongly argue that these institutions are, in fact, not side-lined but rather 'transmitted' into the European Council through the positions held by France. Conversely, the French position is at times almost perfectly reflected in those held by the ECB and the Commission. This issue would require further research into the policy-making in Paris, Frankfurt and Brussels, whereas this book focuses on Berlin.

One of Wessels' critical insights is the tension between the European Council's intergovernmental nature and the EU's democratic legitimacy. The crisis highlighted the challenges of respecting democratic accountability while responding swiftly and effectively. Wessels argues that while the Council's role has facilitated rapid responses, it has also reinforced the EU's 'democratic deficit', as key decisions were made by national leaders with limited transparency and no direct accountability to EU citizens. I fully concur with him on that account, and I agree that the euro crisis reinforces Wessels' fusion theory by illustrating how national and EU-level functions interlock. According to Wessels, the crisis response necessitated further pooling of resources, coordination on fiscal policies, and shared responsibility among Member States. This intensifies the fusion process as national leaders collaborate closely at the European Council level, while EU institutions adjust to new intergovernmental dynamics.

In his work, Wessels often refers to the European Council's evolving role as a 'crisis manager'. He suggests that its actions during the Euro crisis set a precedent for how the EU may approach future crises. Wessels points out that while this role enhances the EU's capacity to handle high-stakes challenges, it also consolidates power in the hands of a few leaders, potentially bypassing more community-based decision-making processes. This interpretation is, however, challenged by the decision-making during subsequent crises such as migration and Covid, when decisions were much more based on national rather than European policies. Also, in light of the Ukraine war, I would argue that a shift back towards national rather than European policy formulation has occurred. This is not always the case, and Brexit yields a good example of another crisis that confirms Wessel's thesis. But the common theme across all different crisis episodes is 'muddling through' and 'incrementalism', not 'fusion'—and the role model is Angela Merkel, not the European Council.

My co-author on the SGP, Amy Verdun, has equally had great influence on my personal reading of the euro crisis. Her book "Political Leadership in the European Union" (2017), co-edited with Ingeborg Tömmel, provides a comprehensive examination of the role of leadership in the EU. Verdun et al. analyse how political leadership operates in the EU's complex multi-level governance system and explore how different types of leaders—whether from EU institutions or Member States—shape policy, decision-making, and the trajectory of European integration. The editors and contributors discuss the evolving nature of leadership, focusing on how it has changed since the EU's early days, especially in response to crises like the euro area debt crisis and the migration crisis. Leadership is examined through both institutional and individual lenses. Institutional leadership refers to how EU structures, such as the EC or the European Council, provide direction and influence policy. Individual leadership, on the other hand, focuses on prominent EU figures, such as the Commission Presidents (e.g. José Manuel Barroso or Jean-Claude Juncker), European Council presidents, and Heads of State and Government from key Member States, and how their personalities and political styles influence the EU's decision-making processes. Verdun et al. also explore the limitations and challenges of leadership within the EU's framework. Given the EU's multi-layered structure, where power is dispersed across institutions and national governments, effective leadership often requires coalition-building, consensus-seeking, and negotiating among diverse stakeholders with conflicting interests. This makes leadership in the EU distinct from national leadership, which tends to have more centralised authority. Crises are another important theme in the book. The euro crisis, the Brexit referendum, and the migration crisis all tested the EU's leadership capabilities, highlighting the tension between national interests and collective European action. The book discusses how leaders at both the national and European levels navigated these crises and the extent to which their leadership influenced the outcomes.

In this book, I concur with the central theme of Verdun et al.: Political leadership in the EU is distinct due to its multi-level governance structure. Leadership in the EU requires managing a delicate balance between national interests, supranational objectives, and institutional mandates. Leaders must be adept at building consensus and negotiating across institutional and national boundaries. This book provides colour to Verdun's emphasis on both institutional leadership (from bodies like the Commission and European Council) and individual leadership (from key figures like the Commission President or influential national leaders like Merkel and Schäuble). Effective European leadership often results from a combination of strong institutional frameworks and charismatic individuals who can drive the European agenda. At this instance, I cannot follow Verdun et al., given that I fail to see charisma in Merkel. But I agree that the various crises the EU has faced have been pivotal in testing the limits of EU leadership. Verdun et al. argue that these crises highlighted both the strengths and weaknesses of EU leadership. In some cases, strong leadership helped stabilise the Union, but in others, leadership was seen as inadequate or reactive, failing to prevent deeper divisions. The central message of this book asserts that Angela Merkel in fact falls into the second domain, contrary to the public image which had carefully been crafted during her overly long term in office.

Turning to other scholars, a work particularly relevant to this book is "The 'Governance Turn' in EU Studies" by Beate Kohler-Koch and Berthold Rittberger (2006). The authors provide an in-depth examination of the shift in EU studies from focusing primarily on traditional integration theories to adopting a governance perspective. This 'governance turn' reflects the growing complexity of how the EU operates, where the analysis of multi-level governance, institutional networks, and non-state actors becomes central to understanding EU policy-making and institutional dynamics. The authors trace the historical development of EU studies, starting with the early theories of integration, such as federalism, functionalism, and intergovernmentalism. They show how these traditional approaches, which focused primarily on the relationships between Member States and the central institutions of the EU, evolved to include governance theories that better capture the EU's decentralised, multi-actor system.

The book defines governance as the interactions and coordination between a wide array of actors—including EU institutions, Member States, regional and local governments, private interest groups, and civil society organisations—who all contribute to the policy-making process in the EU. This perspective emphasises the importance of informal networks and non-state actors, moving beyond the formal, hierarchical structure of EU institutions to understand the complex, decentralised processes of governance. Kohler-Koch and Rittberger argue that the governance turn reflects a more accurate and nuanced understanding of how power is distributed and exercised in the EU. Rather than seeing the EU as a state-like entity, the governance approach views the EU as a multi-level system where authority is dispersed across various levels of governance—supranational, national, and sub-national—and among diverse actors. The authors also explore how this shift in focus from formal integration theories to governance has impacted both academic research and practical policy analysis. The governance turn has broadened the scope of EU studies to include topics such as policy networks, regulatory governance, public–private partnerships, and the role of non-governmental organisations (NGOs) in shaping EU policies.

This present book concurs in principle with Kohler-Koch and Rittberger's claim that the governance turn reflects the complexity and decentralisation of power in the EU, where multiple actors participate in policy-making across various levels. However, it argues that things began to look very different in the period of crisis policy-making, starting with the banking and financial crisis in 2007 and emerging fully during the euro debt crisis. As argued by Wessels, Verdun and others, we have to acknowledge a shift of power back towards high-level politics, i.e. principally Heads of State and Government, Ministers of Finance, their interaction at the European level and their interplay with the key European and international institutions like the EC, the ECB, and the IMF. The political decision-making process through which this occurs is, to my mind, better captured by 'muddling through' or 'incrementalism', rather than the outdated concept of 'governance'. In other words, the multi-level governance entity is superseded by hard power politics at the highest level, engaging in a process best described informally as 'muddling through' or, more formally, as 'incrementalism' (see below). Importantly, this does not weaken Kohler-Koch and Rittberger's diagnosis of 'complexity' as being the prevalent feature of European integration—rather, ruling by incrementalism further adds to complexity.

If true, this shift from governance to incrementalism has important implications for academic research and policy analysis. Kohler-Koch and Rittberger rightly encouraged scholars to explore then-new areas of inquiry such as regulatory governance, public–private partnerships, and the influence of transnational networks. This has made EU studies more interdisciplinary, incorporating insights from political science, sociology, economics, and law. I would now argue to re-focus on top-level decision-making in European capitals and key institutions; and this present book is an example of that. We should retain the interdisciplinary cooperation among scholars, including, for example, ethnography (see below)—but we should focus our enquiry on those actors who matter.

What does this mean for our understanding of the EU polity in crisis? I point towards an interpretation influenced by Ulrich Beck and Edgar Grande's "Empire Europa" (2005). In their article *"Empire Europa: Politische Herrschaft jenseits von Bundesstaat und Staatenbund"* ("Empire Europe: Political Rule Beyond Federal State and Confederation"), Beck and Grande explore the unique nature of the EU's political system. The authors argue that the EU cannot be easily classified as either a traditional federal state *(Bundesstaat)* or a mere confederation of sovereign states *(Staatenbund)*. Instead, they propose a new (in fact, old) concept to describe the EU's form of governance—an 'empire' in the postmodern sense, which challenges traditional notions of political sovereignty and power. Their central thesis is that the EU represents a new kind of political entity that combines elements of both supranational and intergovernmental governance, creating a 'cosmopolitan empire' without clear boundaries of political authority. Beck and Grande describe the EU as an innovative model of governance where multiple levels of decision-making coexist, and sovereignty is shared between Member States and EU institutions. This diffusion of power blurs the lines between domestic and international politics and creates a new form of 'imperial' governance, where control is decentralised and multiple actors, including nation-states, regions, and transnational organisations, contribute to political authority.

The authors distinguish the EU's empire-like characteristics from historical empires by emphasising its lack of centralised coercive power and its commitment to democratic principles, human rights, and the rule of law. Unlike traditional empires, the EU does not rely on military force or domination to expand its influence; instead, it uses economic integration, legal frameworks, and soft power to extend its reach. The EU's governance model, they argue, allows for diversity and pluralism within a unified legal and economic structure, making it fundamentally different from older imperial models.

Beck and Grande also explore the EU's ability to adapt to globalisation and the challenges of the modern world. They argue that the EU's flexible governance system is better suited to deal with transnational issues, such as environmental protection, economic crises, and migration, than traditional nation-states. By sharing sovereignty and allowing for multiple layers of decision-making, the EU can act more effectively on the global stage while still preserving the autonomy of its Member States. However, the authors also recognise the inherent tensions and contradictions in this system. The EU's governance structure creates ambiguity about who holds ultimate authority, leading to a democratic deficit and a lack of accountability in decision-making. This has contributed to the rise of Euroscepticism and political challenges from within the Member States, as citizens question the legitimacy of decisions made at the EU level. Beck and Grande suggest that the EU must address these issues to ensure its long-term stability and legitimacy as a political entity.

I profoundly agree with Beck and Grande's central assertion that the EU does not fit into traditional models of federal states or confederations. Instead, it represents a new form of governance—indeed a 'cosmopolitan empire'—where power is decentralised and shared across multiple levels of authority. Not dissimilar from Kohler-Koch and Rittberger, this multi-level governance blurs the distinction between domestic and international politics and allows for more flexible and responsive decision-making. However, the period of crisis and the particular type of leadership associated best with Angela Merkel has pushed this form of political rule lastingly into a mode of incrementalism or 'muddling through'. For a brief moment in time, it was her who could have transformed the European Empire into a more effective and democratic form of polity. She chose, however, not to do so—or was even unaware of that choice.

Turning to different perspectives, a scholar who challenges conventional narratives about the euro area crisis is Waltraud Schelkle in her book "The Politics of Monetary Solidarity" (2018). She develops the concept of 'monetary solidarity' as a defining feature of EMU and argues that, contrary to widespread criticisms, the euro is not fundamentally flawed, nor is it merely a neoliberal project. Instead, she frames the euro area as a system of mutual risk-sharing that reflects a form of solidarity between Member States, albeit a contested and evolving one. Her book explores how the EMU has functioned as a mechanism for sharing financial risks, particularly during times of crisis. Schelkle asserts that the euro area is not simply about enforcing fiscal discipline or austerity but is also about the collective management of economic vulnerabilities. Through a series of case studies, she illustrates how euro area countries have responded to economic shocks through mechanisms like the European Stability Mechanism (ESM), the ECB's actions, and the various bailout programmes. These are seen as forms of monetary solidarity, where wealthier nations provide financial support to weaker ones, even as this solidarity is often constrained by political limits.

Schelkle also engages with the tensions inherent in the euro area's structure, notably the lack of a Fiscal Union and the political resistance to deeper integration. However, she contends that these constraints are not fatal flaws but features of a union that continues to evolve in response to crises. In her view, the EMU's resilience comes from its ability to adapt and reform rather than from adherence to strict fiscal rules. Ultimately, Schelkle advocates a more nuanced understanding of the euro area, one that sees it not as a doomed project but as a political system built on a complex and evolving form of solidarity, where cooperation is possible even in the face of significant political and economic differences.

This book lends support to Schelkle's view of the euro area as a scheme of 'monetary solidarity', where Member States share financial risks to ensure collective stability. This risk-sharing mechanism, evident in crisis responses, is a form of solidarity even though it is often contested and politically fraught. It is also true, as Schelkle argues, that the euro has demonstrated resilience by adapting to crises. The EMU is capable of evolving in response to economic shocks, and its survival is due to the ongoing reconfiguration of its rules and institutions. Oftentimes, principles and rules are ditched in the heat of crisis and give evidence of 'time-inconsistency' such as the good, old Stability and Growth Pact (SGP). However, the eventual impasse of fiscal stabilisation and the total reliance on monetary stabilisation as of 2012 should not be overlooked. The crisis has triggered some degree of reform—albeit by far not enough. The tragedy of monetary stabilisation is precisely the price of fundamental institutional reform forgone. Rather than deeper 'solidarity', a flood of money is being cast over persisting differences and conflicting interests. One should not confuse a can being kicked down the road with a proper solution.

Vivien Schmidt is another scholar of European integration who has studied the political and economic challenges facing the EU in light of the euro crisis. In her book "Europe's Crisis of Legitimacy: Governing by Rules and Ruling by Numbers in the Euro Area" (2020), she focuses on how the EU's governance model—characterised in her words by strict adherence to rules and numbers—has led to a crisis of legitimacy among its Member States. Schmidt argues that the EU's reliance on technocratic decision-making, which emphasises rules-based governance and fiscal discipline, has alienated citizens and undermined democratic legitimacy. This governance approach, referred to as 'governing by rules and ruling by numbers', was especially evident during the euro area crisis, when austerity measures and fiscal constraints were imposed on crisis-hit countries. Following Fritz Scharpf (2009), Schmidt distinguishes between two forms of legitimacy—output legitimacy (effective policy results) and input legitimacy (democratic participation)—and highlights how the EU's governance during the crisis prioritised output legitimacy through economic stability at the expense of input legitimacy. She contends that the EU's focus on fiscal rules, budgetary oversight, and technocratic control led to poor outcomes for many citizens, fuelling disillusionment and populism.

Her book offers a detailed examination of the policy responses during the euro area crisis, including the role of the ECB and institutions like the European Stability Mechanism (ESM). Schmidt critiques the EU's handling of the crisis, arguing that austerity policies exacerbated social and economic inequality, eroded trust in EU institutions, and led to democratic backsliding in several Member States. Schmidt also explores how these governance failures have given rise to a legitimacy crisis that threatens the future of European integration. According to her, the growing gap between EU institutions and its citizens, coupled with the rise of populism, poses a significant challenge to the EU's long-term stability. To address this crisis, Schmidt calls for reforms that enhance democratic accountability, transparency, and flexibility in EU governance.

I agree with Schmidt's fundamental argument that the EU's emphasis on technocratic governance, which prioritises fiscal rules and numerical targets over democratic engagement, has alienated citizens and weakened its legitimacy. The EU had to rely on rules-based governance during the euro crisis, especially through austerity measures, and had very limited scope for institutional reform—given that Merkel was not willing to engage this strategy. It is true, as Schmidt argues, that this limited course of political action has led to negative social and economic consequences that damaged the EU's credibility.

Scharpf's well-known distinction between output- and input legitimacy is indeed warranted in this analysis. During the euro area crisis, the EU focused on maintaining output legitimacy through fiscal stability but neglected input legitimacy, failing to involve citizens in decision-making processes. This imbalance undermined trust in EU institutions and contributed to the democratic deficit.

As previously stated, I cannot share the standard criticism of austerity measures. These policies, which were designed to restore fiscal stability, indeed had devastating effects on social welfare, deepened economic inequality, and prolonged economic stagnation—but they were inevitable in a situation of insolvency without Fiscal and Political Union. Those who criticise austerity on the grounds of legitimacy generously overlook the legitimacy implications of shifting additional fiscal burdens from Southern to Northern Europe against the democratic preferences of creditor nations.

By contrast, I can follow Schmidt's argument that the EU's governance system, dominated by technocrats and unelected officials, lacks democratic accountability. Decisions during the euro area crisis were often made behind closed doors, with limited input from national parliaments or citizens. Possibly even worse, traditional principles of national and European administrations—such as *Schriftlichkeit*, the use of written, lasting documents—have not been adhered to (see below). This top-down, clandestine approach has alienated the public and fuelled the rise of populist movements across Europe. While the ECB played a critical role in stabilising the euro area, its actions were entirely insulated from democratic oversight—as it is naturally the case for politically independent central banks. The occasional appearance of ECB Board Members before European Parliament committees is a fig-leave and not the same as real democratic accountability. Institutional independence and de-politicisation should simply not be overburdened with eminently political tasks, and a central bank should not make up for the lack of a fiscal backstop. Unlike Schmidt, I would therefore not see the problem in the ECB's independence, but rather in the fact that the ECB had to act politically in the first place—in the absence of Fiscal and Political Union. I concur with Schmidt that the creation of institutions like the ESM further centralised non-democratic power, reducing transparency and public accountability.

I echo Schmidt's calls for reforms that enhance democratic control and transparency in EU governance. However, I fail to see how that should be achieved, as Schmidt argues, through a shift away from rigid rules-based governance towards a more flexible approach that balances fiscal discipline with the needs of Member States and their citizens. This is far too fluffy, for my understanding. For Schmidt, this includes giving national parliaments and citizens a greater voice in EU decision-making processes—which would render them entirely dysfunctional. To my mind, the alternative options are much more drastic and boil down to regaining the legitimacy (input and output) that only a functioning, effective and democratic state can deliver—i.e. essentially a choice between returning to the nation state or moving forward towards a proper European federal state or, for that matter, a European Empire.

More recent contributions to the academic debate include two articles by Erik Jones, Daniel Kelemen and Sophie Meunier: "Failing Forward? The Euro Crisis and the Incomplete Nature of European Integration" (2016) and "Failing Forward? Crises and Patterns of European Integration" (2021). In their 2016 article, the authors analyse the response to the euro crisis through the lens of European integration theory. They introduce the concept of 'failing forward' to explain how the EU addresses crises by advancing integration in a piecemeal and incomplete fashion. According to this argument, crises expose the institutional weaknesses and incomplete nature of European integration, prompting EU leaders to enact incremental reforms that move the process forward without fully resolving underlying issues. The authors focus on the euro crisis, illustrating how the EU's response followed a 'failing forward' pattern. The creation of mechanisms such as the ESM and piecemeal steps towards Banking Union are seen as responses that advanced integration but did not provide comprehensive solutions to the structural flaws prevalent in EMU. These reforms were often partial and reactive, driven by the need to maintain stability rather than a coherent strategy for deeper integration. The central thesis of the article is that the EU's crisis-driven responses tend to institutionalise incomplete solutions, leaving vulnerabilities that can resurface in future crises. This 'failing forward' dynamic highlights the EU's tendency to deepen integration incrementally, but in a way that leaves it perpetually unfinished and prone to recurring crises.

In their 2021 follow-up article, the authors revisit the concept of 'failing forward' in light of subsequent crises, including Brexit, the migration crisis, and the Covid-19 pandemic. The authors expand their framework to explore how crises continue to shape the trajectory of European integration, arguing that the EU's responses to these crises display the same pattern of incremental, incomplete reforms seen during the euro area crisis. Their concept explains the persistence of integration despite repeated crises. The authors suggest that while crises expose the EU's structural weaknesses, they also create opportunities for leaders to push forward reforms that otherwise would not be possible. However, these reforms remain incomplete and continue to leave the EU vulnerable. For example, the response to the Covid-19 pandemic included unprecedented moves like the Recovery and Resilience Facility, which advanced EU-level fiscal policy, but still fell short of full Fiscal Union. The authors argue that 'failing forward' remains a key characteristic of European integration. Each crisis leads to further integration, but in ways that maintain or even deepen the EU's institutional complexity and fragmentation. They also emphasise the role of political leadership, arguing that incremental progress is often driven by necessity rather than a long-term vision for deeper integration.

I fully concur with the authors in their argument that the euro crisis revealed flaws in the EMU, but the EU's response was fragmented, with partial solutions like the ESM, which advanced integration without resolving the fundamental problems. European integration progresses through crises, but the reforms often institutionalise only partial solutions that leave the EU vulnerable to future crises. The concept of 'failing forward' helps to explain EU integration across different crises, from the euro area crisis to Brexit and Covid-19—and, most recently, on defence integration in light of the Ukraine war, I would argue. Crises expose the EU's weaknesses, but also create windows for leaders to push forward reforms, even though these reforms are often incomplete. My central point is that the window of opportunity in 2010 would have been of historic and strategic importance—had Merkel grasped the opportunity, based on Schäuble's proposals and even beyond those. Yet, the progress made in reality remains piecemeal and, despite innovation in areas like Banking Union and fiscal policy coordination, the EU remains institutionally fragmented, with vulnerabilities that persist or are even amplified after each crisis. 'Failing forward' occurs precisely as a consequence of incrementalism.

Incrementalism and Other Approaches

'Muddling through' as a description of decision-making in business, but also in political context, is a subject of social science research but remains hitherto underexplored in its application to European policy-making. It is referred to as 'incrementalism' or 'gradualism' and has led to a scientific model of decision-making that is particularly applicable to management and administration. Charles E. Lindblom coined this term in the 1950s at Yale University and is regarded as one of the most important proponents of this approach. Lindblom's (1959) model, also known as the 'method of successive limited comparisons', is often understood as a counter-approach to rational and comprehensive decision-making. His thesis is that decision-makers who 'muddle through' adjust their policies gradually and in small steps rather than making large, radical changes. Lindblom was not the only one to develop these ideas; other scholars like

Herbert A. Simon (1947), Aaron Wildavsky (1964), and later John P. Crecine (1972) also worked on incrementalism and helped to establish it in political theory and practice.

Lindblom's incrementalism describes a decision-making process in which managers, politicians, and administrators necessarily disregard a multitude of values or goals and their possible consequences. Instead, they rely on a limited number of alternatives, often derived from previous experiences and compared with each other based on the smallest possible decision steps. This step-by-step decision-making is less based on theoretical models and more on practical experience, with the expectation that past actions will serve as a guide for future actions. The weighing of means and ends is not clearly separated but takes place simultaneously. This method assumes that the participants expect to achieve their goals only partially and to constantly adjust their decisions as conditions change and new information becomes available.

At the heart of Lindblom's argument is the belief that a complete theoretical understanding of all political alternatives and consequences is impossible in the short time available. Instead, it makes sense to make decisions step by step, relying heavily on past experience. Lindblom describes this process as continuous: Political decisions are made, reviewed, and corrected if necessary. It is assumed that neither political actors nor public administrations are capable of making clear and comprehensive predictions about the impact of their policies. Incrementalism is therefore a pragmatic approach that considers the uncertainties of the real world—especially when it is marked by crisis.

Lindblom identifies several key characteristics of incrementalism. First, there is a connection between values and empirical analysis, as the selection of values and the analysis of the need for action are closely linked. Decisions are often made without a clear separation between goals and means. Second, there is no attempt to develop a comprehensive theory to assess all possible consequences of a decision. Instead, past experiences are used, and the number of possible alternatives is reduced to a minimum. This second characteristic of incrementalism is consistent with Herbert A. Simon's theory of 'bounded rationality' (1947), which preceded incrementalism and noted that decision-makers are rarely able to consider all possible options and often have to resort to simplified decision-making processes. Simon's theory of bounded rationality already recognised that people are not capable of fully processing all the information necessary for comprehensive decision-making. Therefore, decision-makers tend to use simplified models and make incremental adjustments rather than striving for an optimal solution. Simon emphasised even before Lindblom that incrementalism is a necessary part of decision-making.

A third characteristic of incrementalism is that 'good' policy is often only defined by the fact that it represents a consensus among the decision-makers involved, without any agreement on whether the chosen approach is actually the optimal solution. 'Muddling through' thus relies on consensus wherever it can be found, placing less emphasis on the theoretical proof of the decision. Fourth, any analysis in preparing the decision, if it takes place at all, is drastically simplified. Important consequences and alternative policy options are regularly neglected. This is a consequence of the limited capacity to process information and the need to make decisions quickly, even when not all options have been fully analysed. Fifth, theoretical approaches play a subordinate role, as decision-makers have to rely on practical comparisons and incremental adjustments. Their focus is on pragmatically dealing with uncertainties rather than taking a comprehensive theoretical view.

A central problem of incrementalism is that decision-makers are rarely able to formulate clear values and goals. Lindblom points out that there are usually no precise public preferences on many political issues. Often, specific preferences do not exist because public discussion on certain topics is insufficient, and the attention of the electorate is not directed to the relevant questions—sometimes due to the speed of crisis events alone.

Furthermore, the intensity of preferences should ideally be considered in addition to the number of people who prefer a certain policy—but it is usually not revealed. This uncertainty forces the administration to make decisions without first clarifying the underlying values and goals of the polity. Even when politicians or civil servants use their own values as a basis for decision-making, they often do not know how to rank them when they conflict with each other. Lindblom explains that there is no simple way to determine the relative importance of conflicting values. Values must be weighed against a specific decision situation, and the priority of a value can change from one decision situation to the next. This uncertainty-cum-inconsistency leads political administrations to focus on incremental changes that marginally combine values rather than trying to clarify them fully for once and all.

Lindblom emphasises that, in the absence of clear agreement on values and goals, political consensus becomes the only practical measure of the 'correctness' of a decision. This contrasts with comprehensive, theoretically based decision-making processes, which attempt to take all possible consequences and alternatives into account. Incremental policy is characterised by the attempt to find broad consensus, even if this consensus does not necessarily mean that the best decision has been made. Lindblom's incrementalism thus suggests that political decisions are not and indeed should not be final but, to the contrary, are continuously reviewed and adjusted. The decision-making process is iterative—decisions are made, reviewed, corrected, and made again as the situation evolves and as goals and values adapt. This is reflected in the notion that policy-making is an ongoing process of trial and error. A policy is never considered completely finished but is continuously modified as circumstances change. This repetition and adjustment of decisions serve to avoid serious and lasting mistakes that could result from radical and lasting political changes. Muddling through obviously fails, however, to detect and honour situations in which precedents become path-dependent and lead to lasting policy-changes, contrary to the original wish to retain flexibility.

While Lindblom laid the foundation for incrementalism as a scientific treatment of muddling through, other scholars developed and refined the model. Aaron Wildavsky (1964) examined incrementalism in the context of budget planning and found that step-by-step adjustments in political processes often lead to more stable and predictable results than large breaks. John P. Crecine and Wildavsky (1972) argued that incremental changes are particularly advantageous in complex political systems because they minimise greater uncertainties and unpredictable consequences.

This present book argues that 'muddling through' is what happened habitually under Angela Merkel during the euro crisis. Her style of governance offers a firsthand example of incrementalism. As a case study, the early stage of the euro crisis shows that muddling through in government can be good and right, and even unavoidable under certain circumstances—but that it comes at a high price and is sometimes inappropriate and even highly damaging. Importantly, I argue that Lindblom's notion of incremental policy-making as an iterative process is incomplete. Even when muddling through, policymakers do take decisions (or non-decisions) with lasting effect. At critical junctures, their behaviour does indeed lead to path-dependency. Suboptimal outcomes are locked in, particularly with regard to institutional developments.

Besides incrementalism, there have been important contributions to the academic literature with high relevance for my work. In particular, Frédéric Mérand's book "The Political Commissioner: A European Ethnography" (2021) has provided me with useful guidance on how to rationalise my inside experience in the German government for an academic audience. Mérand presents an in-depth ethnographic study of the EC, focusing on the role and identity of European Commissioners, the powerful bureaucratic and political figures who drive much of the EU's policy-making process. Drawing on his fieldwork and interviews conducted within the Commission, Mérand also provides an insider's perspective on the daily lives, challenges, and political dynamics faced by these Commissioners.

Mérand's study demystifies the European Commission, revealing it as a complex political environment in which Commissioners must balance their national loyalties, political ambitions, and their collective responsibility to the European project. He examines how Commissioners navigate this tension, as they are tasked with promoting European interests while remaining accountable to their home countries and political affiliations. The book also highlights the personal, human dimension of being a Commissioner, exploring how these political figures deal with the pressures of the job, the compromises they must make, and how they construct their identities within the broader context of the EU's political and bureaucratic machinery. Mérand argues that, while Commissioners hold significant power, they are also constrained by the complex institutional structures and political realities of the EU.

Merand's ethnographic approach is highly instructive to my work, and much of what he describes about the Commission can be replicated in my account of the German ministerial bureaucracy. Mérand demonstrates that the EC is not merely a neutral, technocratic institution but a deeply political and human one, where Commissioners must balance competing interests—national, political, and European—while navigating internal and external pressures. His book brings to light the personal experiences and struggles of the Commissioners, showing that they are individuals who experience the same career pressures, ambitions, and ethical dilemmas as other political figures. It underscores the human side of European integration, often overshadowed by the bureaucratic façade. Despite their political influence, Commissioners are not omnipotent. Their power is restricted by the institutional structures of the EC, the broader EU governance framework, and the political realities of negotiating with Member States and other EU bodies. Far from being a technocratic entity, the EC is a site of intense political contestation. Political parties, Member States, and interest groups all exert influence over Commissioners, shaping their decisions and policy outcomes.

While not myself adopting an ethnographic approach, I agree that ethnography can provide a new lens on European—and, for that matter, national—politics. By using ethnographic methods, Mérand offers a fresh perspective on European governance. His in-depth, on-the-ground observations reveal the day-to-day workings of the EC in ways that traditional political science approaches might overlook. They are highly valuable to academic scholars, particularly in political science and integration studies. I have attempted to provide similarly useful insights to an academic audience, offering a nuanced, ground-level view of the German Ministry of Finance in its interaction with the Chancellery, showing the institution as a microcosm of European and national political dynamics and offering new insights into how power, identity, and politics interact.

A more traditional perspective different from ethnography, but no less insightful, explores the intellectual and ideological foundations that underpinned the euro crisis and the divergent approaches to economic policy among European countries. This is the ideational or constructivist route taken by Markus Brunnermeier, Harold James, and Jean-Pierre Landau in their book "The Euro and the Battle of Ideas" (2017). The authors argue that the crisis, which erupted in 2010, was not just an economic or financial issue but was deeply rooted in competing national philosophies about economics and governance, particularly between Germany and France. Their book highlights the 'battle of ideas' between two dominant schools of thought in Europe. Germany advocates a rules-based, ordo-liberal economic model that emphasises fiscal discipline, price stability, and minimising state intervention. In contrast, France and Southern European countries favour a more discretionary, interventionist approach that prioritises economic flexibility, government-led stabilisation, and so-called solidarity among euro area members.

Brunnermeier et al. trace how these philosophical differences influenced policy responses during the euro area crisis. Germany, backed by Northern European countries, pushed for strict austerity measures and structural reforms as the solution, while France and Southern Europe called for more fiscal stimulus, debt mutualisation, and coordinated efforts to promote growth. These tensions complicated decision-making within the EU, particularly around issues like bailout packages, debt restructuring, and the role of the ECB. The authors argue that, while these differences in economic thought created friction, the euro crisis also forced a degree of compromise and convergence in European economic governance. The book explores how these ideas continue to shape the future of the euro and Europe's economic integration.

In my own work, I concur with Brunnermeier et al. and suggest thinking about the euro crisis also as a conflict of economic philosophies, particularly between Germany's ordo-liberalism and France's interventionist approach. I also show in concrete terms how this clash of ideas made it difficult or even impossible to reach consensus on crisis management and reform. Germany's ordo-liberalism emphasises a certain amount of fiscal discipline, monetary stability, and more reluctant state intervention, while France and Southern Europe favour an even more flexible, pragmatic approach that allows for massive state intervention and coordination, allegedly to ensure growth and solidarity—often at the cost of fiscal sustainability and price stability. One of the key issues emerging during the euro crisis was the debate over so-called austerity versus so-called solidarity. Germany and its allies insisted on austerity as a way to contain moral hazard and restore fiscal balance, while France and Southern European countries advocated for policies that would stimulate growth and promote financial transfers from North to South.

I concur also with Brunnermeier et al. in their analysis of the ECB's role in the crisis. Their book reveals the tension between two competing visions: Initially hesitant to intervene beyond its traditional mandate, the ECB eventually adopted more unconventional measures (like massively buying sovereign debt and engaging in quantitative easing) to stabilise the euro area. This shift was a pragmatic solution to brush over the unresolved conflict between divergent economic philosophies. I argue that, short of institutional reform, the ECB was pushed into this essentially political role by the sheer want of leadership from European capitals, above all Berlin.

Economic history is yet another valuable approach to analysing the euro crisis. This workstream is exemplified by books such as "Public Spending and the Role of the State: History, Performance, Risk and Remedies" by Ludger Schuknecht (2021), a close and valued colleague and former superior of mine at the ECB and later-on also at the Ministry of Finance. Schuknecht's book provides a comprehensive historical analysis of government expenditure, tracing the evolution of public spending across different regions and time periods. He evaluates how governments have expanded their roles, particularly in the 20th and 21st centuries, and how this expansion has shaped economic performance, risks, and social outcomes. He examines different models of state intervention, comparing the size and efficiency of governments in various advanced economies. Schuknecht analyses the effects of rising public expenditures on growth, equity, and fiscal sustainability, offering a critique of overly expansive government roles. He suggests that many governments have moved beyond necessary spending in areas such as education, health, and infrastructure, and ventured into inefficient or unsustainable territories. The book discusses how governments can balance welfare state objectives with the need for fiscal prudence and highlights the risks of excessive public debt and unsustainable spending. Schuknecht also explores potential remedies, focusing on strategies to improve government efficiency and ensure that public spending promotes sustainable development. He recommends a return to limited government roles in certain sectors, as well as reforms that prioritise effectiveness and value for money.

My thinking on the origins of the euro crisis borrows heavily from Schuknecht's work and I agree with him that many governments have allowed their expenditures to rise far beyond productive levels, leading to inefficiency and fiscal risks. This has been exacerbated by the euro thanks to low interest rates and capital flows from North to South. The trade-off between government expansion and efficiency has become blatantly clear and Schuknecht rightly emphasises the dangers of excessive government spending, particularly the risks posed by rising public debt against the backdrop of demography. He warns that unsustainable fiscal policies can lead to crises, reduced economic growth, and intergenerational inequality—as has become evident in the euro crisis. The developments discussed in this present book lend support to Schuknecht's plea for a thorough rethinking of the state's role in the economy. He suggests that governments should focus on core functions—such as defence and security, infrastructure, education, and healthcare—while limiting their involvement in areas where private sector solutions are more effective.

Finally, as a yet different scholarly approach, sociologists Jens Beckert and Lukas Arndt examine the role of narratives and 'imagined futures' in shaping the trajectory of the Greek sovereign debt crisis between 2009 and 2015. In their 2024 paper "The Greek Tragedy: Narratives and Imagined Futures in the Greek Sovereign Debt Crisis", they argue that negative narratives about Greece's future, especially in the financial media, contributed significantly to the fluctuations in Greek bond spreads. By analysing over 9,000 articles from prominent publications such as the Financial Times and the Wall Street Journal, the authors identify how these narratives, often filled with uncertainty, drove investor behaviour. The study uses sentiment analysis and machine learning to correlate these narratives with bond market developments, suggesting that the pessimistic views on Greece's future had a real impact on financial markets. The findings underscore how 'imagined futures' in discourse can affect financial decisions, providing a novel contribution to the sociology of financial crises.

I relate to Beckert and Arndt by providing additional colour on the way in which media-driven narratives about Greece's future played a crucial role in shaping market perceptions and actions, influencing bond spreads and investor behaviour as well as, ultimately, political decisions through the sheer pressure of market movements. Investors' decisions were influenced not only by present economic data but also by uncertain and speculative projections about future economic conditions. Their study highlights the importance of integrating sociological perspectives, particularly the role of discourse, in understanding the microfoundations of financial crises. The analysis bridges economics and sociology, showing that imagined futures and collective perceptions can directly impact financial markets during crises.

Applying the 'Flat Politics' Lens

The scholarly debate on the euro crisis encompasses multiple perspectives—incrementalism, institutional complexity, crisis governance networks, integration theory debates, leadership studies, ideational approaches, and sociological insights on narratives. After having charted each work in isolation through sequential mini-reviews, this final section now synthesises key contributions thematically to illuminate the concept of 'flat politics' as the outcome of incrementalism and a style of governance characterised by decentralised, iterative decision-making, consensus-seeking across diverse actors, and pragmatic 'muddling through' under uncertainty. These thematic syntheses reveal how the literature collectively informs our own analytical lens for examining Merkel's political performance in the euro area crisis as well as in other instances of crisis.

Foundational works on incrementalism highlight decision-making through successive limited comparisons—small, reversible steps guided by past experience and bounded rationality. Application to EU contexts shows that policymakers often prefer gradual adjustments over sweeping reforms when uncertainty and complexity loom large. This resonates with crisis governance accounts, where responses evolved through piecemeal packages rather than radical restructuring. From a 'flat politics' perspective, Merkel's crisis approach exemplifies this orientation: successive negotiations among Member States, institutions, and experts produced incremental solutions whose cumulative effect shaped the euro area response. While incrementalism fosters flexibility and reduces the risk of major policy errors, it also risks path-dependency and suboptimal lock-ins when foundational reforms remain deferred. Thus, the literature underscores both the virtues and perils of muddling through—a core dynamic in flat politics.

Analyses of EU institutional architecture emphasise dispersed authority across supranational bodies, Member State governments, central banks, and epistemic communities. Decision-making emerges via continuous negotiation within multi-level networks rather than centralised directives. Crisis governance studies further illustrate how informal expert consultations and ad-hoc task forces operate across these levels. The 'flat politics' lens captures how Merkel navigated this complex terrain: coordinating among other Heads of State and Government, Finance Ministers, ECB officials, Commission actors, and national administrations required lateral bargaining and consensus-building. Institutional complexity both necessitates and arises from incrementalism: each step in crisis management added layers to governance structures (e.g. ESM, Banking Union), reinforcing complexity while operating within a flattened network of actors.

Crisis governance literature examines how networks of experts, international institutions, and political leaders coordinate agile responses. Findings show that effective crisis solutions often emerge from informal consultations and iterative negotiations rather than top-down commands. This network mode aligns with flat politics: authority disperses across nodes that share expertise and bargain over trade-offs, thereby diluting personal responsibility and accountability. Merkel's convening of expert groups, reliance on ECB technical assessments, and iterative crafting of bailout packages exemplify this dynamic. The literature explicitly warns about accountability challenges when decisions diffuse across networks, a tension we explore in subsequent analysis of Merkel's crisis style.

Integration theory debates—intergovernmentalism, neofunctionalism, 'failing forward'—offer competing accounts of how crises shape European integration. Rather than adopting a single school, 'flat politics' suggests that national bargaining occurs within evolving supranational frameworks: preferences form through interaction with institutional norms, while crises drive incremental reforms. The 'failing forward' concept illustrates how crisis-driven initiatives (e.g. ESM, Banking Union) advance integration in piecemeal fashion, institutionalising incomplete solutions that may sow future vulnerabilities. Merkel's navigation of intergovernmental negotiations, constrained by domestic politics and supranational imperatives, typifies this interplay: crisis responses reflect a flattened process where top-level leaders negotiate incremental concessions rather than impose coherent, sweeping integration.

Leadership studies in EU contexts emphasise influence through persuasion, framing, and coalition-building rather than hierarchical command. In a polity lacking a clear executive centre, authority emerges horizontally through negotiation skills and credibility. Merkel's role during the euro crisis illustrates soft leadership: framing proposals to align with heterogeneous domestic constituencies, forging coalitions among sceptical partners, and guiding incremental compromises. Flat politics reframes crisis leadership as a networked, consensus-driven endeavour, where decision-makers exercise power by enabling agreement across dispersed actors. This model highlights the limitations of top-down initiatives in EU governance and the necessity of lateral coordination.

Constructivist and historical accounts explore the ideational roots and structural contexts of the crisis. Debates between ordo-liberal versus interventionist philosophies reveal how conflicting economic ideas shaped policy responses. Historical analyses underline long-term trends in public spending and state roles that predisposed certain outcomes. These insights inform flat politics by showing that decision-making frames (e.g. ordoliberalism) and historical path-dependencies shape the incremental choices available to actors. Merkel's decisions, influenced by domestic philosophic leanings and historical legacies, unfolded within a flattened network negotiating among ideational blocs.

Discussions on monetary solidarity and legitimacy crises examine how risk-sharing mechanisms and technocratic governance affect public trust. Sociological studies on narratives demonstrate how media-driven imagined futures influenced market and political decisions. These works highlight that incremental crisis measures must also contend with perceptions of solidarity and democratic accountability. Under flat politics, legitimacy is negotiated across multiple audiences—national electorates, EU institutions, and markets—through incremental policy adjustments. Understanding narrative dynamics helps explain how consensus is built or eroded in crisis politics.

Across themes, the literature converges on a model of governance marked by decentralised decision-making, iterative adaptation, and networked coordination. Crises prompt piecemeal reforms that accumulate into significant changes yet often institutionalise incomplete solutions. Authority diffuses among diverse actors, requiring soft leadership, consensus-building, and pragmatic muddling through. This 'flat politics' model explains Merkel's crisis management: successive bargains delivered stability but also embedded path-dependencies and complexity, with performance shortfalls and legitimacy risks. Recognising flat politics as the overarching feature of these dynamics provides a coherent analytical lens for the ensuing case studies.

The thematic synthesis equips the reader to:

- Apply the flat politics lens: When examining empirical episodes (e.g. specific bailout negotiations), identify how decentralised actors negotiated incremental solutions, revealing the workings of flat politics.
- Assess virtues and risks: Use incrementalism literature to evaluate the flexibility benefits and path-dependency risks of muddling-through approaches.
- Understand institutional complexity: Draw on multi-level governance analyses to map which actors shaped decisions at each stage, and how complexity both enabled and constrained choices.
- Evaluate leadership dynamics: Employ soft leadership frameworks to interpret how Merkel framed proposals, built coalitions, and influenced partners without hierarchical authority.
- Integrate ideational and narrative factors: Incorporate insights on economic philosophies and media narratives to appreciate how ideas and perceptions affected bargaining positions and public legitimacy.
- Critique incremental outcomes: Leverage 'failing forward' and legitimacy studies to critique incomplete reforms and to anticipate potential future crises stemming from institutional lock-ins.

- Guide further research: The flat politics framework suggests focusing empirical investigation on network interactions among key policy-makers, decision sequences, and legitimacy issues, rather than solely on formal institutional developments.

By weaving these readings into a cohesive flat politics perspective, subsequent chapters will more sharply analyse Merkel's crisis decisions, revealing how incremental, consensus-driven processes shaped the euro crisis trajectory and its lasting implications for EU governance.

The scholarly contributions discussed in this chapter inform our concept of 'flat politics' as both the process and the lasting outcome of a governance style marked by decentralised, iterative decision-making, consensus-seeking across diverse actors, and tactical-incremental adjustments under uncertainty. By weaving together insights on incrementalism, institutional complexity, and power diffusion, we see how 'flat politics' flows from Merkel's crisis management approach. In subsequent chapters, this understanding guides the analysis of concrete decisions during the early euro crisis. Needless to say, we consciously employ the double meaning of 'flat politics': Merkel's political style was 'flat' in terms of process and outcome alike.

CHAPTER 3

Greece: The Weakest Link

How It Started

According to my diary, it was 26 January 2010, a Tuesday, when I wondered for the first time whether we would have to bail out Greece.

But this was a hideous thought at the time. I discussed it over lunch while still being a *fonctionnaire* at the European Investment Bank (EIB) in Luxembourg. My lunch companion, an Austrian economist, would later-on become a staff member of the European Financial Stabilisation Facility (EFSF), set up as a spin-off of the EIB with precisely the task to bail out weak EU Member States.

Little did we sense at the time how much the euro crisis was going to shape our professional lives and thinking. The topic did quickly pick up, however, and became prominent not only for lunch conversations. In fact, a possible insolvency of Greece and the different policy options for the other Member States soon became the number one issue to raise whenever bumping into colleagues in the floors of the EIB on the Kirchberg... or downtown into anybody faintly related to financial affairs, of whom there are many in the streets of Luxembourg.

Before moving on to the Ministry of Finance in Berlin, I remember saying farewell to another colleague in Luxembourg. She was a lawyer from Romania and just then waiting for a bus outside the EIB's so-called 'old building', a rather imposing concrete structure from the 1970s in

M. Heipertz, *Merkelism and the Fine Art of Flat Politics*, Palgrave Studies in European Union Politics,
https://doi.org/10.1007/978-3-031-87592-2_3

brutalist style. The Romanian impressed me by the clarity of her prediction: 'Surely, they will bail out Greece. There is no other way. I think one should buy Greek bonds immediately. You can get them for junk prices now and they will turn out a great investment'. I agreed and somewhat regretted that I could not heed her advice as I was just about to become an insider to that story, also in terms of legal and financial restrictions implied by my new capacity.

Later that week, on Thursday and Friday 28 and 29 January 2010, I attended a conference in Frankfurt at the European Central Bank (ECB), where I had worked as a fiscal economist at the beginning of my career between 2004 and 2008. We started with an opulent dinner in one of Frankfurt's finer restaurants; not an uncommon thing to do for central bankers. As expected, everyone chatted about Greece—and only about Greece. For the first time ever, I heard some colleagues making a rather fine difference between insolvency and illiquidity, arguing that a country can lack liquidity and still be solvent—in principle. By analogy, there would be a difference between a bailout (in the sense of assuming another country's liabilities) and a simple credit. From this line of thought, it quickly emerged that a country which is solvent but encounters only a 'gap' in liquidity (presumably because of stress or hysteria in the financial markets) should simply be given a 'bridge' over that gap…

Conference participants also argued that the perception of risk is self-reinforcing. As new fiscal data comes in and turns out to be bad and, in fact, worse than expected, economic agents pay more attention to it, adjusting their behaviour and thereby causing the next set of data to be even worse—see Beckert and Arndt (2024). There is circular causality between perception and reality, they said—and this was a negative feedback loop. Also, the more you care about risk, the more you detect. The opposite direction of such a circular direction, hence a positive feedback loop, had been true during previous times: Greece, like most Member States participating in the euro area, had, upon adopting the single currency, been sporting an A1 rating by Moody's and an A- by S&P, later to be upgraded even to A+. Those excellent ratings had made credit cheap, and credit had been pouring in massively indeed, above all from Germany where the capital surplus was abundant. In both directions, the circular dynamics were feeding upon themselves, propelled by partial perception and insufficient knowledge—likely leading to untenable disequilibria. The question had always not been *whether* but indeed *when* things would take a different turn.

My ECB colleagues consoled themselves: Over the preceding years, they had done their best to warn about Greece (and other Member States) piling up debt without any hesitation. In its most recent Annual Report,[1] released in April 2010, the Bank had cautioned against a 'sharp worsening in budgetary positions in 2009' and singled out three countries—Ireland, Greece, and Spain—as 'recording double-digit deficit ratios'. Regarding Greece, the ECB took note of a 'significant upward revision of fiscal deficits' after a change in government—not an uncommon thing to happen, but in this case particularly fraught with elements of creative accounting by the preceding government.

More than a few political leaders at the time had been lured into such creative accounting by clever investment banks, using all tricks of the trade of public accounting and suggesting a sort of credit-card mentality along the lines of 'buy now, pay later'. In 2001, during an internship in the *Cabinet des Finances* of the Belgian Minister of Finance, I had personally seen and been tasked to review such proposals, made by a London-based investment bank. (I had opposed them.)

Maybe the Stability and Growth Pact (SGP) was indeed wrong, I had thought already back then in 2001: The Maastricht Treaty still had had a balanced emphasis on a country's annual deficit as well as its overall level of debt, resulting simplistically from the accumulation of preceding deficits and so-called stock-flow-adjustments (debt being 'stock', annual deficits being 'flow'). The SGP, however, had shifted that emphasis away from debt and purely onto deficits—and deficits are far easier to control and, in fact, manipulate.

In any case, in a state like the Greek one, with cronyism and clientele politics (Richter 2015), such offers of investment banks to help governments massage their accounts had obviously proven very seductive: Politicians are in constant need to prove to their clientele the benefits of their being in office. This is true for other countries as well, including Germany—but sometimes the Northerners are more subtle in their proceedings…

It must be said that not only private rating agencies but also Eurostat, the official European statistical body in charge of defining the rules of public accounting and of validating Member States' accounts, is not beyond criticism for having turned too much of a blind eye to this

[1] https://www.ecb.europa.eu/pub/pdf/annrep/ar2010en.pdf.

phenomenon. Eurostat itself had in previous years been embroiled in a massive corruption scandal and had come under fire during the SGP crisis in 2003 (Heipertz/Verdun 2010). As a Directorate-General of the Commission, Eurostat in Luxembourg is not an independent body but works under the political control of Brussels. It was heavily criticised for not detecting and in fact mishandling the problems related to what, among us eurocrats, proverbially became known as 'Greek statistics'. Based on proper data, Greece would not have entered the single currency in 2001.

The 'severe fiscal imbalances' detected by the ECB[2] and revealed especially in Greece had not only to do with fiscal laxity, spurious oversight, and creative accounting. There had of course been another event which had brought Greek's public balance beyond the point of no return: The Greek government, like many other governments affected by the global financial and banking crisis of 2007/8, had shifted the debris of that crisis away from banks and onto the balance sheet of the state, as a direct consequence of having publicly bailed out those banks which had been deemed 'systemic'. Sanitising banks' balance sheets had in many cases been achieved by the injection of public capital and by the setting up of colossal bailout funds, which in turn had to be backed by public capital, hence contributing to the rapid increase in government debt in manifold ways.

Pressure Rising

It took until 8 February 2010, according to my diary, for speculative pressure in the markets to kick in: The yield of Greek government debt—and thereby its spread over the allegedly rock-solid German bunds—started to take off exponentially, and the euro tumbled in the forex markets.

On my new job in the Ministry of Finance, I learned something practical which my previous years at the ECB had not yet taught me: International financial markets, when they (re-)fund a sovereign state, do not care at all about the so-called Maastricht reference values, i.e. a debt ratio of 60% of gross domestic product (GDP) and a deficit ratio of 3% of GDP plus the whole, elaborate edifice of the SGP. Instead, they care about the ratio of interest payments to tax revenue. If actors in the market

[2] https://www.ecb.europa.eu/press/key/date/2010/html/sp100709_3.en.html.

think that the government in question is both willing and able to service its outstanding debt, they provide credit for it to do so. And their best guess, as regards the government's ability to service its debt, is precisely the ratio of interest payments to tax revenue.

Suppose tax revenue goes down, say because of a recession, and interest payments go up because, for example, the market increasingly attaches a risk premium to that state. Then, depending on the maturity profile of the outstanding debt, you look at clearly specified dates in the calendar on which the government's debt agency must fund enough money on the market to roll over whatever tranche is coming due on that day—by issuing fresh debt. The shorter the maturities and the higher the ratio of interest payments over tax revenue, the faster this situation will spin out of control.

In other words, we were starting to hold our breath each time a tranche of Greek public debt had to be rolled over. By that point, the yield only knew one direction: straight up. We were hence looking at the beginning of a balance of payments crisis.

The public discourse across Europe—and particularly in France—very much ran counter to my newly acquired understanding. Whereas I had come to see capital as a shy deer, nervously looking about the plain and ready to leave for the woods at the first instance of danger, politicians and commentators in Athens, Paris or elsewhere (not in London and across the Atlantic, though) complained about 'speculative attacks' on an innocent and defenceless Hellenic Republic.

True, we said, there are such speculators in the market who bet on a falling euro and on a falling price of government bonds, but their activity would be pointless had the government on the other side of the bet not brought itself to the precipice. What politicians call 'speculation' is often nothing else but a sensible market reaction, considering the discrepancies between policy on the one hand and economic reality on the other—notwithstanding the behavioural fact that markets tend to react late and excessively. It is, as stated above, a crisis of faulty policy adjusting to reality.

Uncovered short selling and uncovered credit default swaps (CDS) were the only exceptions of which we thought at the time that market agents were in fact purposefully aggravating the situation, especially if hedge funds were to collude in their positions.

Later-on I learned that such things did of course take place. A former ECB colleague of mine who had moved on to become an investment banker in London once showed me a photograph of the office door of a hedge fund manager, a client of his. The enormous double-door was made of brilliant black Japanese wood and under transparent lacquer, in the middle of the door, there was a beautifully arranged, flower-style pattern in the most incredible shades of blue with a diameter of maybe two metres. You had to look twice to see that the arrangement took the form of a human skull. 'You know what this is?', my colleague asked me and went on to explain: 'Butterfly wings from Latin America, a very rare butterfly. Thousands of them arranged in this pattern'. 'The thought of this gives me nausea', I said. 'Why do you show this to me?' 'Because he bought this door from the money he had made on the first Greek default back in 2010. I wanted you to see it so that you can imagine which type of guys you are up against…'.

We had also heard about a dinner among hedge fund managers in New York, hosted by a company called Moness Crespi Hardt on 8 February 2010. This dinner gave rise to the idea that a conspiracy of hedge funds had been founded against Greece. Later-on, there were press reports that a representative of SAC Capital Advisors at the dinner indeed encouraged his colleagues, including hedge funds run by George Soros and John Paulson, to go short on the euro. These funds had bought cheap CDS contracts on Greece in late 2009 and could now sell them for a multiple of their initial price (Frankfurter Allgemeine Zeitung, 04.06.2010).

Most EU Member States swiftly enacted measures to limit the abusive effects of short selling and CDS in the sovereign bond market, and some resorted to outright bans. In Germany, the banking supervisor BaFin on 18 May 2010 interdicted uncovered short selling of shares in ten significant financial institutions and in sovereign bonds of Euro area Member States as well as CDS on the latter which did not serve the purpose of risk mitigation. Future prohibitions should pertain to derivatives based on CDS or short selling.

However, given that short sales and CDS were hardly traded in continental Europe, these measures were of symbolical effect only. They also resulted in a fragmented approach until an EU Regulation came into force two years later. But the Greek balance of payments crisis in 2010 was of fundamental nature and did not subside because of such superficial restrictions. Furthermore, the effect of the single currency was like that of a fixed exchange rate regime: Greece no more had the chance to defuse the crisis by devaluation. Also, the common monetary policy precluded national inflation as an easy way out of the public debt burden.

Silent Preparations

On February 10th, the decision was taken in Berlin among the Chancellery and the Ministry of Finance to discretely look at and prepare a possible bailout for Greece—just in case and as a political option for the coming weeks and months. Only a handful of colleagues, mainly from the Directorate-General E (responsible for European policy), were involved. The Directorate-General E, under normal conditions, was not central to the workings of the Ministry, compared to the Directorate-General II (budget), IV (taxation policy) or VII (financial markets).

To my surprise, there was no formal set-up for strategic discussion and detailed work on this momentous and highly complex plan with the other branches of the Ministry which should have been principally concerned with Greece, besides Directorate-General E: the Directorates-General I (responsible for economic and fiscal policy strategy), V (dealing inter alia with legal issues) and the above-mentioned Directorate-General VII. I wondered why no formal collaboration or even task force was being set up to bring colleagues together from across the Ministry and, in fact, from different Ministries across the government as in countless other examples.

This was arguably because of confidentiality reasons. With the benefit of hindsight, it could also be one of those cases in which politicians take strategic decisions without bureaucrats even having considered them. Politics and administration are neighbouring spheres with many overlaps—but they are also separate indeed.

The same is true within bureaucratic institutions. Coming from the ECB, I had already experienced friction and struggle between different Directorates-General working more in parallel than jointly on issues of common concern. Usually, it is difficult to settle the initial division of labour, the so-called *Federführung* (defining the unit in charge), and hierarchies are frequently required to sort out differences in analysis, interpretation and interests accruing at working level. But in the case of Greece, the unusually harsh restriction on collegial exchange was baffling to me. Did senior staff at the Ministry have no trust in the discretion of civil servants at working level? Or did they simply not want the experts to have an open-minded debate on the matter? Had the politicians already taken a decision?

To me, the way the administrators embarked upon the narrow question of *how* to bail out Greece—rather than the wider, strategic question of *whether* to bail out Greece—very much smacked of a foregone conclusion;

only faintly assuaged by the understanding that this was to be 'just an option'.

German Bureaucracy at Work

A German Federal Ministry normally works along regular, formal lines—laid down in law and implementing documents such as an elaborate organisational chart, a plan of the division of labour (*Geschäftsverteilungsplan*) and, above all, the common rules of procedure of Federal Ministries (*Gemeinsame Geschäftsordnung der Bundesministerien*), which is usually accompanied by a specific *Geschäftsordnung* for each Ministry. A central principle to the rules of procedure is the involvement of all divisions (*Referate*) concerned by a specific issue—according to the *Geschäftsverteilungsplan*. Likewise, the Ministry itself must involve all other Ministries concerned, as agreed in the rules of procedure of the government itself (*Geschäftsordnung der Bundesregierung*).

According to the rules of procedure of Federal Ministries, complex short-term problems which require experts from several units should be addressed by task forces. As stated above, such a *Projektgruppe* was, however, not set up for handling the impending insolvency of Greece or any of the subsequent operations.

Also, according to the rules of procedure, the Minister would discuss all issues of political relevance at regular meetings at least once a month with all Directors-General of his or her Ministry. For the Ministry of Finance, this was the so-called *Abteilungsleiterkonferenz*. It debated all kinds of issues but not whether to bail out Greece.

It seemed to me as if such things cannot be done if they are properly discussed beforehand. Or as if, from a political point of view, you must want something not to happen if you allow for a broad and comprehensive discussion.

Politicians hardly ever write. By contrast, civil servants are required to produce and work on formally written texts, such as meeting minutes and subject briefings, the so-called *Vorlagen*. The principle of producing written text (*Schriftlichkeit*) is fundamental to the German administration.

A *Vorlage* has a clearly defined template by which an issue is to be presented either for information or for decision to a specific level of hierarchy. If a *Vorlage* is addressed to the Minister, a so-called *M-Vorlage*, it needs to pass all levels of hierarchy from the Division (*Referat*) via the

Directorate (*Unterabteilung*) and the Directorate-General (*Abteilung*) and the State Secretary.

The official in charge of each level of hierarchy can add her or his remarks on the *Vorlage* or send it back with requests for clarification or change. Such remarks are to be made in specific colours: The Head of Division signs the *Vorlage* in black ink, after having obtained agreement among all other divisions involved under her or his *Federführung*, which must all be listed in the bottom line. The Director then signs the cover sheet in brown colour, the Director-General in blue and the State Secretary in red. Frequently, they also add remarks, underlining or stress specific points to the Minister's attention.

Obviously, both formal and informal meetings, phone calls, floor conversations and email traffic take place before, during and after the pinning down of written text—but the *Vorlage* itself is the definitive product of the Ministry at work. Once signed off by the Minister or, depending on the issue, at a lower level of hierarchy, the document is then sent back down the administrative ladder for implementation and will ultimately find its way into the files of the Ministry, subsequently the local archives and, eventually, the federal archives—where, after usually 30 years, it can be accessed by the interested public.

Digital word processing has had a profound impact on the nature of *Vorlagen* texts: Prior to the presence of a network PC or laptop on the desk of each civil servant as of the 1990s, the *Vorlage* would have to be written by hand or, usually, spoken onto a dictating machine and typed by professional typists. As a consequence, there was a certain barrier to changing texts once they had been put into writing by a Division, leading to the old bureaucratic saying that 'he who writes, remains' (w*er schreibt, der bleibt*).

Fellow Heads of Divisions and even superiors would scribble not only their remarks but, in mild cases, even their dissent onto the *Vorlage* rather than sending it back for corrections, and the Minister could be assured that the text before his or her eyes not only was the message that he or she wanted to hear but indeed represented the expert advice of all involved line Divisions.

In formal terms, a Head of Division even has the right to present his or her *Vorlage* to the Minister if the latter asks for a meeting on the issue—obviously in the presence of the respective superiors. In practice, however, Ministers usually do not have a habit of speaking to Heads of Division, and, frequently, meetings of State Secretaries and Director-Generals with the Minister will bundle a whole range of different issues.

Since the advent of digital and interconnected word-processing, a *Vorlage*, before it is signed, is frequently sent around, passing back and forth both horizontally and hierarchically in draft versions. The resulting text is a conglomerate of what the Division in charge has drafted plus the amendments of other Divisions and superiors. Often, the language glosses over differences in opinion, and the whole matter is portrayed as one of consensus. Meanwhile, hard copies of these texts have entirely come out of fashion, having been replaced completely by electronic documents in a shared data warehouse (*E-Akte*).

The facility of contemporary digital word processing often tempts Directors, Director-Generals and even State Secretaries to substantially re-write a *Vorlage* that reaches them electronically in draft format, especially when the issue is sensitive or controversial. A Head of Division then, in extreme cases, gets to put her or his signature under a *Vorlage* that only faintly resembles the original draft produced by his or her Division or, worse still, that contains a few but highly substantial changes to the original judgement—and the nature of hierarchy will usually make it rather difficult to resist or, as it is formally known, remonstrate. In any case, a formal remonstration by the Head of Division is only possible in cases of strictly legal reservations and not for differences in opinion and judgement.

The workings of the German ministerial bureaucracy, dating back to Prussia and beyond, are hence elaborate, collegial, legalistic, comprehensive, thorough, and rigorous—but often enough slow, grinding and even prone to indiscretion, given the large number of civil servants involved in the formal proceedings of an overblown and hypertrophic body politic.

Yet, internal breeches of secrecy are seldom and in fact superseded by a far greater problem, linked to a legal sea change enacted literally during the last days in office of the left-green coalition ruling Germany until 2005: Its freedom-of-information act, the so-called *Informationsfreiheitsgesetz*, effectively did away with the secrecy of ministerial proceedings, including that of any *Vorlage*, which could, from now on, simply be requested for disclosure by any journalist, agency or ordinary citizen. The advocates of transparency might have overlooked the fact that sensitive information and important, controversial decisions—if put into writing at all—require confidentiality.

On top of that, the German government is required by law to hand all written documents on issues of European integration to Parliament[3]—and Parliament can be a notorious place for leaks to the press. This made it impossible for us to officially receive sensitive external documents from 'Europe' or to distribute our own documents to European partners or institutions and fora. Sometimes, however, when we did not like the proposals contained therein, we could point to our obligation to forward them to Parliament—and thereby avoid having to discuss them in the first place.

The pervasive lack of secrecy is the main reason why the Federal archives will contain only part of the relevant records on Greece: The most relevant ones simply do not exist because the bureaucracy of government does not and, in fact, cannot fully adhere anymore to the principle of *Schriftlichkeit*.

Oral decisions on sensitive matters, non-attributable documents, or the destruction of official documents have of course already occurred in the past. It is impossible to say for sure whether such practices have increased over time, but I certainly gained that impression from conversations with older colleagues. Hence, the not only secretive but oftentimes simply non-existent nature of government typework is important for future scholars to bear in mind, when searching ministerial archives. Even more important will be interviews with former administrators, if they are willing to cooperate with scholars.

While numerous *Vorlagen* are still being written in the old-fashioned way, sensitive texts nowadays more and more take the form of so-called 'one-pagers' and 'non-papers'. This is the case not only in Berlin, but also in European institutions and other European capitals, according to my experience. These are informal memos, often without addressee and signatory, sometimes even without a date. Their authors take care to anonymise them and to minimise all data referring to the origin and purpose of the text. They are passed on electronically and hardly ever registered. Such documents have become pervasive both in the European as well as in the German administrations and in the intercourse between Member States.

[3] https://www.gesetze-im-internet.de/euzbbg_2013/BJNR217000013.html#:~:text=%C2%A7%201%20Mitwirkung%20des%20Bundestages,zum%20fr%C3%BChestm%C3%B6glichen%20Zeitpunkt%20zu%20unterrichten.

While the dangers to secrecy are real, contemporary work-arounds often also serve as a useful excuse for restricting the circle of collaboration and shared knowledge to the utmost minimum. This endangers the bureaucratic principle of involving all relevant units (*Beteiligung*) and—by consequence—raises the danger that important elements of a complex matter are overlooked or not sufficiently appraised.

Legal Appraisal

On Greece, this inner circle of deliberations was only sometimes enlarged when highly specific points required special expertise from Directorates-General other than the core team in the Directorate-General European policy. For example, the Division in charge of constitutional law was asked early-on in the process to assess the risks of German citizens or Members of Parliament appealing to the Constitutional Court in Karlsruhe against the Federal Republic extending financial assistance to Greece. This Division proceeded entirely in line with the old-fashioned formal rules: After consultation with the Ministry of Interior Affairs and the Ministry of Justice, it involved all other relevant Divisions in the Ministry of Finance and concluded that there was indeed a significant but manageable legal risk attached to the envisaged bailout.

In its famous Maastricht verdict, the Court had clearly ruled out the transfer of liabilities between participating Member States.[4] No country could rid itself from the consequences of an unsustainable fiscal policy. In fact, German membership to the currency union would be unlawful if the euro area were to become anything else than a *Stabilitätsgemeinschaft:* literally a 'community of stability'. Hence, Karlsruhe's Maastricht ruling gave, from the point of view of German constitutional law, a very clear and indeed restrictive interpretation of the so-called no-bailout clause laid down in Article 125 of the Treaty itself, which prohibits the Union or a Member State from assuming the liabilities of another Member State.

The open question in constitutional terms was, whether 'assuming liabilities' meant the same as 'extending credit lines' or 'granting a loan'. In other words, would it be legally possible to do what my former ECB

[4] http://www.bverfg.de/e/rs19980331_2bvr187797.html.

colleagues had anticipated a few weeks earlier: Circumvent the Maastricht Treaty's no-bailout-clause without breaking it, regardless of what the spirit of that clause had originally implied?

As it turned out, the Legal Division in February 2010 in its analysis correctly predicted the first of a whole string of legal proceedings before the German Constitutional Court as well as before the European Court of Justice, proceedings which were to accompany our efforts at stabilising the euro over the next couple of years. But our legal experts also correctly predicted that the no-bailout clause would *not* preclude bilateral assistance of the form we were envisaging—a repayable loan—simply because the Treaty did not cover that eventuality. It also pointed to the German budget law as enabling the federal government to assume guarantees with future budgetary implications if required by 'specific public interest to the Federal Republic', implying that the stabilisation of the euro area could be seen as being in Germany's own best interest. It cautioned against the precedence which would be set and criticised the Treaty for failing to provide a legal basis for state insolvency. The EU's rules-based framework on fiscal deficits and debt were seen as a feeble substitute for the missing treatment of state insolvency: They had arguably the purpose to prevent state insolvency and, by 2010, they had most evidently failed to do so. Interestingly, the Bundesbank, in its 1998 convergence report prior to entering the final phase of monetary union, had already anticipated that the no-bailout clause would not safely preclude measures of bilateral financial assistance.[5]

As much as bilateral assistance hence appeared possible from a legal point of view, the Ministry's lawyers saw no chance to apply EU resources to the Greek bailout. They pointed to Article 122 of the Treaty which, in Paragraph 2, envisages union financial assistance to a Member State in case of 'severe difficulties caused by natural disasters or exceptional occurrences beyond its control'—but applying this provision to the case at hand seemed out of the question: The budgetary emergency of Greece was self-inflicted and could have been prevented by less reckless fiscal policy in the past. Even the preceding banking and financial crisis was only one—and not the principal cause—of the current impasse. The principal cause indeed, according to the Ministry's experts, was Greece's deplorable

[5] https://www.bundesbank.de/resource/blob/691524/47af4189b2d15ae6c9edbae0f63091c6/mL/1998-04-konvergenzlage-data.pdf.

track record of years and years of wrong economic, budgetary, and financial market policies. I do not recall any colleague at the time doubting whether this narrative was correct and complete—despite the fact that there had already for a decade been a wide-ranging debate in academia on the systemic origins of imbalances in the euro area (e.g. Scharpf 2002, Enderlein 2004).

In any case, Article 122 would only allow taking recourse to the existing EU budget envelope. Taking on credit on behalf of the EU could be envisaged on the basis of Article 352, the so-called flexibility clause—but this would require a consensus decision by the Council, subject to an enabling law in the German Bundestag:

The German *Integrationsverantwortungsgesetz*, the 'law on responsible integration', had been adopted in the previous year following the ruling of the Constitutional Court on the ratification of the Lisbon Treaty. It stipulates with regard to Article 352 that the German government could only agree to a proposed measure if specifically allowed to do so by a national law to be passed both by the Bundestag, the Federal chamber, and the Bundesrat, the representation of the *Länder*.

This law interacts with the above-mentioned legal duty of the government to report to both Bundestag and Bundestag about its European dealings "comprehensively, as early as possible and continuously"—an issue giving rise to several defeats of the government against the Bundestag before the Constitutional Court over the years to come, pushing the administration to seek at least informal secrecy about its dealings in European affairs, as discussed above.

As regards the credit-funding of possible EU financial assistance to Greece, the Legal Division concluded that Germany's domestic legal requirements would be insurmountable: Given that sufficient assistance was to be already extended bilaterally, additional EU assistance would simply not be necessary and hence run counter the principle of subsidiarity. It was also argued that EU assistance would set a dangerous precedent towards institutionalisation, ending up in a permanent European financial transfer and equalisation scheme akin to Germany's *Länderfinanzausgleich*—something dreaded by every federal civil servant working in the field of public finance.

It is important to understand that, looking at Athens and Brussels, the Federal Ministry of Finance in Berlin was already painfully acquainted with decades of financial and legal struggle between the federal and the

Länder levels in Germany herself. In fact, the Ministry's Legal Division belonged to exactly the Directorate-General V which was primarily occupied with these intricate domestic financial relations...

Banks at Risk

Besides the legal dimension, there was another point of highly specific interest requiring expert advice. This issue was arguably even the core motivation for embracing the bailout in the first place: the exposure of German and other European banks to Greek public debt.

Europe was still reverberating with the financial and banking crisis of 2007/8, triggered by the excessive accumulation of bad assets in banks' balance sheets on the back of global bubbles in bad credit, such as US subprime mortgages. Were Greek sovereign credits and bonds going to be the next bubble to burst, from a banking point of view?

This was an issue for the Ministry's Directorate-General VII (financial market policy). It had presided over the setting up of Germany's bailout fund for banks, the *Sonderfonds Finanzmarktstabilisierung* (SoFFin), which mustered a capacity to guarantee banks with up to 400bn EUR and to inject up to 80bn EUR in capital.

Ten banking institutions had taken recourse to the SoFFin and required approximately half of the available guarantee envelope and about a fourth of the capital available for injection. In other words, the SoFFin had kept most of its powder dry—as it was in fact meant to be. The by far largest engagements were Hypo Real Estate, West LB and HSH Nordbank, and the SoFFin eventually closed its doors in 2018 with a loss to the German taxpayer of 22.6bn EUR.[6] This compares rather unfavourably with the tougher measures enacted by other Member States in defending the public interest against the bonfire of private credit sprees turned bad (Bertelsmann Stiftung 2010; Zohlnhöfer 2011; Schuknecht and Siegerink 2020; Schuknecht 2021).

One had to assume that the so-called bad banks already in resolution under the auspices of the SoFFin would probably have Greek bonds on their balances—as it turned out to be the case, this was primarily true for former Hypo Real Estate and West LB assets. But how about the banking sector at large? Wouldn't a Greek default mean a sudden,

[6] https://www.deutsche-finanzagentur.de/fileadmin/user_upload/finanzmarktstabilisierung/Bericht_Geschaeftsjahr_2018_FMS.pdf.

automatic, and unavoidable recoil into financial nemesis, as bad or even worse as in 2007/8, when nobody in the market knew their counterparts' exposure to bad assets, precipitating a meltdown first in the interbank money-market and subsequently leading to the fall of Lehman Brothers?

'Greece will be ten times worse than Lehman', was a message sent many times a day to Berlin, particularly from New York, Washington, and London but also from the skyscrapers and certain twin-towers in Frankfurt. But how bad could it really be?

Colleagues in Directorate-General VII had no means to give a precise and reliable answer. First, one would need to know the direct exposure. I was surprised how difficult it already seemed to obtain this factual point of information. We looked at a rough overview by the Bank for International Settlements (BIS) in Basel, the self-declared 'central bank of central banks'.

According to the BIS, total foreign banking claims on Greek debtors (public and private) at the end of 2009 amounted to 298bn USD, of which 107bn USD were owed by the Greek state. I was wondering how this could really be ten times worse than the Lehman balance in 2008, which had amounted to 639bn USD. But I was told and accepted that a sovereign default would be a significantly worse shock to market sentiment than a banking default. Sovereign debt is, in simple terms, commonly used to build the bedrock component of low-risk assets held by banks and corporations against which they in turn can borrow from the market: Among their risk-weighted assets, sovereign debt stands for very low risk and high liquidity.

By consequence, one would need to investigate the different holdings of Greek public debt, and here the BIS data was incomplete. We only knew that French and Swiss banks each held about 80bn USD in Greek debt (public and private), of which well over 20bn USD were held by French banks in public debt and less than 10bn USD by Swiss banks. German banks were exposed like the French ones with about 20bn USD in public debt and, less than those in France, with about 40bn USD in total debt. Significant exposure to Greek public debt was also accrued by US banks (roughly 5bn USD), as well as Dutch and Irish banks (each about 8bn USD).

Despite frequent exchanges with the national banking supervisor, the *Bundesanstalt für Finanzdienstleistungsaufsicht* (BaFin), we did not know exactly how these sums would subdivide among the individual institutions—and we had to assume that, if we did not know, they would not know either about each other's exposure and could therefore not measure risk precisely. These were Rumsfeld's 'known unkowns' mentioned above.

Hence, there seemed indeed to be a situation akin to the frightening wave of uncertainty that had washed across financial markets in the preceding crisis: A Greek default would immediately cause a so-called 'first-round effect' by drilling a hole in each bank's assets to the extent that this bank was directly exposed to the Greek state or to Greek debt in general. The second-round effect would consist of that bank subsequently encountering trouble in refinancing itself and thereby starting to fail. The magnitude of the second-round effect would be defined by the combined size of the affected banks' balance sheets. The dreaded third-round effect would then consist of a general meltdown in market confidence and mutual trust, getting us back to square one of the financial crisis with the danger of wide-spread bank runs and a sudden partial or even total collapse of the system. The magnitude of the third-round effect was anybody's guess, but we did remember from 2008 that, eventually, everything is connected to everything else, and, by consequence, there would be unexpected correlations of unexpected events of the largest scale—the 'unkown unkowns'...

Two years later, I had the chance to ask a very senior advisor to the Federal Chancellor about his thoughts at the time. Did he not think that we already had put all necessary preparations in stock to weather this renewed storm, the SoFFin and all legal provisions, including the *Patronatserklärung* of 2008 by which the German government had guaranteed all private saving accounts (a successful bluff committing in fact a multiple of annual tax revenue)?

Yes, he replied, according to his judgement, our financial market stabilisation package would have carried the day also in 2010—with a likelihood of 90%. But he went on to say to me: 'A 10% tail risk is too much if you bear the political responsibility. The Chancellor was not going to have it'. And why, I insisted, did he then not recommend ramping up the precautions for financial market stabilisation rather than entering the business of sovereign loans? 'That would have taken too much time', was his reply. 'And it seemed back then that it would be even more costly than the sovereign bailout. After all, we were expecting our money back from Greece—in full and with interest'.

Policymakers were also acutely aware that Greece could well be only the beginning of a much more serious landslide in geographic terms. It was considered the weakest link in a chain of euro area Member States with a position of public finances which had either already been unsustainable before the banking crisis or was quickly becoming so as a result thereof.

Hence, the fear of contagion was palpable. While lamenting the lack of rules and procedures for state insolvency, nobody wanted to risk one in the first place: Talking about rules-based state insolvency is, in a way, time-inconsistent. You want it in principle but not in practice.

Allowing Greece to go bankrupt and fending the financial shockwave off by countermeasures in the banking sector was, from this point of view, suboptimal because other countries would likely follow suit and thereby push the overall second and third-round effects in financial markets beyond any limit of control. If contagion were to happen, one would rather have it in the public sector than elsewhere, given the comparatively lower order of magnitude.

Kicking the Can Down the Road

On February 11th, the day following the internal German decision to prepare a bailout option, the Heads of State and Government of the EU convened and declared: 'Euro area Member States will take determined and coordinated action, if needed, to safeguard financial stability in the euro area as a whole. The Greek government has not requested any financial support'.[7] It was clear to all market participants that Greece required about 10bn EUR in April to roll over its debt due in that month alone. Bond issuances in March were helped by the declaration as well as by Greek domestic austerity measures, but it was far from clear whether market confidence could thereby be restored in a lasting manner.

I privately thought that one thing could be even worse than no market demand at all for fresh Greek debt: a single buyer, in the form of China. While there were no indications whatsoever that China could contemplate becoming a major creditor to Greece, I wondered whether that scenario was only in the back of my mind alone.

At the same time, I thought it unwise to hint at possible German support to Greece only to assuage markets. We should not offer help in the hope of not being asked to help, I noted in my diary. Market participants would smell this attitude and punish our lack of credibility. It did

[7] https://www.consilium.europa.eu/media/20485/112856.pdf.

not seem wise to go for a lurching course. I wrote down: 'We will be taken at our word on the part of Greece as soon as the markets stop taking us at our word'. And if we had to pay anyway, we should better think of some strategy what to ask for in return. The consequences of our current approach, I believed, were to be contagion and the further building up of debt, ultimately also on our balance. This, in the long run, could only lead to inflation—and we would get nothing 'strategic' in exchange.

In any case, the Ministry was launching the necessary legal procedure required to back up a possible bilateral loan through a guarantee by the federal budget. It proposed an amendment to the draft annual budget law for 2010, which was delayed in that particular year because of the federal election in 2009. The bilateral loan was to be extended by Germany's state bank, the *Kreditanstalt für Wiederaufbau* (KfW).

In legal terms, the government would be asking Parliament to approve taking on its books guarantees of up to 50bn EUR for loans to euro area Member States for emergency measures sustaining their solvency. The law was to be accompanied by an explanatory paragraph stating that such loans would secure the functioning of EMU and the stability of financial markets in the euro area. It also stipulated that these loans would represent the German contribution to a coordinated effort and would be contingent on the financial contribution of other euro area Member States. The budget law was planned to come into effect in early April 2010, retroactively for the whole year.

The financial market experts saw that this formal and transparent budgetary procedure as preferable over any emergency legislation at the last minute: Waiting until the danger of a state bankruptcy had become imminent would trigger hefty reactions on the financial markets. By contrast, precautionary action should be taken while this was still possible. The legal experts shared this preference and argued that the alternative—i.e. emergency measures—would also show a lack of respect for the other constitutional organs involved in the proceedings.

The proposed amendment of the budget law was reported by the press on 22 February 2010 but then subsequently shelved upon request of the Chancellery. When the budget came into effect on 6 April 2010, it did not contain the provisions recommended by the Ministry's experts.

In line with the Ministry's legal judgement, a possible rescue package for Greece did not entail an EU component. However, another multilateral donor did come into play, in addition to the bilateral loans of euro area Member States: This was the International Monetary Fund (IMF), and IMF involvement became a highly political issue by early March.

At the outset, and from a strictly legal point of view, it posed the least of problems, given that a classical IMF programme was in principle available to all IMF members in the event of a balance of payments-crisis—with the drawback that, originally, IMF programmes had been designed to deal with shortfalls in *foreign*, not domestic, currency. The Bundesbank did not fail to point this out in its monthly bulletin of March 2010, stressing the 'monetary character' of the IMF.[8]

Proponents of IMF involvement argued that only the 'Fund', as it was commonly called, had the expertise to structure a programme of reform for an entire country, in macro- and microeconomic terms. This view was held by those colleagues in the Ministry who worked on international financial relations as well as by a very small but influential group of Christian Democrat Members of Parliament. As it turned out, this view was also held by the economics staff at the Chancellery.

Opponents of IMF-involvement fell into two camps: There were those, usually of left-wing political persuasion, who criticised the neoliberal worldview held by the Washington-based institution, a worldview epitomised by the saying that the acronym 'IMF' stood for 'it's mostly fiscal'. Others, and those included the German Minister of Finance Wolfgang Schäuble, saw the political clout of non-European IMF Member States, above all that of the USA, coming to bear unduly on intra-European affairs if the IMF were to provide a loan and to structure and run the corresponding reform programme.

Furthermore, Schäuble saw the historical chance to fix the institutional deficiencies of the single currency. Even though he had to undergo medical treatment and was hospitalised, Schäuble declared on 7 March 2010: 'We should look at improvements to the institutional framework. (…) The euro area wants to solve its problems on its own. (…) For the internal architecture of the euro area, we need an institution with the experience of the IMF and corresponding powers of execution' (Welt am Sonntag, 07.03.2010, own translation).

The Ministry had already prepared the concept for a future European Monetary Fund (EMF). In case of a euro area Member State running into a debt crisis, the EMF should provide liquidity assistance under

[8] https://www.bundesbank.de/resource/blob/706992/b7025649902da9f90a9bd88f04c8348b/mL/2010-03-monthly-report-data.pdf, page 60.

strict conditions—including a prohibition against accepting money from the IMF. In addition, there would be rules on state insolvency if the country concerned did not comply with the reforms prescribed by the EMF. Finally, a non-complying country could be expelled from the single currency or leave on its own accord. Decision-making on loans, reform programmes, insolvency and exit would be made upon proposal by the EMF and subject to consensus by the Eurogroup, without the vote of the Member State concerned. As a precautionary measure, sanctions of the Stability and Growth Pact (SGP) would be reinforced and made more 'biting'—with the aim to avoid debt crises in the first place. For example, a country not complying with the SGP rulebook would lose its vote in the decision-making bodies of the single currency.

The press hailed the German EMF-initiative as 'Berlin's masterplan for the euro area' and Commission Vice-President for Economic and Monetary Affairs Olli Rehn declared his readiness to table the legislative proposal. Within the government, the liberal party, coalition partner of the ruling Christian Democrats, was also in full support—expressed by Economics Minister Rainer Brüderle who made additional proposals for the governance and funding of a future EMF. However, the legal experts of the Finance Ministry pointed to the need for Treaty change if Schäuble's initiative was to see the light of day.

Worse still, Chancellor Angela Merkel appeared to be at best lukewarm about the idea. After a state visit of Greek Prime Minister Giorgos Papandreou in Berlin, she declared that Greece needed no financial assistance (Frankfurter Allgemeine Zeitung, 12.03.2010, own translation). Any future EMF would not be connected to the current issue at hand and was rather a conceptual idea for the very long term. Following a meeting with the Prime Minister of Luxembourg and Chairman of the Eurogroup, Jean-Claude Juncker, she said to a puzzled audience:

> From my point of view, it is such that we see that a region, which has its own and common currency, is not in a position to react in all cases, which may turn up, adequately when you look at it in terms of readiness for the future. You can perhaps construct a projection. We have felt to be politically responsible. But a European reaction is not foreseen. If we want to have a common currency, we should envisage this possibility. Today we do not have it as such. It is hence about a further development of the Treaties, which in no way is going to soften the Stability and Growth Pact, but in fact sharpens its instruments. After all, the sanction that you

> pay money to the EU turns out as not particularly sensible in the case of Greece, because this concerns a shortage of money and not an abundance of money. Hence, this is a learning process. (ibid.)

On 10 February 2010, the German Chancellor met with French Prime Minister François Fillon. Both applauded the success of recent Greek policies and said that any future EMF, if it would come into being at all, could not be seen as a support measure in favour of Greece currently. Merkel declared:

> We spoke about the issue and which lessons we should possibly draw from such a situation as it currently exists with Greece. But we have to think beyond that. And I say that the possibilities of sanctions have to be sharpened and that the possibility, as ultima ratio, to create an EMF, is indeed a good idea, which we must discuss in detail. This is a big task, and it will only be possible with Treaty change. But Germany and France will have intensive discussions about this. It is such that we have to realise in the face of the problems in connection with Greece that the instruments, for example of sanctions in the Maastricht Treaty and in the Stability and Growth Pact, are not sufficiently given. (ibid.)

Merkel also spoke about the ambition of the 'Euro-family' to solve its problems internally and added:

> This is the goal of the EMF, including the issue of state insolvency in an orderly procedure, in order to avoid a situation which we know from the banking side, growing into a systemic risk. (…) The experts have to work out the details, but the EMF so to speak stands at the end of a chain of what I think are necessary reactions in such a situation. The highest duty is to do everything necessary to prevent such a situation in the future. (ibid.)

The ECB throughout the debate kept a low profile, neither endorsing nor rejecting Schäuble's initiative. Schäuble, still in hospital, conceded that his idea was 'in no way' meant to deal with Greece but wrote in the same op-ed: 'Without doubt, it will take a great deal of political willpower to adapt the rules of monetary union speedily to suit the new realities. Yet there is no alternative to monetary union' (Financial Times, 12.03.2010).

Looking, first, at the unsuccessful attempt to amend the budget law and, second, at the floundering EMF-initiative, the press was quick to detect a deep rift between the German Chancellor and her Finance

Minister and uncovered that Merkel had even tried to stop Schäuble from going public about the EMF (Handelsblatt, 12.03.2010). On 19 March, the Minister, just out of hospital and visibly weakened, delivered his closing speech for the budget debate before the Bundestag.[9] There was not even a mention of Greece or the EMF anymore, only an appeal to respect the SGP.

In my diary, I noted about the debate of EMF vs. IMF: 'On the great march towards inflation, this question is a mere footnote'. I was sceptical about the prospect of institutional change anyway. The status quo was path-dependent and backed by insurmountable vested interests. Did Schäuble not see this, I wondered, or did he just pretend to believe in the possibility of strategic reform? And which of these two possibilities would I find more worrying?

As far as Merkel was concerned, she had irritated European and international observers in her budget speech, delivered to the Bundestag two days earlier, on 17 March.[10] She had floated the idea of not extending 'premature help' but rather expelling a non-complying country from the single currency: 'We need to have an agreement under which, as a last resort, it's possible to exclude a country from the euro zone if again and again it doesn't fulfil the requirements' (Wall Street Journal, 18.03.2010).

While this was geared at pleasing a domestic audience, it ran against strong resistance elsewhere. ECB President Jean-Claude Trichet, for example, declared that membership to the single currency was about sharing a common destiny and that the notion of expelling a Member State was 'absurd' (ibid.).

France and other European countries also became more vocal in blaming Germany's export dependency for the crisis, combined with her refusal to increase spending and reduce tax levels and thereby stimulate domestic demand. But within the German administration, there was only one predominant view: Greece had to consolidate its budget and conduct structural reforms to increase its competitiveness. The causes of the crisis had nothing to do with Germany or, for that matter, with systemic imbalances in the euro area. Against that worldview, French Finance Minister Christine Lagarde, among others, suggested: 'Germany could perhaps (...) lower taxes to encourage internal consumption. (...) Those with

[9] https://dserver.bundestag.de/btp/17/17032.pdf.

[10] https://dserver.bundestag.de/btp/17/17030.pdf.

deficits need to reduce them (…) and those with a surplus should accept considering the idea of moving beyond a single source of growth to find other sources of growth' (ibid.).

In fact, the balanced budget, nicknamed "*schwarze Null*" (black zero) was reached in 2012 and became a widely perceived trademark for Schäuble's reign in the Ministry of Finance, akin to a political heritage—notwithstanding that it had been his predecessor Peer Steinbrück who in fact had coined the phrase of 'black zero'. On a strict expenditure policy, Schäuble enjoyed Merkel's public backing when she stated in her budget speech before Parliament: 'Germany will not forfeit its export strength' (ibid.). In other words, Germany would not accept any form of European coordination of trade balances inside the common currency.

It is important to understand that domestic German politics had come to bear heavily on the issue of a Greek bailout. The most important of all regional elections was due on 9 May 2010, the one in North-Rhine-Westphalia (NRW), being the most populous among the *Länder* and the largest economic building block inside Germany with an economy commensurate to that of the Netherlands.

The NRW election is traditionally seen as a 'small federal election'. The ruling Christian Democrats were trailing in the polls and the incumbent Prime Minister, Jürgen Rüttgers, was tarnished by a fund-raising scandal. Defeat in NRW would have dire consequences from a viewpoint of federal politics: The Christian Democrats would thereby lose their majority in the *Bundesrat*, the second legislative chamber and representation of the *Länder*.

While European issues hardly ever dominate regional or federal elections in Germany, Greece had the potential to do so. Already for weeks, the tabloid BILD had run a campaign against the hard-working German taxpayer being held to ransom for the profligate Greek scapegraces who didn't pay taxes and went into retirement in their fifties. German citizens were made to understand that, as far as personal net wealth is concerned, they do not enjoy high ranks by comparison to other EU countries. Hence, why should they bail out Southerners who simply could not keep their public house in order? This view also had some sympathy with us civil servants and, in private conversations, with more than just a few politicians.

Some Taste of *Ordnung*

Economic thought in Germany is special, compared to Anglo-Saxon and Mediterranean views. In simplified terms, the latter trusts more in demand-side policy, whereas the traditional German emphasis leans much more towards the supply-side of the economy.

Inspired by academic thinkers of Schumpeterian persuasion, old-school German economic policy is required to respect the requirements of *Ordnungspolitik*, quite literally the 'policy of order'. Such policy will typically look at increasing productivity, reducing costs (wage and non-wage, e. g. taxation), spurning innovation and facilitating a business-friendly investment climate. It will generally not embrace Keynesian demand stimulation, deficit spending and the like.

While, from an empirical point of view, both schools of thought can rightfully claim to be appropriate—supply-side policy in the long-term and demand-side policy in the face of short-term challenges—a dogmatic rather than pragmatic approach in Germany used to gear the political system on average profoundly in favour of supply-side policy, preferably based on rules and semi-independent institutions. This tendency became particularly stark when applied to foreign debtor countries who received policy prescriptions with the aim of ensuring the repayment of German loans—according to German economic thought.

Germany and France persistently and systematically disagreed or at least misunderstood each other when discussing measures to spur economic growth and looking for the best way forward considering the debt crisis. Personally, I gained the impression that senior interlocutors from both countries were inadequately conscious of their intellectual disparity which permeates from academic debate through the political echelons right down to the various hierarchical levels of their respective bureaucracies. Both sides were not reflecting the peculiarities of their own position, clinging rather staunchly to the belief that their respective view of the world was the only sensible one to adopt.

This situation, I thought, was maybe not much of a problem as long as economic integration had remained rather limited—by now, however, the profound difference in economic culture between France and Germany had become the very essence of the European malaise. Given our financial leverage at the time, the German point of view prevailed momentarily—provided that the debt crisis could primarily be resolved through fiscal means. Inevitably, our dominance vanished as soon as monetisation through the ECB became the preferred and then only course of action. Hence this book argues that Merkelism has undermined Germany's predominance over economic policy in Europe. Had, instead, fiscal stabilisation been followed by institutional reform—the outcome would have been lastingly different.

There is also a striking contrast between the role of public finances in German and French politics. As civil servants, we sometimes envied our French colleagues for the largesse with which they could conduct financial diplomacy, comparatively undisturbed by domestic concerns of public opinion or Parliamentary proceedings or, for that matter, legal challenges before the Constitutional Court. No wonder that the international coordination of creditor countries in international financial relations is called the 'Paris Club' and convenes in the French capital, we thought.

By contrast, much has been said about Protestant ethics and the linguistic connection in German between 'debt' (*Schulden*) and 'blame' or 'guilt' (*Schuld*). 'Forgive us our trespasses', in the Lord's Prayer, is in German: '*Vergib' uns unsere Schuld*'. Also, a 'currency' in German is a *Währung* and thereby, linguistically, something lasting and solid. In terms of etymology, *Währung* is linked to *Gewährleistung*, which meant a sort of assurance that a coin contained the rightful amount of precious metal and was worth what it stood for.

Schäuble once said to us privately that one can win an election in Germany by promising the consolidation of public finances—but it will be extremely hard to implement, given the nature of German politics. In France, by contrast, the President could easily decide and implement austerity but would never be popular for doing so.

Financial diplomacy *à la française* to us seemed a branch of foreign policy and guided by the national interest and strategy of statecraft. In Angela Merkel's Germany, we sighed, we even lack the notion of national interest and strategic statecraft—but, instead, the people will ultimately hold the state accountable for how it treats private property through its economic, financial, and monetary policy.

Reaching the End of the Road

Back to the story: Mainly domestic considerations—NRW and the risk of being taken before the Constitutional Court—led the Chancellor to favour an IMF loan over the bilateral assistance package already drawn up by the Ministry of Finance in conjunction with the other euro area

Member States in the Eurogroup. It must be said that, compared to the Commission, there was also considerably more trust in the ability and impartiality of the Washington-based IMF to run a 'proper' programme on Greece.

At a meeting of the EU Heads of State and Government on 25 March 2010, Angela Merkel strongly resisted the European rescue plan and told Greece to turn to the IMF instead, if necessary. She did not prevail. The concluding summit statement combined both approaches, the bilateral one and the IMF loan[11]:

> Euro area member states reaffirm their willingness to take determined and coordinated action, if needed, to safeguard financial stability in the euro area as a whole, as decided the 11th of February. As part of a package involving substantial International Monetary Fund financing and a majority of European financing, Euro area member states are ready to contribute to coordinated bilateral loans. This mechanism, complementing International Monetary Fund financing, has to be considered ultima ratio, meaning in particular that market financing is insufficient. Any disbursement on the bilateral loans would be decided by the euro area member states by unanimity subject to strong conditionality and based on an assessment by the European Commission and the European Central Bank. We expect Euro-Member states to participate on the basis of their respective ECB capital key. The objective of this mechanism will not be to provide financing at average euro area interest rates, but to set incentives to return to market financing as soon as possible by risk adequate pricing. Interest rates will be non-concessional, i.e. not contain any subsidy element. Decisions under this mechanism will be taken in full consistency with the Treaty framework and national laws.

Merkel had sought also to enshrine in the statement the notion that a country should leave the single currency in cases of extreme non-compliance with the fiscal rule book. But there was no mentioning of that, only a commitment to revisit the SGP, as follows:

> The current situation demonstrates the need to strengthen and complement the existing framework to ensure fiscal sustainability in the euro zone and enhance its capacity to act in times of crises. For the future, surveillance

[11] https://www.consilium.europa.eu/media/21429/20100325-statement-of-the-heads-of-state-or-government-of-the-euro-area-en.pdf.

> of economic and budgetary risks and the instruments for their prevention, including the Excessive Deficit Procedure, must be strengthened. Moreover, we need a robust framework for crisis resolution respecting the principle of member states' own budgetary responsibility.

The President of the European Council, the first one under the Lisbon Treaty, Herman Van Rompuy, was asked to set up a task force with the Commission, the ECB and the rotating Council Presidency with the aim to 'explore all options to reinforce the legal framework' before year-end. But this was just a side-show to the overall outcome of the summit: As of 25 March, the scene was ready for a coordinated public bailout of Greece by the other euro area Member States in conjunction with the IMF.

The SGP reform foreseeably would not lead to much, given that substantial progress required legislative changes to primary law. French Finance Minister Christine Lagarde had already declared: 'It is not desirable to fundamentally reform the Treaty of Lisbon' (Handelsblatt, 19.03.2010, own translation). This was not even surprising, given that, unlike Germany, France is a democracy which can and indeed does hold a referendum upon ratification of European Treaties. While such a referendum is constitutionally required only in Ireland and technically optional in France, it seemed politically impossible to dodge it: The French people in 2005 had already rejected the Treaty establishing a Constitution for Europe—a lasting trauma for any politician in favour of enhanced European integration. Therefore, most European politicians at best paid lip-service to the need of Treaty change—with Wolfgang Schäuble being one of the notable exceptions to lay out concrete proposals and elements of Treaty change.

Commission Vice President Rehn sketched his views on euro area governance reform during a Eurogroup meeting in Madrid on 16 April. Like Germany, the Commission favoured a strengthened SGP, albeit short of Treaty change and thereby incorporating the caveat of France and other Member States. The EDP should get 'teeth' primarily from additional sanctions. These should be applied to non-complying Member States by cutting their receipts from structural and cohesion funds. The Commission wanted to enhance economic policy coordination by monitoring macroeconomic imbalances and divergences in competitiveness. Under the SGP, Brussels should get powers for a so-called ex ante coordination of budgetary policies of euro area Member States. Finally, Rehn took up Schäuble's EMF proposal and suggested a permanent mechanism for crisis resolution instead of ad-hoc assistance.

Schäuble welcomed Rehn's proposals, especially those on strengthening the EDP. But some of Rehn's ideas fell entirely on deaf ears in Berlin. Germany outright rejected any notion of ex-ante coordination of national fiscal policies which was seen as a national and, for that matter, Parliamentary prerogative. Germany also rejected any more binding treatment of macroeconomic imbalances—which would likely have touched upon the already controversial German economic policy strategy based on balanced budgets and export-driven growth. As concerned the new mechanism—or institution—for crisis resolution, Germany doubted the Commission's view that this initiative could be based on Article 136 of the Treaty. Here, Berlin saw the need and indeed the lever for Treaty change. Under a reform of primary law, Germany would have pushed for a general suspension of voting rights of Member States in non-compliance with the EDP, as well as for the ultimate option of forcing their exit from the single currency. It was clear that the Van Rompuy Task Force, which was to start work on 21 May, would not easily agree on governance reform.

Would the EU statement of 25 March be sufficient to calm markets and to allow for a regular roll over? We looked at the calendar of Greek obligations coming due: 5bn EUR would have to be raised by 10 April, and a total of 22bn EUR was required by the end of May. The yield had risen to over 6%, bringing the spread above the Bund to over 3 percentage points. At some point, the increase in interest payments would outweigh any discretionary cuts to primary spending—and the deficit would spiral out of control.

Not only Merkel, but also Greek Prime Minister Papandreou had a domestic policy problem: His austerity measures were hugely unpopular and, obviously, the public understood that all hard-earned savings would be consumed by the ever-growing burden of debt service. Public sector pay cuts and a new pension law were coming into force, accompanied by a new tax law that did not even spare the Orthodox Church anymore. Ordinary people were losing benefits, loopholes, and dearly held privileges by the minute and were being asked to contribute ever more—but for what? For the coffers of international financial investors, evidently.

In that situation, Papandreou obviously thought that external assistance could maybe assuage the political storm as well as market pressure. He therefore increasingly vocally called on his European partners to prepare it. An offer for assistance on the table, according to Papandreou, could be enough to tell the markets: 'Hands off, no speculation. Let this country do what it is doing' (Wall Street Journal, 19.03.2010).

On Monday 29 March, Greece placed its 5bn EUR bond on the market. Despite a duration of only seven years and an interest rate of staggering 5.9%, investor appetite was remarkably low. According to market observers, French state banks were among the biggest bidders (Frankfurter Allgemeine Zeitung, 30.03.2010). The transaction had an overall signalling effect, with Greek sovereign and CDS rates rising only slightly upward. The immediate sense of crisis receded somewhat—but only for one week. Already during the second week of April, Greek bond yields resumed their steep climb upwards as, obviously, the market had returned to requiring ever higher risk premia. The rating agencies reduced Greece's status to BBB- (Fitch), BBB+ (S&P) and A2 (Moody's).

To still allow Greek bonds as collateral for central bank liquidity, the ECB decided to keep the minimum credit threshold in its collateral framework at investment-grade level (i.e. BBB-) beyond the end of 2010 but announced a so-called 'graduated valuation haircut' as of 2011, more rigorous than the previous uniform 5% haircut applied to such assets.[12] This was a compromise in the ECB Governing Council between those who argued that Greek assets could no longer be counted as collateral and those who pressed for continued leniency.

The Finance Ministries of euro area Member States worked out the financial details of the bilateral aid package during the first two weeks of April and agreed on the terms in a telephone conference on Sunday, 11 April 2010. Conference calls and emergency meetings on Sundays became a habit for the next couple of years, usually driven by the urgency to present results to the public before financial markets in Tokyo would open for business.

The press was directly informed in time and reported widely on 12 April: Bilateral loans would amount to up to 30bn EUR in 2010 and cover more than the refinancing needs for the remainder of the year. The overall ceiling beyond 2010 was not specified; observers expected it to be at some 80bn EUR. The size of the IMF loan was yet to be defined but was expected to amount to roughly a third of the overall package, which was intended to surprise and impress financial markets by its size. The German component of the first 30bn package would amount

[12] https://www.ecb.europa.eu/press/pr/date/2010/html/pr100408_1.en.html.

to 8.4bn EUR, commensurate to Germany's 28% share in ECB capital. Loan duration was set at 3 years. Greece was supposed to pay 5% interest. The calculation was based on Euribor plus 3 percentage points and an administrative fee of 0.5 percentage points.

Commission Vice President Olli Rehn argued that the interest rate was in line with market prices and hence did not represent a subsidy, thereby paying respect to the no-bailout clause. This completely counterfactual claim was frequently repeated in German political circles.

Greek Prime Minister Papandreou committed to only ask for assistance if market developments would push him to do so. But: 'The gun is loaded now', he said, 'and I can use it against the speculators' (Frankfurter Allgemeine Zeitung, 12.04.2010, own translation). German government spokesman Christoph Steegmans commented, somewhat differently: 'There is a fire extinguisher on the wall. This does not imply anything about the likelihood that it will be used' (Frankfurter Allgemeine Zeitung, 13.04.2010, own translation).

Greek bond rates failed to drop significantly after the package was announced, and the risk premium over German bunds rose to 3.7 percentage points. According to market commentators, investors doubted the ability of the German government and others to quickly surmount all political and legal hurdles before the loans could be made available.

True enough, Berlin was now haunted by the fact that the budget law did not include the necessary provisions. To make matters worse, Finance Minister Wolfgang Schäuble was back in hospital since early April, and there were rumours that he would resign after the NRW election. Also in the Netherlands, Parliamentary approval for the loan seemed far from assured. Greece appeared to have enough resources to roll over bonds maturing on 20 April on the order of 8.2bn EUR. But another 8.7bn EUR would come due on 19 May, and this was starting to become the focal point on the timeline ahead. To avoid default, Greece would need to ask for assistance well ahead of that deadline, allowing Parliamentary procedures and technical preparations to be cleared on the donor side.

On Thursday 15 April 2010, Greece asked for talks with the Commission, the ECB, and the IMF—what came to be called the 'Troika'—about the details of the structural adjustment programme which would accompany the loan package. This official request was generally perceived as a clear sign that the bailout was now imminent. Greece was paying more than 7% interest on 2-year bonds and, by comparison, the conditions of the bailout package looked financially attractive.

The Commission announced that it was ready to engage in the talks requested by Greece and that the definition of a possible programme would certainly help to finally reassure the markets: While these wanted to 'see' the programme, it would still not necessarily imply the activation of the loans (Frankfurter Allgemeine Zeitung, 16.04.2010). ECB Director Jürgen Stark said: 'We have possibly already reached the next phase of the crisis: a sovereign debt crisis' (Welt, 16.04.2010, own translation).

To me, the situation felt like a strange reversal of causality: While the bailout, as one option among several, had emerged from the financial situation, it now looked as if the situation itself was evolving purposefully and exclusively in direction towards the bailout. The emergency loans to Greece had become a cognitive focus on which all actors were starting to home in through mental convergence. Policymakers who previously had staunchly rejected even the notion of a bailout were now defending the rescue plan for Greece as the only sensible thing to do—a remarkable change in attitude to which I had difficulties adjusting myself.

During one of those days, a friend showed me an antiquarian book about the history and politics of Greece, printed in France in the late 1850s. There was a section about public finances which opened with the remarkable sentence: '*La Grèce est toujours en faillite*' (Greece is always bankrupt). I glanced over the pages and read about nineteenth-century loans from Great Britain, France, and Russia, most notably even from the Kingdom of Bavaria—none of which were ever paid back in full. So much political benefit lies in the ignorance of history, I thought. And would we fare any better this time?

Talks about the adjustment programme were set to last for roughly two weeks. Work would be based on the recommendations which Greece had received as part of the SGP's excessive deficit procedure (EDP). But individual measures would be spelled out much more concretely and implementation would be monitored strictly. Furthermore, the individual tranches of the loan package would only be paid out on the condition that specific milestones of the programme had been implemented—standard IMF policy, notwithstanding the possible time-inconsistency of making pay-outs conditional on reform implementation.

The technical preparations on the German side concerned mainly the state bank KfW. It would act on the order of the government by taking on a short-term loan on the interbank market, backed by a federal guarantee. The KfW would be involved in setting up the loan contract. Given that Germany paid much less interest than 5%, there would be a profit margin of commensurate size. The guarantee would take the form of an amendment law to the budget and needed to pass by a majority vote in the Bundestag.

As far as legislation was concerned, the national budget law had been missed on purpose. The Ministry now proposed to piggy-back the legal amendment onto another law in the legislative pipeline, a law which was to abolish Germany's Financial Planning Council. This procedure, known as the so-called 'omnibus', was quite common for uncontroversial issues. In the present case, however, it raised suspicion even among the ranks of the ruling parties. The Parliamentary fraction of the Christian Democrats decided to enact the bailout guarantees by a separate law instead, to ensure full procedural transparency. Also, the Liberal coalition partner voiced criticism about approving the guarantee as if it were a mere formality.

The rumblings in Parliament were an indication as to the sensitivity and unpopularity of the measure. For example, Georg Nüßlein, spokesman of the Bavarian Christian Democratic CSU caucus in Parliament, stated: 'Greece sneaked her way into the euro area. This should not be rewarded with honest German tax money' (Handelsblatt, 22.04.2010, own translation). Despite his ongoing medical problems, Finance Minister Schäuble on 21 April 2010 spent several hours in various Parliamentary committees, working hard to soften up the Members of the governing parties and the opposition alike.

In colloquial talk, when preparing such meetings, we frequently used medical connotations such as 'massaging' or 'ventilating' sceptical Members of Parliament. Members were also put under considerable hierarchical pressure within their fractions. As far as the Christian Democrats were concerned, the remaining dissenters, such as Klaus-Peter Willsch, were treated like outlaws and later-on removed from influential positions within Parliament. This treatment of democratic representatives is not in line with the spirit of the Constitution, I thought, but it seemed natural to all involved.

On Thursday 22 April 2010, Greek bonds crashed on the capital markets, sending jitters through many other asset classes as well. Greek ten-year bonds fell by about 5%, bringing accumulated losses since the beginning of the month to a staggering 15%. The rate rose to 8.7%, which was higher than the rates of some developing countries. The crash had been triggered by new data on public debt and deficits, Eurostat announcing that the 2009 deficit had been 0.7 percentage points higher than the previously reported 12.9% of GDP. This compared shockingly badly to the less than 4% which had been announced officially by Athens in the previous year.

Market commentators now openly discussed a haircut on Greek debt like the one experienced in Argentina during 2005. The envisaged bailout for Greece was seen to rise significantly beyond the announced 30bn EUR, likely tripling that amount. Alarmingly, the rate on Portuguese bonds was rising and approached the 5% threshold which had marked the start of the Greek debt crisis in early 2010. It seemed inevitable that Greece would now take recourse to the bailout package—less than one week after German Finance Minister Wolfgang Schäuble still had declared: 'We yet believe that the Greeks are on the right path and that, in the end, they may not even need our assistance' (SWR2 Tagesgespräch, 16.04.2010, own translation).

I was hence not all too surprised when, in the late morning of Friday 23 April 2010, I received a phone call from the office of Greek Finance Minister George Papaconstantinou. My Greek counterpart Eleni informed me that Athens' request for financial assistance was now to come. I confirmed my email-address to her once more and said that I would be on stand-by, and I informed my superiors. At precisely 12.40 hrs, Eleni sent a copy of the activation letter, addressed to Messrs Juncker, Rehn, and Trichet. It read as follows:

> Dear Sirs,
> In accordance with the Statement of the Heads of State and Government of 25 March 2010 to provide financial support to Greece, when needed, and the follow up Statement of the Eurogroup, Greece is hereby requesting the activation of the support mechanism.
> Sincerely,
> George Papaconstantinou

CHAPTER 4

A Tough Call

Bailout Choreography

While not being surprised about the letter itself, my colleagues and I were somewhat disappointed about the style. The event felt historic, and we were quite excited indeed—however, the wording seemed trivial and certainly not up to this moment of drama. Greek Prime Minister Papandreou found more emotional words when giving his press conference in the enviable beauty of Kastellorizo Island, amidst the effortless grace of the Aegean Sea and the bright light of a shining blue sky, broadcast live across the globe: 'We believe our European partners will act decisively and provide Greece with a safe haven to rebuild our ship of state with strong and reliable materials'.[1] And there we were, watching from a grim, Nazi-style ministerial building amidst the comparatively more limited charms of central Berlin, wondering what such an arrangement of material transfers into a realm of bucolic, paradiscal beauty has to say about the fairness of life.

Subsequent events surrounding the IMF spring meeting in Washington and the accompanying communication made for a play with carefully rehearsed choreography. On Sunday 25 April 2010, IMF Managing Director Dominique Strauss-Kahn received Greek Finance

[1] https://www.ft.com/content/35fe6cfe-4ec7-11df-abb5-00144feab49a.

M. Heipertz, *Merkelism and the Fine Art of Flat Politics*, Palgrave Studies in European Union Politics,
https://doi.org/10.1007/978-3-031-87592-2_4

Minister George Papaconstantinou. Speaking to the press, Strauss-Kahn said that he was impressed by the Greek reform package and confident that Greece and her European partners would agree in time to cover the financial needs of Athens. Papaconstantinou hinted at early May as the probable date for enacting the programme. This was confirmed by Commission Vice President Olli Rehn. Papaconstantinou categorically rejected debt restructuring—a measure which, in fact, nobody in official function dared to seriously consider at the time. There was consensus in Washington not even to talk about debt restructuring in public (Frankfurter Allgemeine Zeitung, 26.04.2010).

Furthermore, Papaconstantinou declared that Greece would stay 'forever' in the Euro area, rebuking exit demands which had been voiced most vocally in Germany from the quarters of the Bavarian Christian Democrats, the CSU. Resistance against the rescue policy was pronounced in Germany not only by CSU politicians but also by prominent Liberals, in ruling coalition with the Christian Democrats at the federal level. Prince Hermann Otto zu Solms-Hohensolms-Lich, who was said to have eyed the Finance Ministry for himself, criticised German Finance Minister Wolfgang Schäuble: 'It was a blatant mistake to offer help to Greece in the first place' (ibid., own translation). Following the Greek request, it would now be impossible to decline the loan. He thereby alluded in everything but name to the time-inconsistency of applying strict conditionality.

From Washington, however, there was uniform embracement and, in fact, a sentiment of relief palpable in all instances of public communication. US Secretary of Treasury Timothy Geithner welcomed the 'greater sense of urgency' which the Europeans now finally showed and French Finance Minister Christine Lagarde declared belligerently that France would 'defend the territory of the euro' (ibid., own translation).

Schäuble was not in Washington for the IMF/World Bank Spring meeting but had stayed in Berlin, because of his health and to spend time in Parliamentary committees, still busy convincing the sceptics among the governing and opposition parties alike. He also gave a flurry of press and TV interviews in those days to convince the public at large that the European strategy was justified. A typical line of his reasoning in such meetings and interviews ran as follows:

Greece had been 'strangulated' by 'excessive' interest rates on international financial markets. Germany's KfW would provide a loan guaranteed by the Federal Republic, but no money was required from the Federal budget. The ambitious adjustment programme was 'indispensable' and an 'absolute condition' for Germany's assent and, thanks to the adjustment, 'we can assume that Greece will pay the loan back'. The German guarantee would amount to up to 8.4bn EUR, and these would only flow if Greece 'bowed to the harsh restructuring measures' imposed by the creditor states. The German government could also refuse to advance funds and individual tranches, and it now all depended on Greece adhering to strict austerity over the next couple of years. As regarded the scandals about 'Greek statistics' in the past, the country was now forced to be fully transparent and was paying the price for having lived beyond its means. By contrast, demands for exit were not helpful and in conflict with the Treaties. Defending the stability of the euro was not wasting German tax money but instead serving Germany's national interest (all quotes from Bild am Sonntag, 25.04.2010, own translations).

Sigmar Gabriel, head of the Social Democrats, the main opposition party in Germany, meanwhile attacked directly the Chancellor: 'Mrs Merkel has lied to the Germans and duped them. A few weeks ago, in Brussels, she played the Iron Chancellor and pretended to defend the German taxpayer. In reality, Angela Merkel knew already that Germany could do nothing else but help Greece'. He also demanded a contribution by the banking sector which should bear some of the cost of saving Greece (Bild am Sonntag, 25.04.2010, own translations).

The opposition's demand for a contribution by the banking sector, at least by those banks which were creditors to Greece, became quickly very vocal and was also supported by many in the ranks of the governing parties.

How About Debt Restructuring?

I was wondering how a contribution by creditor banks could be affected other than through debt restructuring or at least rescheduling. In that way, the banks would take a hit on their asset side. But restructuring or rescheduling continued to be shunned by everybody at the political level. It was only—yet intensively—discussed among civil servants, think tanks and the financial press.

For example, Daniel Gros, director of the Centre for European Policy Studies, stated: 'Some kind of rescheduling must now be the central scenario' (International Herald Tribune, 26.04.2010). Most financial analysts concurred, based on the calculation that total Greek government debt amounted to 273bn EUR with interest payments running at 97bn EUR over the next five years. Rescheduling was the only option if international aid was not going to pass way above the 30bn EUR officially announced. Daniel Gros proposed extending the maturity of Greek bonds by five years at stable interest rates, rather than outright defaulting.

This option was widely debated among civil servants in the Ministry although it entirely lacked political backing. But was it so unthinkable to devise a restructuring plan which would maintain the credibility of monetary union, avoid financial panic and contagion to other countries and at the same time redress Greece's situation of over-indebtedness?

Key would be to convince (or force) bondholders to exchange their holdings for longer-term debt. This idea, applied with considerable success frequently in history, was liable to complicated legal proceedings but seemed much more promising than the exit option: By exiting, Greece could of course redenominate its debt and devalue the Drachma, thereby alleviating the debt burden massively—but this would mean immediate default and was certainly not in Germany's interest. By contrast, debt restructuring seemed an avenue worth further investigation, at least conceptually.

At the request of the Chancellery, the Ministry of Finance and the Ministry of Justice investigated state insolvency issues more generally, starting from established elements such as Paris Club proceedings or the so-called Sovereign Debt Restructuring Mechanism (SDRM) proposed by the IMF in the year 2001, based on US insolvency law. The experts argued that a framework for state insolvency would need to be legally binding at the international level and should be discussed by the G-20 Member States.

Short of an international rulebook, there was increasing recourse to so-called Collective Action Clauses (CACs): Sovereign debt was being issued with CACs, according to which both the emitting state as well as the holders of the debt agreed to handle default situations and problems of payment through specified super-majority votes of bondholders. In fact, EU Member States had committed in 2003 to include CACs in all sovereign bonds brought to the market. Greek bonds, for instance, as of 2004 regularly contained provisions for a qualified majority of creditors to adopt rescheduling measures binding on all bondholders. CACs, however, did not apply to most bonds due for roll-over in 2010—this solution was hence out of reach.

In sum, rescheduling played no role in the political decision-making and, to the extent that it came up in public discourse, the issue was talked down rather than encouraged.

Crunch Time

Financial Markets were seriously unimpressed by the preparations for the rescue loans or by the fact that the German government was about to launch an emergency legislative procedure for passing the underlying budget guarantee for the KfW-loan. The Ministry initiated the inter-ministerial approval of the guarantee law at State Secretary level on 27 April 2010. The law had the official title 'Law to create the foundation for enabling the taking over of guarantees in connection with emergency measures for the preservation of solvency required for the stability of the monetary union'—in short: 'Law for the preservation of the stability of the monetary union'.[2]

The law consisted of only two paragraphs and stipulated that the Federal Ministry of Finance would be empowered to give guarantees of up to 8.4bn EUR in the first year and of a yet unspecified amount in the following two years for loans to the Hellenic Republic. It also stipulated that the government would report to the budget committee of the Bundestag about the activation and use of the guarantee.

A Cabinet decision was planned for 3 May 2010. Squeezing all deadlines to the utmost with the cooperation of the Parliamentary opposition, the law could enter into force on 7 May 2010. This would be legislation at record speed, akin to the emergency measures adopted during the banking and financial crisis.

Standard & Poors downgraded Portugal to A- with negative outlook on Tuesday 27 April 2010. Portuguese two-year bonds now definitely exceeded the critical 5% interest rate which had marked a point of no return for Greece back in March. The news from Lisbon was a *déjà-vu* in that the government rushed to announce emergency austerity measures—only to encounter domestic strikes and violent street protests.

On the same day, S&P downgraded Greece by three notches to BB+ with negative outlook. The interest rate on Greek two-year bonds rose by 417 basis points to mind-blowing 18.11%, one of the highest yields

[2] https://www.gesetze-im-internet.de/wfstg/BJNR053700010.html.

on short-term debt in the world, with the bond price down at roughly 80%. The new S&P rating for Greece counted as 'junk' and was below the BBB-rating required as a minimum standard by the ECB for collateral.

Even by its already lowered collateral standards, compared to the original A-, the ECB could no longer accept Greek debt as collateral should Moody's and Fitch follow suit with the downgrade. Avoiding this, the ECB delivered a textbook example of time-inconsistency a few days later by suspending its ECB collateral framework for Greek sovereign debt altogether, declaring:

> The Governing Council of the European Central Bank has decided to suspend the application of the minimum credit rating threshold in the collateral eligibility requirements for the purposes of the Eurosystem's credit operations in the case of marketable debt instruments issued or guaranteed by the Greek government. This suspension will be maintained until further notice. The Greek government has approved an economic and financial adjustment programme, which has been negotiated with the European Commission, in liaison with the ECB, and the International Monetary Fund. The Governing Council has assessed the programme and considers it to be appropriate. This positive assessment and the strong commitment of the Greek government to fully implement the programme are the basis, also from a risk management perspective, for the suspension announced herewith. The suspension applies to all outstanding and new marketable debt instruments issued or guaranteed by the Greek government.[3]

International pressure on Germany to decide in favour of the bailout had become intense. The government was furiously criticised for allowing the crisis to roil on, raising the cost of the bailout even further. Both ECB President Jean-Claude Trichet and IMF Managing Director Dominique Strauss-Kahn flew to Berlin on Wednesday 28 April 2010 to see the Chancellor and the Minister, separately. They also presented the rescue strategy to the key decision-makers of the governing and opposition parties. Angela Merkel had proposed their visiting the Bundestag to usher in the adoption of the guarantee law.

Trichet spoke in plain terms: A bond redemption amounting to 8.2bn EUR plus interest was due for Greece on 19 May and it was unlikely that Greece would be able to fund this on the market. Bond spreads were very high and rising, harming financial stability in the euro area as a whole.

[3] https://www.ecb.europa.eu/press/pr/date/2010/html/pr100503.en.html.

Market reactions threatened to shut out other euro area countries from external financing, leading to large losses in investor portfolios and a flight to safety. Banks were particularly exposed to risks and to an overall loss in confidence. While German banks were exposed with approximately 32bn EUR to Greece, their exposure to Spain amounted to 170bn EUR. The crisis could trigger a self-reinforcing divergence among euro area Member States which would be difficult to reverse. At the same time, any calls for banks to accept haircuts would increase the tension. Strauss-Kahn elaborated on the envisaged programme and expressed his confidence that the Greeks would enact whatever austerity was required.

Trichet and Strauss-Kahn, jointly with Finance Minister Schäuble, then held a press conference in the Ministry, aiming to pacify market sentiment and displaying confidence that Germany would not waver but stand fast by Greece. Alas, Spain was now downgraded to AA, and panic rose rather than retreated in the market. Liquidity drained by the minute from Greek banks which received less and less funds on the backing of their Greek sovereign collateral and depended almost entirely on ECB liquidity. The debt crisis had spilled over into stock markets and sent Germany's Dax index down as well, having lost 2.7% in value already on the preceding day.

Schäuble, whom we internally just called 'Chef' or with the formal bureaucratic short form 'M', looked somewhat lost and fragile in his wheelchair among the two Frenchmen who were sitting beside him. It all seemed to depend on him—but did M have a choice, according to what the other two had said in private and in public and according to what the Chancellor had already announced?

After the press briefing, I took Jean-Claude Trichet down the old-fashioned Paternoster elevator in the Ministry. He recognised me as a former ECB Staff Member, took me by the arm and said: 'Cher ami, good that you a here. We must act now. This is otherwise financial Armageddon'. Strauss-Kahn, by contrast, had no eye for ordinary civil servants and exuded an air of power and arrogance. From close by, I felt uneasy and a sense of doubt whether he had the public interest in mind and whether, therefore, we should at all listen to the man.

Schäuble strove for clarity and confirmed that Greece would receive the loan, that no haircuts would be imposed on creditors, that debt rescheduling would not take place and that the banking sector would not be forced to contribute (Handelsblatt 28.04.2010). In doing so, he rebuffed all critics in Germany who were burning with rage at the government. Ignoring their cries, Schäuble delivered the clear line that was expected internationally and, above all, by the markets. After all, Chancellor Merkel had already put her full political weight behind the decision to bail out Greece, de facto asking Parliament to enact the guarantee law within a week. I was amazed: Our leaders were right to simply assume final consent by the opposing Social Democrats to the urgent legislative procedure.

But according to opinion polls, 86% of Germans rejected the bailout, matching and even exceeding the levels of popular resistance against the introduction of the single currency twelve years ago (Der Tagesspiegel, 13.02.1998). Democracy can obviously mean not to heed the will of the people in all cases, I mused. In public fora, the generous Greek pension system caused most of the fury—as well as the fact that the taxpayer had to chip in rather than the banks (Financial Times, 27.04.2010).

A Contribution by the Banking Sector

The NRW election on 9 May was looming large. Not only the opposition, but also leading members of the governing parties now insisted on a contribution by the banking sector. Merkel had declared that she 'understood' such demands and that the Minister of Finance should deal with them—but that the current situation required public guarantees, which would happen within days (Börsen-Zeitung, 27.04.2010).

In his exchanges with the different Parliamentary fractions, the Finance Minister reiterated why debt rescheduling was out of the question: The real danger for financial stability in the euro area was a general loss of confidence. Debt rescheduling would aggravate this problem, given that rescheduling amounted to default, magnified by contagion, a situation far worse than 'Lehmann'. A renewed financial and banking crisis would derail the real economy, and costs would be far higher than the envisaged loan. In the absence of a state insolvency regime, there would be drawn-out legal proceedings, cutting Greece off from financial markets for years to come, as had been exemplified by Argentina. Only CDS speculators and vulture investors would benefit from that scenario. By contrast, fiscal consolidation and a comprehensive economic and institutional restructuring programme would lay the groundwork for recovery and fiscal sanity with subsequent years of primary surpluses, following the example of Belgium.

On the other hand, if rescheduling was out of the question, how about a 'voluntary' contribution by the financial sector? It was no secret to the public that banks were among the main drivers and beneficiaries of the bailout. The Chief Executive Officer (CEO) of Deutsche Bank, Josef Ackermann, had declared: 'If we do not manage to stabilise Greece, the banks will have the next problem' (Frankfurter Allgemeine Zeitung, 19.03.2010, own translation).

Already in early March, Deutsche Bank had proposed a private sector consortium to buy Greek bonds, covered by a German state guarantee. This idea had been a complete non-starter as it had shown an all too well-known pattern: Profits for the private sector, risks for the public sector. Nevertheless, by late April, there were talks behind the scenes, mainly conducted in London, and partially hosted by Her Majesty's Treasury at senior civil service level. The UK Treasury seemed keen to broker a 'club-deal' ahead of the British general election on 6 May 2010, aiming to impress markets and voters alike.

The new idea was to pool public and private resources into a so-called Common Currency Stabilisation Fund (CCSF), the private sector contributing a tranche commensurate to the initial tranche foreseen by Member States' bilateral loans, i.e. roughly 30bn EUR topped up by the IMF tranche of 15bn EUR. The total volume of the CCSF would hence be around 75bn EUR, allowing to take Greece off the market for roughly two years. The IMF should govern the CCSF and ensure conditionality between disbursements of the fund to Greece, verified against the Greek government implementing the restructuring and reform programme. The 30bn EUR private sector piece would subdivide along national lines, foreseeing 7.5bn each for the German and French private sectors, 5bn each for the British and Swiss ones and 2.5bn each for the Spanish, Italian and Dutch ones. On the German private sector side, Deutsche Bank took a leading role in these talks and organised initial support from Allianz, Münchner Rück and Siemens. But the idea of an CCSF did also not take off:

First, the private sector representatives involved required the three pieces of the CCSF to rank *pari passu*, hence without differences in seniority among the three contributing groups. This would have been unacceptable to the IMF which, as a matter of principle, only lends with preferred creditor status, implying that the IMF is always the most senior lender and thereby gets its money back first. Given the risk of a later restructuring of Greek debt, the private sector institutions involved in the talks shunned the fact that they would bear the brunt of the losses if they ranked lower than the IMF and the euro members.

Second, the CCSF would have given a too powerful role to the IMF in handling the programme, compared to the European scheme which foresaw the 'Troika' of IMF, Commission, and ECB in equal partnership.

Third and last, the European scheme was, by that point in time, far too advanced—leaving only a binary choice between this option and a disorderly default. It would simply not have been possible to realign the political compromise behind anything else, given that no other government was on board and that the communication effort had now intensely been focussed on the European plan. This left the German government longing for at least a symbolic contribution of the banking sector.

On Sunday, 2 May 2010, the Eurogroup convened in Brussels with the IMF and agreed to provide an overall package of 110bn EUR to Greece, covering its financing needs for three years, and issued the following statement:

> Eurogroup Ministers concur with the Commission and the ECB that market access for Greece is not sufficient and that providing a loan is warranted to safeguard financial stability in the euro area as a whole. Following a request by the Greek authorities, euro area Ministers unanimously agreed today to activate stability support to Greece via bilateral loans centrally pooled by the European Commission under the conditions set out in their statement of 11 April. Parliamentary approval, needed in some Member States prior to the release of the first tranche, is expected to follow swiftly. The Eurogroup is confident that the ambitious fiscal adjustment and comprehensive structural reforms under the Greek authorities' programme are appropriate to stabilise the fiscal and economic situation and address the fiscal and structural challenges of the Greek economy in a decisive manner. The programme is supported by strong conditionality. It will thereby also help restore confidence and safeguard financial stability in the euro area. In the context of a three year joint programme with the IMF, the financial package makes available € 110 billion to help Greece meet its financing needs, with euro area Member States ready to contribute for their part € 80 billion, of which up to € 30 billion in the first year. The first disbursements will be made available before the payment obligations of the Greek government fall due on 19 May. Euro area financial support will be provided under strong policy conditionality, on the basis of a programme which has been negotiated with the Greek authorities by the Commission and the IMF, in liaison with the ECB. The programme has been approved by the Greek Council of Ministers on 2 May and endorsed

> by the Eurogroup on the basis of a Commission and ECB assessment. In this context, the Eurogroup welcomes the efforts to date by the Greek Government to resolutely address the fiscal imbalances as well as the new measures announced today in the framework of a three-year programme agreed with the European Commission, the ECB and the IMF, which is also announcing its staff-level agreement with Greece on a standby arrangement. The main elements of policy conditionality, as endorsed today, will be enshrined in a Council Decision under Articles 126 and 136 TFEU to be formally adopted in the coming days and further detailed in a Memorandum of Understanding, to be concluded between the Greek authorities and the Commission on behalf of euro area Member States.[4]

On the same day and per email from Brussels, I was tasked with organising at short notice a meeting of the Minister with leading representatives of the German financial sector. With the help of colleagues from the Directorate-General VII (financial markets), I compiled a list of CEOs from banks and insurance companies, representing a cross-section of commercial banks, cooperatives, savings banks, Landesbanks, insurers, re-insurers, and the like, altogether fourteen gentlemen under the leadership of Josef Ackermann of Deutsche Bank and Wolfgang Kirsch of DZ Bank who at the time presided over the German banking association. On our side, Bundesbank President Axel Weber and BaFin President Jochen Sanio would participate as well as the top echelons of the administration in Chancellery and Ministry.

My colleagues were sceptical as to what we could expect from the bankers, but, having spoken to the Minister as well as to Ackermann on the phone, I sat down and drafted a declaration. I wrote down that the financial sector in Germany would be 'flanking the public measures aimed at stabilising economic and monetary union in Europe'. The key sentence read: 'We commit to maintain existing credit lines and other exposures to Greece over the lifetime of the programme'.

My colleagues objected and argued that such a commitment was entirely impossible—after all, a CEO was liable to the shareholders of his or her institution, not to the whims and wishes of the German taxpayer. Holding onto Greek debt in the current circumstances could easily amount to breach of trust and bring the CEOs behind bars. After

[4] https://www.consilium.europa.eu/media/25673/20100502-eurogroup_statement_greece.pdf.

some back and forth with Ackermann's team, we developed compromise language according to which the institutions would hold onto Greek debt 'to the extent possible' and aim at even expanding their engagement in Greece.

The Minister's summit with the bankers took place on Tuesday 4 May 2010 and went well. I remember the discussion as frank and outspoken. Only Ackermann seemed to see things as serious and as strategically as Schäuble saw them, pointing to the danger of a complete financial collapse. The other CEOs were still more afraid of their shareholders and of state prosecutors but agreed to support the declaration and an ensuing press conference of the Minister with Ackermann and Kirsch. The bankers committed publicly to sustain their holdings of Greek debt 'to the extent possible', while Schäuble explained the legislative process of our guarantee law which had been adopted in a special meeting of the Cabinet on Monday and was going to pass the first reading in Parliament on Wednesday—the Social Democrats having accepted the urgency procedure, as expected.

We published the bankers' declaration immediately. To my delight, it resonated well in the press—but markets were entirely unimpressed. There were rumours about Spain, Portugal and even Italy going down; especially Spain was associated with ever wilder fears. I started to doubt that we could still stem the tide, and, late in the evening, there was a sense of panic on the floors of the Ministry. Everybody was tense and highly nervous as we approached a Ministerial phone conference with France, Spain, Italy, and Portugal about the market situation. The following day saw the Parliamentary debate on the guarantee law and, as far as I was concerned, the preparation of a technical follow-up meeting with the German financial sector about their holding commitment.

The Parliamentary debate on the *Währungsunion-Finanzstabilitätsgesetz* (law on the financial stability of the monetary union), as it was now referred to, took place on Wednesday 5 May 2010[5] and started at 8.30 hrs with a government declaration by the Chancellor on the law itself and on the upcoming special meeting of Heads of State and Government, scheduled for 7 May.

In her speech, Merkel said that the law was *ultima ratio*, addressing an immediate emergency. She then laid out the parameters of the

[5] https://dserver.bundestag.de/btp/17/17039.pdf, quotes in own translation.

programme, as they had been fixed over the previous days: A total amount of 110bn EUR for three years, 30bn EUR by the IMF, 80bn by euro area Member States, the German contribution being 28%, hence 8.4bn in 2010 and 14bn in 2011 and 2012. The fact that the original number, 8.4bn EUR, had almost tripled in total by defining the time frame, went largely unnoticed. In any case, she said, this was not about numbers: 'This is about nothing more and nothing less than the future of Europe and hence the future of Germany in Europe'.

She went on to stress the political and historic dimension of the situation and appealed to Germany's responsibility—and she recalled that it had been the Schröder government under Social Democrats and Greens which had admitted Greece into the euro area in the year 2000. Her remark triggered uproar among the ranks of the opposition, but she went on to say that Europe now was at a crossroads, requiring no backward-looking but forward-looking, ruthless analysis and therapy.

Merkel listed four conditions for the bailout: First, a comprehensive and demanding programme of consolidation enacted by Greece herself, to regain competitiveness and access to market finance. She stressed that this programme had not been possible without Germany holding back her agreement to the assistance package, otherwise giving rise to moral hazard and other countries preferring assistance over consolidation. Second, involvement of the IMF—which would also not have been possible without German insistence. The third condition was that Greece had effectively lost market funding—as confirmed by the Troika. And the fourth condition, equally based on Troika judgement, was that the assistance was 'without alternative' to safeguard financial stability in the euro area.

To my recollection, this was the first time that what we called the 'TINA-dogma' was declared in public, TINA standing for 'there is no alternative'. Merkel elucidated the *ultima ratio* nature of the law by pointing to the danger of a chain reaction in European and international markets and a rerun of the 2008 crisis with tangibly more economic damage. She stated that the four conditions were now fulfilled, which is why the decision could and would need to be taken swiftly.

She then spoke about creditor participation and said that the federal government wanted a decision in the same week, a decision which reflected the responsibility of the banks and other creditors. She went on to say that the Finance Minister had held talks with the financial sector and reiterated that banks and other creditors must not escape their responsibility. 'And therefore I welcome that, obviously, there is a readiness by banks and other creditors. It is of particular importance in that context that the financial sector plans to maintain its credit lines to Greece and to Greek banks until 2012 and beyond'.

The second part of her speech was devoted to the issues of bank levy, financial transaction tax, and the primacy of politics over the financial system. She also mentioned the need for a new growth strategy in the EU, based on competitiveness, and the need for tougher SGP sanctions. She did explicitly not exclude Treaty change.

Ending on a historical note, she alluded to Germany's place in Europe and called it a *Schicksalsgemeinschaft*, a community of fate, to which we owed peace, prosperity, and harmony with our neighbours. War was now absent from Europe and therefore we should work for a strong Europe—and Members of Parliament should now vote in favour of the law, which was a necessary decision for the future of Europe.

In their replies, most speakers of the opposition did not criticise the government for the law itself but rather for presenting it so late in the process—and for being too soft on the banks. It was clear that the law would pass the second reading, scheduled for Friday 7 May, with a solid majority but that the opposition would try to benefit as much as possible from the situation, considering the upcoming election in NRW.

Meanwhile, I urged the Directorate-General VII to summon the Chief Financial Officers (CFOs) of the banks and insurance companies we had spoken to on Tuesday, scheduling a meeting at the Bundesbank headquarters in Frankfurt for Thursday 6 May. My political task was to produce a number, a significant number, something close to 10bn EUR. As the German taxpayer was asked to provide for guarantees of 22.4bn EUR, we needed something tangible and clear from the financial sector for the purposes of political communication. The bankers' verbal commitment was not enough and risked creating more doubt rather than respect in public—during this crucial phase of legislative decision-making, just ahead of the NRW election.

Conceptually, this pushed me back to an old issue relevant since February: the exposure of our financial sector to Greece. By now, thanks to the work of Bafin and Bundesbank, we had much better data but still no full overview. Deducting hedges and safeguards such as CDS, there seemed to be a net exposure of German banks to Greece at 34.5bn EUR overall, of which roughly 22bn EUR to the Greek state. About three quarters of that was in government bonds. Exposure to Greek banks was comparatively low at around 3.5bn EUR. Deutsche Bank, in fact, was not heavily exposed; the situation was more serious for Commerzbank and HRE, both already under SoFFin protection. Some cooperative banks and Landesbanks were also significantly exposed. Regarding insurers' investment funds such as Allianz Global Investors or MEAG Munich Ergo, we looked at an exposure of roughly 8.7bn EUR. An additional 9.1bn EUR was sitting on the books of the insurance companies themselves.

A wild thought crossed my mind: These numbers seemed manageable. Should we not rather take the hit in the financial sector? But who was I to judge that situation? And, in any case, it was far too late—the decision in fact had been taken long ago. A colleague found drastic words when we talked about it on the way to the airport: 'The monster was conceived long ago; what we behold now is but the agony of its birth.'

So, I focused on the task at hand—producing a number which could be sold to the public. Overall exposure was not going to do the trick, but we zoomed in on the level of exposure to government and bank debt with a remaining duration of three years, commensurate with the length of the programme. This figure, but we were not sure, had to be in the range of 9bn EUR.

I was not aware at the time, but this experience was just one example of a deep and structural phenomenon: Policy-making is increasingly driven by communication, not vice versa, as it used to be. The Chiefs of Staff of Ministries in Berlin as well as of Cabinets in Brussels are no longer former career civil servants from the rank and file but usually ones with a background in press offices or journalism directly. This explains an emphasis on tactics, opinion polls and public effects rather than substance and strategy.

We arrived in the famous Bundesbank building, like the EIB another fine example of brutalist architecture and an epitome to *Stabilitätskultur*, the culture of stability, overlooking the skyscrapers of Frankfurt. The institution exuded a delusion of importance and of still being somewhat more than a mere subsidiary of the ECB downtown, at that time still without permanent premises of its own.

We were ushered into one of the top floors, and the meeting commenced almost instantly. I soon gathered that the CFOs did not know the details of their exposure: What was the precise maturity structure, and how much of it was hedged, and how was it hedged in fact? A top-level representative of BaFin leaned over to me and said: 'Good that you see this, from the Minister's Office. This is our regular ordeal. These guys can be pretty useless, you know'.

Individual CFOs were repeatedly on the phone, speaking either with their subordinates to obtain more reliable data as it emerged in a piece-meal fashion from back offices and inadequate data bases, or with their CEOs to report live from our on-going meeting and to ask for their approval to agree to the wording of a text under negotiation, the draft of which had been discretely sent to me by a senior lawyer from Deutsche Bank.

In operationalising Tuesday's agreement, we had also added a European dimension by asking Madame Lagarde's office in Paris to hold parallel talks with the French financial sector. To my delight and in constant exchange with my French counterpart, this progressed as well, based on the agreements we had already reached in Berlin and were now achieving in Frankfurt. In Paris, it seemed a lot easier to sign on the dotted line of such lip-service statements. We hence delightfully added the term 'European convoy' to the wording.

In a mix of negotiation, fact-finding, and drafting, we pinned down that the participating companies agreed (within the margins of their legal and economic possibilities) to maintain credit lines as of 6 May 2010 at least until 6 May 2013 with a total volume of 3.3bn EUR by refraining from terminating existing arrangements (other than for good cause) and to renew maturing credit contracts (at market prices), retaining constant or even expanding the overall amount of finance. Furthermore, they agreed to hold on to Greek sovereign bonds (again within the margins of their legal and economic possibilities) with a total volume of 4.8bn EUR at least until 6 May 2013 and to purchase new bonds in those volumes to replace bonds that would reach maturity in the meantime. Our technical statement also foresaw biannual reports of the participating companies to the financial supervisors but also specified that it was a declaration of intent only and did not bind the signatories in legal terms. After some eight hours of deliberation, we cabled the statement back to Berlin and added a cover note to the press that this concerned an overall volume of more than 8bn EUR. Mission accomplished.

Later-on, however, it became clear to anyone who cared to check the numbers that the financial institutions did not feel bound by the commitment at all. Not even one month after the agreement, a first bank was in the news for not having prolonged its exposure in Greece, encouraged behind the scenes by BaFin (Handelsblatt, 01.06.2010). Whenever asked by Members of Parliament, the government answered evasively.[6] And when Greek debt was eventually rescheduled in 2012, I was in fact relieved that most of the German banks and insurers had silently got rid of it meanwhile—with the notable exception of the HRE bad bank under SoFFin resolution, where it fell to the taxpayer to foot the bill once more.

In the summer of 2012, I met Joe Ackermann at an evening reception in a garden palais Unter den Linden. We chatted about the army, both being officers of the reserve, and then came to the banking crisis. Talking about the bank rescues of 2008, he said proudly: ‘I have never taken a penny from the state’. I replied: ‘But when it came to Greece, you also didn’t pay a penny, I believe’.

Most analysts detected within days the purely political nature of our gentlemen’s agreement with the financial sector. It was a bluff. But it did the trick: The agreement, its technical operationalisation, and the fact that it was paralleled in France and subsequently also in other countries, were all well received by the press—and while it lasted, this effect gave us some breathing space to allow the guarantee law to pass rather smoothly in Parliament.

Crossing the Rubicon

Before that, the Troika had to provide its assessment on the Greek programme. From our point of view, the ECB’s verdict was the most relevant one, given the respect and standing that the central bank in those days still enjoyed in the eye of the German public.

Attached to a letter addressed to the President of the Eurogroup, Jean-Claude Juncker, on 2 May 2010, ECB President Jean-Claude Trichet forwarded the Bank’s assessment.[7] Based on the premise that ‘restoring fiscal sustainability and international competitiveness are necessary to lay the foundation for the return to sustainable growth’, it determined in a purely non-technical and shallow manner that ‘fiscal adjustment will be the cornerstone of the programme’. It concluded that ‘overall, the ambitious fiscal adjustment and comprehensive structural reforms under the

[6] For example, question 7 in the following: https://dserver.bundestag.de/btd/17/063/1706312.pdf.

[7] https://www.tweedekamer.nl/downloads/document?id=1ee72c0c-4d2e-4aec-9626-2b2be0e5e03a&title=Assessment%20of%20the%20programme%20parameters%20underlying%20the%20external%20financial%20support%20to%20Greece.pdf.

programme are appropriate' and that the programme was 'comprehensive and supported by strong conditionality'. The ECB finally declared about the programme: 'It addresses the relevant policy challenges in a decisive manner. It will thereby help restore confidence and safeguard financial stability in the euro area'. That's it, I wondered, not even a fake justification in terms of economic analysis? Purely political propositions, declarations, dogma? It was obvious that only the ECB Press Office had drafted this document and not my former shop, the Directorate General Economics.

Clearly, the Bank left it to the other two institutions, the Commission, and especially the IMF, to risk their economic credentials by providing the underlying analysis. On 5 May 2010, the IMF tabled its so-called Staff Report on Greece, entailing the Washington-based institution's verdict on the programme.[8] This was a lot more solid and honest, to my mind. It stated: 'Risks to the programme are high. The adjustment needs are unprecedented and will take time, so fatigue could set in. Any unforeseen shock could weigh on the economy and the banking system even if the fiscal programme is on track'.

The core of any IMF programme assessment of that kind is a so-called Debt Sustainability Analysis (DSA) which featured among the exhaustive analytical materials provided by the IMF. On that basis, the Fund concluded: 'While risks regarding debt sustainability are undeniably high, the Fund's support is nevertheless justified given the new government's strong initiatives and the substantial cofinancing by the euro area countries, coupled with the systemic concerns arising from spillover effects if Greece were not given an opportunity to improve its economic policies'.

The largest international loan in history was going ahead. We jokingly borrowed a quote from Churchill, saying: 'Never before in history was so much owed by so few to so many'.

Our national guarantee law[9] was adopted on Friday 7 May 2010 at noon by the 622 Members of the Bundestag with 391 voting in favour, 72 voting against, 139 abstaining and 20 not casting a vote. Of the governing coalition, there were four notable dissenters and one vote not cast among the Christian Democrats as well as one dissenter among the Liberals. The Social Democrats abstained with a few exceptions, the far Left voted

[8] https://www.imf.org/external/pubs/ft/scr/2010/cr10110.pdf.

[9] https://dserver.bundestag.de/btd/17/015/1701544.pdf.

against and, surprisingly, the opposing Green party voted largely in favour. The governing parties also passed a resolution, against the votes of all other parties, asking for a strengthening of the SGP.[10]

A subsequent vote in the Bundesrat on the same day was not necessary, given that none of the *Länder* requested the law to pass to the so-called conciliation committee between the two chambers. But a formal debate took place also in the Bundesrat and Schäuble, as government representative, had to rush there from the Bundestag, while the Bundesrat plenary had been waiting in suspension for the Bundestag vote to pass.

In his speech to the Länder representatives, Schäuble mentioned the agreement with the financial sector that I had helped to broker: 'Meanwhile, we know that the volume of credit and bonds of the financial sector towards Greece amounts to roughly 8bn EUR. This number is provisional, but we can say that the financial sector has made a commitment equivalent to more than a third of the maximum loan volume which we extend through KfW, backed by federal guarantee, to retain the solvency and liquidity of Greece—so that our credit line ideally would not even have to be used'.[11]

Schäuble also alluded to the need for institutional lessons to be drawn from this crisis and, at the end of his speech, like Merkel, referred to the Second World War which had ended 65 years before the decision at hand. To me, this seemed somewhat far-fetched—but it shows the spell under which political decision-makers in Germany think they must act.

It was early afternoon on Friday, 7 May 2010, and the law had passed both legislative chambers. We now had to rush through a whole menu of formalities, keeping especially the drivers busy. The President of the Bundesrat had notified the Chancellor by letter with handwritten signature, driven by courier from Bundesrat to Chancellery. The text of the law underwent final linguistic, orthographic, and legal checks and was then printed on vat paper in the Ministry of Justice, to be driven by courier to the Ministry of Finance. The vat copy reached my desk by special messenger in the late afternoon for signature by the Minister. Having obtained Schäuble's signature, I dispatched it by courier to the Chancellery for Merkel's signature. It was after sunset when the law finally

[10] https://dserver.bundestag.de/btd/17/016/1701641.pdf.

[11] https://www.bundesrat.de/SharedDocs/downloads/DE/plenarprotokolle/2010/Plenarprotokoll-869.pdf?__blob=publicationFile&v=4, own translation.

reached Federal President Horst Köhler, who, I was told, had sat waiting in Bellevue Castle.

Before becoming a highly popular Federal President of Germany, Köhler had been Managing Director of the IMF and a long-standing civil servant at the Ministry of Finance. As Finance State Secretary, he had been one of the key negotiators of the Maastricht Treaty. He might have held private views on the matter of Greece, but now his role was purely ceremonial as he put the last signature under the law before it was published in the Official Journal and entered into force on the following day.

Köhler resigned from office only three weeks later. His resignation occurred after a minor controversy on security policy, and Köhler staunchly rejected rumours that his resignation had to do with personal reservations about the Greek bailout and what followed. Weeks later, Finance Minister Schäuble made a snapping comment about Horst Köhler that 'he, sorry, obviously has not really understood his office'. Schäuble went on to say that 'it is fine if you want to be popular with the people. But that popularity should be gained through authority and not by denouncing the political class as terrible' (Tagesspiegel, 04.07.2010, own translation).

In the evening of Friday 7 May, we had to move on quickly from the law to other documents which urgently required finalisation. This included the so-called Intercreditor Agreement between the fifteen creditor countries.[12] This text had been drafted by the Troika and agreed at Eurogroup level and now had to be initialled on every page and signed on the last page by the Minister. The Intercreditor Agreement stipulated in detail the coordination and management of the pooled bilateral loans, such as the opening of a special account in the name of the lenders with the ECB by the Commission, to be used for processing all payments on behalf of the parties, or the calculation and distribution of individual payments. It also laid down that all lenders ranked equally and *pari passu* among themselves and that the conditions of the loan could only be changed by unanimous consent. The parties agreed to take their decisions at meetings within the framework of the Eurogroup, excluding Greece.

[12] https://www.irishstatutebook.ie/eli/2010/act/7/schedule/1/enacted/en/html.

In addition, there was the Loan Facility Agreement between the lending Member States and Greece.[13] This was the legal basis of the bailout and laid down the rights and obligations of the lenders, details of drawdown and disbursement, rules on interest, costs, and expenses as well as repayment, early repayment, cancellation, and the like. It also regulated events of default, undertakings on information, fraud prevention and inspection.

Furthermore, there was Council Decision 2010/320/EU of 10 May 2010 addressed to Greece with a view to reinforcing and deepening fiscal surveillance and giving notice to Greece to take measures for the deficit reduction judged necessary to remedy the situation of excessive deficit.[14] This was the comprehensive definition of the adjustment programme to which Greece had to commit in exchange for the loan. It defined an adjustment path for the levels of deficit and debt in proportion to GDP as well as the precise policy measures deemed suitable to achieve it: tax legislation including a VAT rise, budget cuts, pension reductions, abolition of bonuses etc., including deadlines by which specific measures had to be taken.

Finally, there were additional documents,[15] above all a Memorandum of Economic and Financial Policies, a Memorandum of Understanding on specific economic policy conditionality and a Technical Memorandum of Understanding, each signed already on 3 May 2010 by Greece, following a so-called Staff Level Agreement between the IMF and Greece on the programme in conjunction with the 30bn EUR Stand-by Arrangement, as the IMF loan was called. These documents contained economic appraisals, the objectives of the programme and its specificities in line with the abovementioned EU Council Decision.

By comparison between the Commission and the IMF documents, the ones from the IMF were more elaborate on financial market policy, including supervision, and structural policy such as modernising public administration and improving the business environment. The IMF Executive Board was to approve the Stand-by Arrangement on Sunday 9 May 2010.

[13] https://www.irishstatutebook.ie/eli/2010/act/7/schedule/2/enacted/en/html.

[14] https://eur-lex.europa.eu/legal-content/EN/TXT/?uri=uriserv%3AOJ.L_.2010.145.01.0006.01.ENG&toc=OJ%3AL%3A2010%3A145%3ATOC.

[15] https://www.imf.org/external/pubs/ft/scr/2010/cr10111.pdf and https://ec.europa.eu/economy_finance/publications/occasional_paper/2010/pdf/ocp61_en.pdf.

Needless to say: Nobody in the political sphere of decision-making can possibly have read (and understood) this plethora of highly technical documents at the speed which developments had acquired by that time. This holds especially for the lawmakers in the Bundestag, most of whom were entirely unfamiliar with the subject matter.

I remember only very few Members of Parliament from among the governing parties to ring up at the Ministry and ask for explanations beyond the Committee hearings. To the extent possible, the Minister himself would devote time and speak to them in person. In some instances, I was asked to provide additional information and documents. It turned out that then a yet smaller subgroup of these Members voted against the law. Many more complained openly that nobody could possibly have digested the piles of documents on their desks during just a few days—only then to vote in favour of the law.

A final technical matter in that week concerned the Ministry's interaction with KfW as our agent. The Directorate-General VII prepared a letter of the Minister to the CEO of KfW, Ulrich Schröder, which had to be dispatched at short notice on Saturday 8 May 2010. By this letter, the government tasked KfW to sign the Loan Facility Agreement and to provide for the German contingent of the loan package. Furthermore, the government committed to cover any losses, according to a separate guarantee agreement between the Ministry of Finance and KfW, in turn based on the guarantee law which had just cleared all Parliamentary hurdles.

On this Saturday morning, 8 May 2010, it fell to me (and it did feel somewhat strange) to send the letter off by email to Frankfurt, thereby telling KfW to get ready to transfer up to 22,336,133,611.30 EUR to the Bank of Greece. I used a handheld device for doing so because, at the same time, I was privately busy looking for a house to buy in Berlin, and I quickly calculated that my mortgage was some 0.001% of that sum which I had just instructed KfW to muster.

Another piece of news popped up on my handheld device on that day: The Constitutional Court in Karlsruhe had dismissed an urgency procedure which had been brought to it right after adoption of the guarantee law in the Bundestag and before its treatment in the Bundesrat, still on Friday 7 May 2010.[16]

[16] http://www.bverfg.de/e/rs20100507_2bvr098710.html.

A group of five professors of law and economics had complained about the Federal Republic's bailout of Greece as violating fundamental rights and principles of the Constitution, such as the free mandate of Parliamentarians (who theoretically are subjected only to their personal conscience free from party-political pressure) and the plaintiffs' personal right of property. They had requested the Court to interdict the Federal President to sign the law and the government to implement it—as a matter of urgency to prevent the bailout becoming a *fait accompli*.

But the Court argued that the consequences of stopping the law could be graver than the infringements on the rights of the plaintiffs and transferred the case to a normal procedure—the first of a whole string of Constitutional Court proceedings with which the government was to be confronted.[17] Hence, the government was free to implement the law for the time being, as I texted my superiors with an overall sense of relief, yet not without a tinge of disappointment at seeing the Court so servile to political expedience. This aspect of Germany's 'juristocracy' is hardly surprising, given the party-political nature of judicial appointments to the Court.

The real verdict was spoken by the sovereign one day later, on Sunday 9 May 2010: The Christian Democrats lost the election in NRW smashingly, dropping by more than ten percentage points down to 34.6%—still 0.1 percentage points ahead of the Social Democrats, but no longer able to form a government by coalition. This might have weighed on Merkel's mind considerably, but probably still less than the Brussels summit she had lived through two days earlier.

[17] http://www.bverfg.de/e/rs20110907_2bvr098710.html.

CHAPTER 5

Weathering the Storm

Doubling Down

Markets drove politics—no doubt about that. They continued their collapse on Friday 7 May 2010, and the fact that Greece was about to be saved did not calm them in the slightest. Instead, it seemed to set the fire even more ablaze.

In the afternoon, when New York opened, and right after his speech before the Bundesrat, Finance Minister Schäuble participated in a G7 telephone conference. Contagion was now real: Portugal was going down the same path as Greece only months before.

The Chancellor travelled to Brussels on Friday 7 May 2010 for a meeting of the Heads of State and Government of the euro area. They had planned to endorse the aid package for Greece and make solemn declarations about economic reform, strengthening the SGP, regulating financial markets and fighting speculation.

But the summit turned into an epic crisis meeting as market volatility continued to mount despite the Greek bailout. Now, according to some participants, the entire euro area was at risk and the Greek crisis was transforming into a general collapse. There were rumours about a coordinated attack of American and Asian hedge funds on the euro, and the risk premia on Portuguese and Spanish debt were rising rapidly.

M. Heipertz, *Merkelism and the Fine Art of Flat Politics*, Palgrave Studies in European Union Politics,
https://doi.org/10.1007/978-3-031-87592-2_5

It was reported that US President Barack Obama in phone calls (ahead of the meeting) as well as French President Nicolas Sarkozy and ECB President Jean-Claude Trichet (during the meeting) urged the summit participants to enact a much larger and more comprehensive package than the bilateral loans mustered for Greece. Allegedly, there was sheer panic in the markets. Trichet spoke to the summit in the most alarming terms, repeatedly using the phrase that he had told me in the Paternoster elevator a week earlier: *financial Armageddon*. He explained that the ECB saw the interbank market collapsing as in 2007/8 and that the crisis would be even worse this time.

Sarkozy, like Obama, had also held one-to-one talks before the meeting and subsequently declared in a press conference that 95% of the outcome corresponded to French proposals and that the decision implied that 'we now finally have a real *gouvernement économique*' (Focus and Frankfurter Allgemeine Zeitung, 10.05.2010, own translation). He thereby referred to the following line of the summit statement:

> Taking into account the exceptional circumstances, the Commission will propose a European stabilization mechanism to preserve financial stability in Europe. It will be submitted for decision to an extraordinary ECOFIN meeting that the Spanish presidency will convene this Sunday May 9th.[1]

This so-called 'mechanism' was indeed a breakthrough after some nine hours of negotiation. Additionally, there were announcements that the ECB would purchase government bonds of failing states, something which it had until then avoided to do other than through so-called open market operations (OMOs)—but the ECB intervention was not mentioned explicitly in the summit statement, respecting at least symbolically the independence of the central bank. The 'mechanism' on its own was surprising enough, and, in the Minister's Office, I in fact heard about it for the first time on Monday morning and literally almost fell off my chair.

I only knew that still one day ahead, on Sunday, Finance Minister Wolfgang Schäuble had flown to Brussels at very short notice for the said emergency meeting of ECOFIN. But during the negotiation, his health degraded alarmingly, and he had to be taken to a local hospital.

[1] https://www.consilium.europa.eu/media/21430/20100507-statement-of-the-heads-of-state-or-government-of-the-euro-area-en.pdf.

In this crucial moment, Germany was represented by the State Secretary until, at least formally, Interior Minister Thomas de Maizière, who had been hiking in the countryside, flew in and took over—understandably unprepared on substance.

France was pushing for *gouvernement économique* in anything but name. There was no official definition of what that meant, but to my mind it in essence consistently implied a combination of debt mutualisation and political dominance over the ECB (ideally by Paris) for as long as French politicians and civil servants had pondered the design of monetary union.

Germany, by contrast, made no strategic demands. We could have used the historic chance to advance our previously long-held strategic aims of Political Union or, at least, Fiscal Union (see Heipertz 2001 and 2005). But these aims were dropped after the era of Helmut Kohl, Federal Chancellor from 1982 to 1998. Long forgotten were the days of the famous 'Schäuble-Lamers-Paper' from 1994 which had demanded radical institutional reform with France and Germany at the centre (allowing for 'variable geometry' and 'flexible integration' around that core) and seeing the single currency as defining the membership of a future Political Union. This Political Union was to merge not only monetary and economic policy but also foreign policy, security, defence, and other relevant fields into a federal European core state.[2]

Under Angela Merkel and one-and-a-half decades later, Germany no longer strove for the political unification of Europe and arguably missed a historic chance of doing so—65 years after the much-referenced end of World War II. In fact, following the Brussels summit, Merkel flew to Moscow to help Wladimir Putin celebrate the anniversary of Germany's capitulation.

Meanwhile, decision-makers at the ECOFIN level were suddenly under extreme time pressure to produce the results promised by the Heads of State and Government. Ministers had to deliver before financial markets opened in Tokyo on Monday. Paris, Brussels, and Frankfurt had a plan—Berlin did not. Her position as veto player would have given Germany a strong hand in the negotiation, had the Chancellor not already capitulated on Friday night.

[2] https://eu-asia.essca.fr/wp-content/uploads/sites/4/2014/09/schaeuble-lamers-paper-1994.pdf.

At the beginning of the negotiation, the only offer on the table was the Commission's conspicuously well-prepared legal proposal for a European Financial Stabilisation Mechanism (EFSM) by which it would borrow funds on financial markets under an EU budget guarantee to on-lend them to failing euro area Member States.[3] The EFSM would reproduce and magnify the already existing mechanism of the Balance of Payments Regulation, in place for non-euro area Member States in balance of payments crises.[4]

Among colleagues in the Ministry, we saw the EFSM as the intended breakthrough to debt mutualisation, the realisation of the so-called euro-bond, long sought by the Southerners and the European institutions, even more so by the financial markets. Common European debt had existed since the setting up of the European Investment Bank in 1958, and common European debt was also already issued by the Commission for the cash management of the EU budget—but the EFSM would open the door to an entirely new dimension of *Schuldenunion*, literally the 'union of debt'.

Limiting the Damage

Germany's main demands were, as stated above, not strategic, but tactical: First, Member States should intensify fiscal consolidation where required. Second, the EFSM of the Commission would be limited to an amount which could be borrowed against the *existing* EU budget framework; hence Germany resisted an increase in the EU budget against which the Commission could have borrowed the entire amount foreseen.

This limited the scope of the EFSM drastically because there was only a small margin available in the existing budget to fund the guarantee against which the debt would be issued. This margin resulted from the difference between the spending authorisation granted to the Commission by the Council in the EU budget framework and the actual spending.

Because of this much smaller size, the EFSM would have to be complemented by a far larger but *intergovernmental* rather than *communal* instrument, a special purpose vehicle which later came to be called the

[3] Commission Proposal: https://eur-lex.europa.eu/legal-content/EN/TXT/?uri=COM%3A2010%3A2010%3AFIN. Final: https://eur-lex.europa.eu/legal-content/EN/TXT/?qid=1484663483987&uri=CELEX:32010R0407.

[4] https://eur-lex.europa.eu/eli/reg/2002/332/oj.

European Financial Stabilisation Facility (EFSF). Its amount was defined at 440bn EUR, and the duration was limited to three years. Importantly, the EFSF was to be guaranteed by the contributing Members States *pro rata*. By consequence, Germany would not be jointly liable for the entirety of EFSF obligations but only severally for the size of her own subscription.

In other words, the German delegation thought about the financial damage and thereby overlooked the strategic opportunity associated with the proposal. Later-on, I had the opportunity to ask a top negotiator of our delegation as to whether anybody had wondered about the possible future of European integration on 9 May. While we were crossing a busy street in Brussels, he halted, looked me in the eyes, shook his head and sighed: 'Nobody had any time whatsoever to think about such issues'. Maybe Schäuble would have thought about such issues, I fancied silently, but Schäuble had been laying in hospital.

By consequence, the outcome of the 9 May ECOFIN meeting was merely financial in nature and differed markedly from the preceding statement of the Heads of State and Government. It read as follows:

> We have decided to establish a European stabilisation mechanism. The mechanism is based on Art. 122.2 of the Treaty and an intergovernmental agreement of euro area Member States. Its activation is subject to strong conditionality, in the context of a joint EU/IMF support, and will be on terms and conditions similar to the IMF.
> Art. 122.2 of the Treaty foresees financial support for Member States in difficulties caused by exceptional circumstances beyond Member States' control. We are facing such exceptional circumstance today and the mechanism will stay in place as long as needed to safeguard financial stability. A volume of up to EUR 60 billion is foreseen and activation is subject to strong conditionality, in the context of a joint EU/IMF support, and will be on terms and conditions similar to the IMF. The mechanism will operate without prejudice to the existing facility providing medium term financial assistance for non euro area Member States' balance of payments. In addition, euro area Member States stand ready to complement such resources through a Special Purpose Vehicle that is guaranteed on a pro rata basis by participating Member States in a coordinated manner and that will expire after three years, respecting their national constitutional requirements, up to a volume of EUR 440 billion. The IMF will participate in financing arrangements and is expected to provide at least half as much

> as the EU contribution through its usual facilities in line with the recent European programmes.
> At the same time, the EU will urgently start working on the necessary reforms to complement the existing framework to ensure fiscal sustainability in the euro area, notably based on the Commission Communication to be adopted on 12 May 2010. We underline the importance that we attach to strengthening fiscal discipline and establishing a permanent crisis resolution framework. We underlined the need to make rapid progress on financial market regulation and supervision, in particular with regard to derivative markets and the role of rating agencies. Furthermore, we need to continue to work on other initiatives, such as the stability fee, which aim at ensuring that the financial sector shall in future bear its share of burden in case of a crisis, also exploring the possibility of a global transaction tax. We also agreed to speed up work on crisis management and resolution.
> We also reiterate the support of the euro area Member States to the ECB in its action to ensure the stability to the euro area.
> The Council also adopted a regulation establishing a European financial stabilisation mechanism. In addition, the representatives of the governments of the euro area member states adopted a decision to commit to provide assistance through a Special Purpose Vehicle that is guaranteed on a pro rata basis by participating member states in a coordinated manner and that will expire after three years, up to EUR 440 billion, in accordance with their share in the paid-up capital of the European Central Bank and pursuant to their national constitutional requirements. The representatives of the governments of the 27 EU member states adopted a decision allowing the Commission to be tasked by the euro area member states in this context.[5]

The Commission Proposal for the Regulation establishing the EFSM had been adopted at a special meeting of the Commission ahead of the ECOFIN, and Commission President José Manuel Barroso had declared: 'We will defend the euro, whatever it takes' (The Telegraph, 08.05.2010). The formula 'whatever it takes', which was also used by Commission Vice President Olli Rehn in that context, was hence coined by the Commission in 2010—not by ECB President Mario Draghi two years later, who brought it to full prominence.

In its original form, the EFSM proposal by the Commission foresaw two steps for the raising of funds. First, the EFSM would borrow against

[5] https://www.consilium.europa.eu/uedocs/cms_data/docs/pressdata/en/ecofin/114324.pdf.

a guarantee from the existing budget, and the draft Regulation read accordingly:

> **Article 2**
> **Form of the Union financial assistance**
> 1. Union financial assistance for the purposes of this Regulation shall take the form of a loan or of a credit line granted to the Member State concerned.
> To this end, in accordance with a Council decision pursuant to Article 4, the Commission shall be empowered on behalf of the European Union to contract borrowings on the capital markets or with financial institutions.
> 2. Subject to Article 3, the outstanding amount of loans or credit lines to be granted to Member States under the present stabilization mechanism shall be limited to the margin available under the own resources ceiling for payment appropriations.

Crucially, Article 3 then foresaw an open-ended guarantee by Member States, which is worth also quoting in full:

> **Article 3**
> **Guarantees**
> 1. Loans and credit lines above the ceiling referred to in Article 2 (2) shall benefit from the joint and pro-rata guarantee of the euro-area Member States.
> 2. Each euro area Member State shall guarantee the amounts above the ceiling referred to in paragraph 1 according to its share in the paid-up capital of the European Central Bank.
> 3. In the cases covered by this Article, the Commission may rely on the services of the national debt offices of the euro area Member States, which offices shall be at the disposal of the Commission to this end.
> 4. A Member State receiving a financial support decided by the Council under the present Regulation shall not provide a guarantee. The guarantee to be provided by the other Member States shall be recalculated accordingly.
> 5. Member States shall take the measures necessary to ensure that the guarantee is provided within ten days following the Council decision taken in accordance with Article 4.

Article 3 would have been the decisive step towards a fiscal equalisation and transfer scheme—unlimited in size. It would be made available in the form of loans or credit lines to every euro area Member State experiencing or seriously threatened with a severe economic or financial disturbance caused by exceptional occurrences beyond its control (Article 1) upon a Council decision with qualified majority and subject to an economic policy adjustment programme (Article 4). Needless to say: Through the backdoor of debt rescheduling and debt restructuring, the loans could be converted into transfers at a later stage.

Basing the EFSM on Article 122 of the Treaty—foreseen for natural disasters—allowed for a decision under qualified majority. For as long as the EFSM would be taking recourse to the EU budget in the first instance, it would implicate all EU Member States. This included the UK, which was just in the formation of government after a general election. No wonder then that London sided with Berlin in trying to limit the financial damage caused by the EFSM. Both ensured that Article 3 was deleted and that the bulk of the assistance would instead be channelled through the new special purpose vehicle, the EFSF, limited to 440bn EUR and topped up by additional IMF loans which were expected in a size commensurate to half the EFSF volume, hence 220bn EUR.

Somehow, I Have to Make This Final Breakthrough

I was flabbergasted when the news hit Berlin on Monday in the very early morning—and little credit did I give to de Maizière's words in Brussels that the money would ideally not be needed (Focus, 10.05.2010).

The total size of the package, having in mind the financing needs of at least Spain, Portugal, and Ireland for the next two years, amounted to 720bn EUR. Including Italy, however, this would suffice for only one year. Would it be enough to calm the waters? I recalled that German mortgage banks alone were exposed with 87bn EUR to Greece, Portugal, Spain, Ireland, and Italy (Frankfurter Allgemeine Zeitung, 19.02.2010). European banks were exposed to Greece, Portugal, and Spain with about 935bn EUR, according to the BIS.

But it was clear that a momentous breakthrough had occurred, and many saw it as the 'final breakthrough' like in Freddy Mercury's lyrics—final in institutional terms and on substance, certainly not yet in volume. We clearly sensed that this was what one would call a critical juncture—and from here on, developments would be path-dependent.

If necessary, volumes or secondary features could be adjusted later-on. The rather momentous institutional innovation was a joint but intergovernmental body which would be set up with the aim to incur tremendous financial liabilities for the support of floundering Member States. It would stand ready for a change of creditors, should private or non-European creditors of Euro area Member States drop out. While its size was limited, it was equally clear that such caps could be lifted. The importance lay in the precedent. The additional announcement that the ECB would buy sovereign bonds on the secondary market beyond the traditional OMOs was, to my mind, an even more important watershed—as it pushed the door fully open to monetising state finance in the euro area.

I wondered how the combination of these factors would go down in legal as well as political terms in Germany, where planned tax cuts had just been postponed for the sake of creating fiscal buffers on the course to budget balance. More importantly, the prohibition of bailouts and the independence of the central bank had been the cornerstones of German assent to monetary union.

ECB President Jean-Claude Trichet admitted that the Governing Council vote on the decision to purchase government bonds had not been unanimous. He claimed that his new Security Markets Programme (SMP) did not impinge on central bank independence, but commentators in Brussels stated clearly that the ECB's move had occurred under political pressure from some European capitals and Washington (Frankfurter Allgemeine Zeitung, 11.05.2010).

In its press statement, the ECB intended to create a 'tit for tat' situation (on the ECB playing 'tit for tat' games, see Hübner 2019). It connected the SMP to Member States' fiscal consolidation measures:

> The scope of the interventions will be determined by the Governing Council. In making this decision we have taken note of the statement of the euro area governments that they "will take all measures needed to meet [their] fiscal targets this year and the years ahead in line with excessive deficit procedures" and of the precise additional commitments taken by some euro area governments to accelerate fiscal consolidation and ensure the sustainability of their public finances.[6]

But I doubted how this policy line should overcome time-inconsistency in the actual event—would the ECB really withhold its support when Member States failed to consolidate? Or would it rather not succumb increasingly to a situation of fiscal dominance, where the monetisation of

[6] https://www.ecb.europa.eu/press/pr/date/2010/html/pr100510.en.html.

state finance would slide more and more out of the bank's discretion and control (Sargent and Wallace 1981)?

In the current real-word example and all related incidents, the academic notion of time-inconsistency translated into *Realpolitik* whenever institutions like the ECB, the Council, the Commission and Member States alike threw their rules, commitments, and principles overboard as and when required by immediate and insurmountable pressure. The insight that they do so systematically when muddling through a crisis belongs to the essence of this book.

The ECB justified its extreme step by 'severe tensions in certain market segments which are hampering the monetary policy transmission mechanism and thereby the effective conduct of monetary policy oriented towards price stability'. The rather opaque reference to 'transmission' would reappear time and again from this day onward, allowing in terms of communication to nicely link whatever the Bank was doing to its official mandate of price stability.

Few dared to put the notion of transmission into question—it sounded technical enough to justify what was happening, as if the sovereign debt market was a black box in malfunction which would now be fixed by the magic of central bank money. I felt a certain unease and apprehension about this as I personally wondered whether the officially unintended side-effect of compressing spreads—the monetary financing of public balances—was not the real motivation, at least for some.

The market effects were indeed profound—but also short-lived: Spreads fell initially, the Greek two-year rate for example from 18.3 to 5.5%, stocks rose, and the euro gained 0.8% in external value to 1.2820 USD. Spanish and French banking stocks rose by about 20%. Markets remained nervous, however. They picked up on 'good news', such as Spain enacting austerity measures, aiming to reduce its deficit from 9.8% of GDP to 9.3% in 2010 and to 6.5% in 2011, and they fell equally quickly on 'bad news', such as Ackermann alluding to the need of ultimately rescheduling Greek debt. Rumours were also ripe that Schäuble would resign on account of his health.

At the same time, we had start work immediately on a new legal project: The EFSF with its 440bn EUR would require new Federal guarantees, if not capital directly. Initially, we expected an additional burden of 123bn EUR coming our way—not including our share in the EU budget and in increased IMF obligations.

The EFSM, cut down to the existing budget frame and hence limited to 60bn EUR of EU support, to my surprise, had already passed the legislative hurdle, based on the Council decision of Sunday night. It entered into force on Tuesday 11 May.

It was startling to me that the Commission had dared to base it on Article 122—but the move worked. In the case of Greece, Article 122 had not been deemed appropriate, given that the Greek insolvency was hardly caused by events beyond Greece's control. Now, arguably, the daunting contagion to other countries was something akin to *force majeure*, explicitly compared to a natural disaster and thereby the original motivation behind Article 122.

In a similar vein, the ECB's decision on the SMP also required no legislative follow-up—if, for the moment, one disregarded the array of legal proceedings brought against the different elements of the overall aid package.

I noted in my diary: 'We have raised the stakes immeasurably in order to save monetary union and thus the European project. In the process, we have thrown overboard all the principles that were once dear to us—especially in the area of monetary policy and national responsibility'.

When work set in after some moments of amazement on Monday 10 May, it was focused on the setting up of the EFSF. A special cabinet meeting was held already on the following day to initiate a new guarantee law: The German EFSF contingent of 123bn EUR should be equipped with a 20% safety margin, so the ceiling rose effectively to 148bn EUR. The law was scheduled to pass the Bundestag on Wednesday 19 May and the Bundesrat on 4 June.

The Social Democrats made their possible support contingent on the government also advancing a so-called financial transaction tax (FTT). This demand was echoed by the Christian Democrats. The FTT was also a popular request in some other Member States and had found its way implicitly into the summit statement of 7 May, demanding 'a fair and substantial contribution of the financial sector to the costs of crises'. The Services at the Ministry of Finance, however, had always been sceptical about an FTT for technical reasons to do with the global mobility of capital. Short of an international or even just European agreement on such a measure, they cautioned strongly against a unilateral national approach as this would only drive financial transactions abroad.

The EFSF negotiation itself was far more complex than the national guarantee law. An international treaty had to be devised from scratch.

This was the task of the Eurogroup Working Group (EWG), the euro area subset of the Economic and Financial Committee (EFC) which meets at the State Secretary level and reports to ECOFIN.

The EWG held a first telephone conference call on 12 May 2010. The core German demands were threefold: First, loans could only be granted under tough conditionality in the form of a joint IMF/EU adjustment programme. Second, EFSF loans would only be applicable if EFSM resources were insufficient. Third, EFSF decision-making would be unanimous, granting a veto right to Germany. In addition, Germany objected to equipping the EFSF with a large capital base of its own. Finally, Germany sought to limit EFSF membership to euro area countries but encouraged other EU Member States to contribute bilateral loans to the overall effort. Such offers had in fact been aired by Sweden and Poland, building on earlier examples when Iceland and Latvia had received bilateral loans by individual EU Member States during the banking crisis.

Governance Reform?

Meanwhile, work on the governance reform of the euro area took off in meagre form. The Van Rompuy Task Force met for the first time on 25 May 2010. France had made clear once more that Treaty change was out of the question. The Commission was hence preparing secondary legislation to strengthen the SGP—with a level of ambition far below German expectations.

Berlin was seeking more effective sanctions and a more binding framework to increase competitiveness and was still hoping for changes to primary law. Treaty change would be required to strengthen the Commission's role in the EDP and to establish the loss of voting rights as a political sanction for violating the deficit rule. Additionally, Berlin was seeking an international legal basis for state insolvency.

However, once Germany had agreed to set up the EFSF and EFSM, it did not have any leverage to extract more far-reaching concessions on governance and institutions. Angela Merkel had given away Germany's excellent hand in the game for rather little, even by Berlin's own standards of thinking non-strategically about European integration. To elaborate this further, it is worth looking at the German analysis and understanding of the crisis:

According to the Ministry's experts—in close exchange with the Chancellery, the Foreign Office, and the Ministry for Economic Affairs—there were three main institutional deficiencies in EMU: First, the SGP was not flawed by design but simply insufficient and too weak to prevent lapses in fiscal policy. Second, economic policy coordination was equally too weak to prevent imbalances and divergences in competitiveness, leading to asset price bubbles, excessive private debt, current account deficits and overall lack of competitiveness (notably not: current account surpluses as in Germany herself). Third, there were no provisions for the extreme case of sovereign liquidity or solvency crises.

There were multiple underlying sources of these deficiencies, according to the experts, and they amounted to a damning verdict of the euro: The empirical and statistical basis of policy formulation was unreliable, and Eurostat was powerless against the manipulation of public accounts by Member States. The Commission and Member States failed to implement financial and economic policy recommendations and enforce the rules, and the recommendations themselves were often too weak, sketchy, incomplete, and insufficient. The Commission was too political and did not play its role as impartial guardian of the Treaty (on the 'political Commission', see Mérand 2021).

In fact, Jean-Claude Juncker, who in 2014 promised to lead a 'political Commission' told me with disarming honesty why he would rather not open an EDP against France: '*Parce que la France, c'est la France*'.

Four years earlier, the staff of the Finance Ministry already believed that there was too much diplomatic consideration in Brussels and a lack of frankness in the debates of EMU fora, hence not enough peer pressure. Ultimately, in their view, there was a lack of understanding both by Member States and by the Commission that economic and monetary policy were not part of financial diplomacy but in fact the core of European interior policy. There was no appreciation that monetary union in essence had created a *Schicksalsgemeinschaft*, a community of fate and destiny, and there was no respect for the common good of monetary stability. Ultimately, countries should leave the euro area if they continued to disrespect this fundamental character of EMU.

In concrete terms, Germany devised a dozen proposals for strengthening the governance of the euro area, including stricter budgetary surveillance through tougher appraisals of national stability programmes and a more focused debate on deficit procedures, more accountability towards national Parliaments, the introduction of national fiscal rules akin to Germany's zero structural budget deficit rule (the so-called *Schuldenbremse* or 'debt brake'), withholding structural and cohesion fund transfers for EDP sanctions and an enhanced economic policy surveillance.

Berlin also repeated its demand for political sanctions in the form of loss of voting rights, albeit now only for those Council votes that pertained to economic policy matters in the euro area. Given that Member States in that context already do not vote on decisions which concern themselves, the 'political sanction' would now only imply the loss of voting power over other Member States. But beyond that, for extreme cases and under a set of clear criteria, the ultimate sanction still should be a forced exit from the currency union.

Finally, Germany returned to earlier ideas about an international state insolvency regime plus a European Monetary Fund (EMF), now in conjunction with a restructuring facility. Both would provide emergency assistance under strict conditionality and should replace the EFSM and EFSF, seen only as interim solutions.

Dispatching the German proposals to his colleagues in the Van Rompuy Task Force, Minister Schäuble wrote on 20 May 2010: 'We need to take steps to enhance the political dimension of the Monetary Union'. This was the essence of the thinking in the Ministry at the time—but events had moved on and had embarked upon a different trajectory.

Preparing the EFSF

Towards mid-May, risk spreads were on the rise again and the euro returned to its previous downward trend against the dollar. Market developments hence put the EFSF negotiations under acute time pressure. The EFSF was perceived as the missing link between the EFSM and the ECB's SMP, both of which had been put in place with immediate effect.

The ECB had started to purchase sovereign bonds of affected Member States already on Monday 10 May, accumulating 16.5bn EUR of securities in 'dysfunctional markets' by the end of the first week. The amount of public debt on the balance sheet of the ECB has been rising ever since, until the time of writing, albeit in different purchasing programmes: The SMP was terminated in 2012.

According to the breakdown history provided by the ECB,[7] the nominal debt holdings at the end of SMP purchases amounted to 14.2bn EUR for Ireland, 33.9bn EUR for Greece, 44.3bn EUR for Spain, 102.8bn EUR for Italy, and 22.8bn EUR for Portugal; all bonds to be held until maturity. To prevent an impact on monetary policy, the ECB promised to sterilise its SMP asset purchases by draining liquidity in commensurate volumes from the banking system, e.g. through interest-bearing tenders.

The operation was seen to help with compressing sovereign spreads initially, but it did nothing to stop the fall of the euro's external value. Rather to the contrary, market commentators feared that the SMP would tarnish the ECB's independence and set the central bank on a slippery slope towards fiscal dominance (Frankfurter Allgemeine Zeitung, 18.05.2010). As it turned out, full sterilisation proved not even possible already in June (Wall Street Journal, 30.06.2010).

The euro had lost more than 11% of its value against the dollar since 1 February 2010. Furthermore, there were allegations that the purchase of Greek debt helped French banks get rid of their holdings at elevated prices (Der Spiegel, 31.05.2010). Bundesbank President Axel Weber, German ECB Board Member Jürgen Stark and the President of De Nederlandsche Bank Nout Wellink had voted against the SMP in the ECB Council (Frankfurter Allgemeine Zeitung, 04.06.2010). Weber even criticised it in public (Börsen-Zeitung, 11.05.2010). However, he subsequently acquiesced and was known to harbour ambitions to succeed Jean-Claude Trichet at the helm of the ECB.

As the Ministry was advancing the national guarantee law for the EFSF, the details of the international treaty were yet far from clear. Based on the ECOFIN result of 9 May 2010, the negotiation reached or confirmed the following terms over the subsequent week:

The EFSF would only come into play when the EFSM funds were depleted. Any EFSF finance would be conditional on the recipient country agreeing to an adjustment programme with the Troika of IMF, ECB, and Commission. EFSF support would be decided unanimously if the Troika confirmed that the recipient Member State risked losing market access and that this situation would put at risk the stability of the euro area as a whole. The overall limit remained at 440bn EUR, and

[7] https://www.ecb.europa.eu/mopo/pdf/SMP_breakdown_history.csv?2383121633ce6b0629a608d3091e9f6e.

support would only be given in the form of loans or credit lines—with conditions like those used in the Greek bailout. A special purpose vehicle (SPV) would be set up in order to administer the loans, and the 16 euro area Member States would act as shareholders of this SPV. Operational aspects of the SPV would be outsourced to service providers so that the personnel headcount would be reduced to the absolute minimum. The cost of the external services would be borne by the shareholders directly. The SPV would issue bonds only to raise the money required for a concrete loan and in fact only for the immediately planned tranche of that loan—it would hence not be hoarding liquidity or grow in financial volume beyond actual needs. Euro area Member States would guarantee the bonds issued by the SPV pro rata, not jointly, according to their ECB capital share. The guarantees would be issued for specific bonds which in turn would be associated with specific loans. The SPV would charge the recipient country a premium on the loan, to be distributed to the issuers of the guarantee according to their share. Loans could be granted until end 2013, and the SPV would wind down as soon as all outstanding loans were repaid. Bonds issued by the SPV would only serve the purpose of refinancing and carry no credit risk of the recipient Member State, as bonds and guarantees would be legally separate from the loans extended by the SPV. Furthermore, the loan tranches would be made conditional on the recipient Member State implementing the adjustment programme, but the bonds and guarantees would be valid regardless of fulfilment of conditions by the recipient Member State, in order not to deter EFSF bond investors. The disbursement of each tranche would be subject to a unanimous vote by all shareholders, based on a positive recommendation by IMF, Commission and ECB. The SPV should have no capital subscription and no banking licence.

Two important issues were still open: The seat of the SPV would be determined according to the most beneficial tax and legal regime (which is a somewhat paradoxical thing to seek, from a Ministry of Finance point of view), and an already existing institution would be identified to take care of treasury functions such as payments and the administration of loans and bond issuances.

It soon became clear that Luxembourg's agile financial market and the European Investment Bank (EIB) located there fulfilled those requirements in the most pragmatic and convincing way, and some of us civil servants came to see the EFSF as a spin-off of the EIB, not least in terms of the personnel it recruited as EIB secondees—including former close colleagues of mine, as alluded to earlier in this book. With the help of legal experts from the EIB and a couple of high-end law firms, all necessary treaties, contracts, the statute of the EFSF, and other documents were now drawn up swiftly.

German Chagrin

The political debate in Germany was heated. The wider public but also most Parliamentarians felt overwhelmed by the new move, just after having digested the Greek bailout. But senior politicians of the ruling coalition repeated the mantra-like justification of the government and strongly identified themselves with it also personally, as far as I could tell:

They would go back to the global financial and economic crisis of 2008 and the Lehman bankruptcy, stressing the loss in economic output and jobs caused by the ensuing recession and arguing that a recurrence would cause substantially higher costs than the rescue package. According to them, a core lesson from the banking crisis was that politics had to trump markets and surprise them in terms of financial volume, countering the bets of speculators. Speculative attacks would have caused contagion to fiscally 'innocent' Member States like Spain or Ireland which had respected the SGP. It was all about restoring trust as a prerequisite for more orderly developments in the future. The measures were in the German interest because the euro was in Germany's interest and had helped to create our successful model of export-led growth. Conditionality would ensure adjustment and adjustment would assure repayment of the loans—with interest. This, arguably, was the opposite of the much criticised 'transfer union'. Germany would continue to insist on the independence of the ECB, and all measures were in line with the no-bailout clause of the Treaty and rightly based on the legal provision for disaster assistance. And, last but not least, Germany would insist on strengthening the SGP and fiscal discipline in the euro area.

The first reading of the EFSF guarantee law in the Bundestag took place on Wednesday 19 May 2010. Chancellor Angela Merkel delivered a second government declaration, less than two weeks after the one on Greece.[8] 'We protect the money of the citizens of our country', was her opening line before stressing the exceptional test which

[8] https://dserver.bundestag.de/btp/17/17042.pdf#P.4125.

the single currency was facing. The euro was in danger and if that danger could not be averted, the consequences would be incalculable for Europe and beyond. The turbulences on financial markets were 'hysterical' and dramatic. But this was only the economic dimension—the political consequences were beyond imagination. Brushing aside the technicalities, one should see the *Schicksalsgemeinschaft* of currency union (literally the communion of destiny) and that this was about preserving and proving the European idea. It was a historic task: 'If the euro fails, Europe fails'. If we managed to deter this danger, then both the euro and Europe itself would grow stronger as before. The whole of Europe would have to subscribe to *Stabilitätskultur*.

Merkel claimed that she had prevented attempts to set up a *Transferunion* (union of transfers) through joint EFSF liability. She stressed the role of conditionality so that 'deficit sinners' could not escape their duty to make efforts themselves. The government would be able to decide each individual use of the EFSF. (To this, the Green opposition replied that only the government could decide, not Parliament—pointing to yet another future legal battleground before the Constitutional Court. They also criticised that the EFSF contract was not yet ready.)

Merkel insisted that the prerogatives of Parliament were being respected. Returning to the issue of *Stabilitätskultur*, she argued that ECB independence was unquestionable and in fact helped by budgetary consolidation: 'Long-term stability is unthinkable without healthy state finances'. Paying tribute to the recent consolidation measures in Spain and Portugal, she demanded more stringent fiscal policy in all Member States—including Germany herself, where the *Schuldenbremse* (the structural balanced-budget rule) had broken the vicious circle of overspending and indebtedness.

Europe needed a new *Stabilitätskultur*, hence the government was seeking to strengthen the SGP—after it had been weakened in 2004 under a Social Democrat and Green government. She listed some examples of German demands for governance reform, including the loss of voting rights, triggering disbelief among the ranks of the opposition, and confirmed that her government was working towards Treaty change. Merkel concluded by postulating the primacy of politics over markets and presented a long list of financial market reforms on which the government was working.

This list, drawn up at very short notice between the Chancellery and the Ministry of Finance, was designed as a counterweight to the state-sponsored European rescue effort. It was intended to demonstrate to the public that the government would not even wait for the EU to regulate financial markets better and would press ahead its reform agenda in its quest to defend the public interest. In reality, however, most relevant legislative projects concerned the Common Market and where necessarily located at EU level, such as the European Market Infrastructure Regulation, the Markets in Financial Instruments Directive and the Directive on Alternative Investment Fund Managers.

The list also included the delicate issue of a financial transaction tax (FTT), although a public hearing of the Financial Committee of the Bundestag on 17 May 2010 had just demonstrated the common scepticism of representatives of the Bundesbank, the financial sector and academia. The Ministry itself consistently pointed to the need for international cooperation on a possible FTT.

Finance Minister Schäuble spoke two days after Merkel, on 22 May 2010, at the second and final reading of the guarantee law which was again passing under an emergency procedure within a single week.[9] He had to defend the government against the claim that Parliament had not been properly informed about the emergency measures under discussion and was now being presented with a *fait accompli*.

This argument was, as mentioned above, advanced again and more vocally than ever before by the Green party and gave another foretaste of the legal battles before the Constitutional Court which were to follow. The issue of Parliament's rights allowed the Greens to support the EFSF proposal in substance while voting against it for formal reasons in defence. Beyond this topic, it also became clear in the exchange between Schäuble and the Greens that the opposition was seeking Parliamentary votes on each single EFSF loan to be decided—something which the government at that time rejected outright. This tug of war between the legislative and the executive powers of the state would only be settled at Karlsruhe, the site of the Constitutional Court.

In his conclusion, Schäuble stated that stabilising the euro was not without alternative—a remarkable difference to the TINA-sound of the Chancellor—but that it was in Germany's enlightened national interest:

[9] https://dserver.bundestag.de/btp/17/17044.pdf.

'The national interest means to stay bound into a further integrating Europe'. And he reiterated that the proposed measures referred to loans, not transfers.

The EFSF guarantee law was approved on the same day with 319 to 73 votes and 195 abstentions. Six members of the ruling coalition voted against, four abstained and three did not participate in the vote—this was a small but noticeable increase in opposition from within the ranks of the governing parties.[10] Like the Greek guarantee law, it sailed through the Bundesrat immediately after the Bundestag vote. Federal President Horst Köhler, who had just returned from Afghanistan, put his signature under the law before 4.00 pm. Some Parliamentarians, including the Christian Social Democrat Peter Gauweiler, wondered whether the government had exerted influence on the President—who resigned a week later, as mentioned above.[11]

The next important regional election, Baden-Württemberg, was less than a year away. Losing Baden-Württemberg after NRW would be catastrophic for the Christian Democrats, given that this Land had always been considered their stronghold. Inside the party, an authoritarian organisation by any standard, Merkel started to earn criticism in conservative backroom circles. Her course of re-orienting the political profile of the Christian Democrats towards centre-left was anathema to most ordinary members at the grassroots level.

But the last one of the conservative champions and a long-standing rival of Merkel, Roland Koch, the Prime Minister of the Land Hessen, resigned in those days. It had become obvious that the Federal Ministry of Finance, should Schäuble have to resign on account of his health, would rather go to the Merkel loyalist Thomas de Maizière than to Koch. His resignation left Merkel with one competitor less, given that Schäuble was dependent on her support and that the former Head of the Christian Democrat fraction, Friedrich Merz, had left political life already years ago and would not return during Merkel's reign. Christian Wulff, Prime Minister of Lower Saxony, was seen as the last possible Merkel contender. When Federal President Horst Köhler resigned after Merkel's bailout decisions, Wulff became his successor in the highest office of the

[10] https://www.bundestag.de/parlament/plenum/abstimmung/abstimmung?id=113.

[11] https://dserver.bundestag.de/btd/17/022/1702223.pdf.

state and was thereby also neutralised politically. Merkel ruled alone and uncontested thereafter for more than a decade.

The EFSF debate in the Bundestag had shown the political attraction of a financial transaction tax (FTT). Understandably enough, the public longed for a retribution from the world of finance, sensing the ever-growing support which financial markets extracted from the taxpayer. But, in the Ministry of Finance, nobody believed that an FTT would be possible. Capital was globally mobile, and competition was fierce among geographic clusters associated with financial services. Any FTT worth its name would simply cause evasion by relocation to other jurisdictions. Demanding a national FTT was either not very smart or sheer populism. Nevertheless, the government had to be seen to be actively working for an international and, for that matter, global solution—hopeless as the cause may be (see Schäuble 2024).

We set up an international financial market conference at the Ministry to discuss matters of banking regulation, to take stock of the banking crisis and to send a domestic policy signal that we were at least putting FTT on the agenda. To that end arranged a string of very senior political speakers as well as expert panels, the usual workshops, and an elaborate dinner. This conference took place in the same week as the EFSF guarantee was passing Parliament, and the combination of the two events literally caused me sleepless nights. Chancellor Merkel spoke at our conference—my first opportunity to gain a personal impression of her. One-on-one, she did seem to have a very good sense of humour. At the conference, she said that Germany would lobby at the G-20 level for international rules on bank levies and for an FTT (Financial Times Deutschland, 21.05.2010). However, a global FTT, at least internationally based on the G-20 framework, was out of the question. Representing the G-20 chair nation, Canadian Finance Secretary Tiff Macklern made outright clear that his government would resist both—an international agreement on bank levies as well as an FTT.

Finalising the EFSF

More important and intricate than both the national guarantee law and our fruitless attempts on FTT, from our civil service point of view, was the finalisation of the EFSF documents in Brussels and Luxembourg over the following days.

After protracted negotiations in the Eurogroup meeting of Monday 17 May, a so-called term sheet was being devised to define further modalities of the EFSF, adopted on 7 June.[12] At the time of incorporation, Luxembourg was the only shareholder of the EFSF. The other Member States would follow suit as soon as their national proceedings would allow. Their shareholding would correspond to their capital share in the ECB.

As Germany had prevented joint liability and capitalisation, the EFSF required an over-guarantee to attain AAA ratings. Member States therefore agreed that each pro rata guarantee would cover 120% of each bond issue. Also, a cash buffer was foreseen, and experts were looking at possible other market requirements that would need to be observed in order to satisfy the rating agencies.

In terms of governance, the EFSF would have a CEO and a Board. The CEO was still to be appointed, and Germany had made clear that the position should be given to a German national. Eventually, Klaus Regling was chosen, a former civil servant of the Ministry of Finance who had later-on turned into a hedge fund manager and had then served in the highly influential post of Director-General for Economic and Financial Affairs in the Commission (DG-ECFIN) until 2008.

The EFSF Board would consist of the Finance State Secretaries of the Member States in their capacity as shareholders. The EIB was now officially tasked with treasury management and 'administrative support' through a service contract. Behind the scenes, the EIB was engaged in one of its many power struggles with the Commission, the latter securing for itself the task to negotiate and monitor the loan conditions of the EFSF as well as overall consistency between EFSM, EFSF and other bailout measures.

At the beginning of June 2010, most contentious issues in the EFSF negotiation had been resolved. Germany had successfully resisted the demands of France and other partners to waive the strict ceiling on the volume of the EFSF, set at 440bn EUR, and to foresee a so-called 'stepping-in'. Stepping-in would have meant that guarantees given by a Member State which later-on would turn out to require EFSF support itself would be transferred onto the remaining shareholders. These would then 'step in' for their failing companions. In the extreme case, the combination of these two measures could have implied a potentially unlimited

[12] https://www.consilium.europa.eu/uedocs/cms_data/docs/pressdata/en/misc/114977.pdf.

liability shifting ultimately onto the strongest public balance sheet in terms of size and financial standing, hence that of Germany.

It had taken a direct exchange between French Finance Minister Christine Lagarde and Germany's Wolfgang Schäuble before France dropped this demand—the two got along very amicably and we had organised a one-to-one meeting in the form of a breakfast in the Minister's office, a Spartan place compared to her opulent office in Bercy. In turn, the Minister and thereby Germany had accepted secondary measures to enhance the rating of the EFSF as well as the possibility for the EFSF to emit bonds in foreign currency and to engage in hedging operations to cater for foreign exchange risk and interest rate risk, also to be covered by the guaranteeing Member States and subject to their unanimity.

Of those questions that were still unresolved after this ministerial breakfast, the first pertained to the date at which the so-called Framework Agreement[13] on the EFSF should enter into force. Germany had demanded that all shareholders should step in on the same date. However, elections were due in Belgium and Slovenia and their respective governments faced political as well as legal difficulties in tying their hands. In any case, their contributions were small, hence France and other countries demanded that the Framework Agreement should enter into force as soon as 90% of the so-called Commitment Confirmations had been received. This implied that a possible first engagement of the EFSF would take place without the lagging shareholders. Germany accepted this under the condition that the laggards would contribute a commensurately higher proportion in the subsequent engagement.

The second issue concerned Germany's demand that AAA shareholders should receive beneficial terms in the pay-out of the cash buffer of the EFSF. The buffer would be accumulated over time by accruing fees for guarantees and service. It should be invested in high-quality liquid debt instruments and paid out to the shareholders in the case of default or at the end of the maturity of the EFSF. Germany had argued that the buffer should be distributed not pro rata but at a higher rate according to better ratings, given that the top rating lowered the refinancing cost of the EFSF and thereby enabled the accumulation of the cash buffer in the first place. This was logical, but Germany was isolated and even the other AAA shareholders did not support this somewhat stingy claim.

[13] https://www.esm.europa.eu/sites/default/files/20111019_efsf_framework_agreement_en.pdf.

It did also feel odd to me personally to put 148bn EUR in tax money on the fence and then to be wrangling over peanuts. But, after all, the German Ministry of Finance was a place that, at least in those days, used to charge its employees 10 Cents extra if they added milk to their filter coffee in the canteen and that would invite them to a summer party where they had to pay for their beer themselves…

Schäuble dropped both of these two ludicrous demands on 2 June 2010 in a situation when markets were once more deteriorating and when the ECB was calling behind the scenes for immediate readiness of the EFSF. Over the next couple of days, commercial banks deposited 351bn EUR with the ECB, rather than lending to each other—a clear sign of confidence collapsing. At an inconclusive G-20 meeting of Finance Ministers in Busan, South Korea, it became clear that there would be no international agreement on banking levies nor on an FTT.[14] Equally inconclusive was the first meeting of the Van Rompuy Task Force on governance reform on 7 June 2010 on all issues requiring Treaty change.

But at the Eurogroup meeting on the same day, the EFSF was formally set up—equipped with the desired AAA rating. Germany's debt agency, the *Finanzagentur*, stood ready to issue an emergency bond for on-lending to the EFSF, if required before the new bailout fund would be operational. Peter Gauweiler, a Member of Parliament of the Christian Social Democrats from Bavaria, had appealed to the Constitutional Court against Germany's EFSF guarantee law—and, once more, Karlsruhe on 9 June 2010 declined to take immediate action.[15]

The Sparpaket

Two days before, the German government had announced a *Sparpaket* (budget cuts) of 80bn EUR until 2014.[16] It included a new tax on air traffic and a cut particularly in social spending and defence. The government announced that it would reduce the Bundeswehr by 40.000 troops and for the first time put into question Germany's traditional conscription to military service—hitherto a cornerstone of Christian Democracy.

[14] http://www.g20.utoronto.ca/2010/g20finance100605.html.

[15] http://www.bverfg.de/e/rs20100609_2bvr109910.html.

[16] https://www.ardmediathek.de/video/tagesschau/tagesschau-20-00-uhr/das-erste/Y3JpZDovL2Rhc2Vyc3RlLmRlL3RhZ2Vzc2NoYXUvODBkOTc4MmEtNTNlNC00OTUwLThjYzItNjY1OTI3ODc3NTA1.

We unsuccessfully tried to label the *Sparpaket* as *Zukunftspaket* ('future package', instead of 'savings package'). Semantically, the concept of saving seemed to me already far removed from its original meaning, which is to take in more money than one spends and thus create a stock of savings. 'Saving' in government finances, however, means increasing revenues above the increase in expenditures, possibly also a slower increase in expenditures, but hardly their reduction (in nominal terms). I found the application of this watered-down term to mere planning particularly questionable and was relieved when Schäuble acknowledged in private: *"Wir sparen ja gar nicht."* ('We don't even save, really.'). With great fanfare, the medium-term financial planning was adjusted—80 billion EUR were to be 'saved', most of it but by no means all of it on the expenditure side, 'saved' only in the sense of a reduced planning value, however. Of course, savings must begin in the planning stage—but in terms of communication, the decision was deliberately exaggerated in order to suggest the ability of a government in crisis to act.

Regardless of its name—this *Sparpaket* was our ticket to achieving the strategic target of 'black zero', the *Schwarze Null*. It was firmly embedded in the economic worldview prevalent among those who formulated economic policy in Germany, including myself.

During the public unveiling of the *Sparpaket*, I had been asked to prepare 'juicy' bullet points for one of our Parliamentary State Secretaries, in addition to the extensive technical preparation which the Minister and he had received from the specialists. Hence, I sat down, ticking boxes of a narrative that presented our policy as a textbook case of growth-friendly expenditure contractions—a theme I had worked on a few years before as a fiscal economist at the ECB (Hauptmeier, Heipertz and Schuknecht 2007). And a textbook case it was, despite the exaggeration in display:

We were frontloading the consolidation effort, placing the emphasis on reducing expenditure rather than raising revenue, aiming to reduce long-term debt in light of our demography and implicit debt burden, reducing government consumption—particularly on wages—sparing public investment and raising only indirect taxes or direct ones with low elasticity of demand. Our approach was contracyclical as we were saving during an economic upturn and not in conjunction with monetary contraction. We were strengthening institutions—in particular the zero-structural-deficit-rule in the constitution, the so-called *Schuldenbremse* ('debt brake'), which had been adopted in 2009.

The only two textbook boxes I was unable to tick for the presentation by the Parliamentary State Secretary pertained to the lack of flanking structural reforms to lift potential growth and to an unheeded recommendation often made by political economists: If you impose hardship on your economic constituency, hurt everyone—not just particular segments of society. A specific case at hand was the novel tax on air traffic which turned out to be particularly harmful to the business model of Air Berlin, the second biggest carrier in Germany—which was in fact forced to close business in the year the tax was introduced.

Untainted by such remorse to come, I noted the following core messages for our PR strategy: First, solid state finances are the precondition for growth—not vice versa. It's the confidence, stupid! By contrast, deficit spending would lead to debt and reduce fiscal policy effectiveness rather than enhance it. We made clear that the political capital of this government was invested in the consolidation strategy—bound to say what we do and to do what we say. We would set clear strategic objectives, be reliable, allow for long-term planning by economic agents and create, above all, confidence through our wholesale, comprehensive approach.

On the evening of the day when the *Sparpaket* was announced more or less along these lines, I met a fellow officer of the reserve who served in the Ministry of Defence. The recently introduced smoking ban in Berlin was still widely ignored, and we enjoyed our cigars in *Clärchens Ballhaus*, a place famous for ballroom dancing since the roaring 1920s. Judging by the glances of prospective dancing partners, I regretted that I was not also wearing my uniform.

My comrade leaned over to me, referred to the *Sparpaket* and said that the Bundeswehr, cutting another four divisions to free money for the continued effort in Afghanistan, would now become smaller than the Reichswehr of the Versailles Treaty—and as a military not even faintly as good. 'You are ruining the Bundeswehr beyond repair. There is money for Greece and everybody else but not for military capabilities. Forget Afghanistan if we cannot even stand up to defend our own country. What will happen if, one day, we will have to stand against Russia?' I sighed and quoted Angela Merkel who had just declared to the press: 'These are serious times. These are difficult times.' (Frankfurter Allgemeine Zeitung, 08.06.2010, own translation)

CHAPTER 6

Testing the Limits

Discussing Governance

The EFSF was a watershed in more than one way. In stark contrast to the Commission's original proposal, Germany and other Member States had insisted on an intergovernmental approach instead of the so-called 'community method'. The EFSF arrangement was based on an international treaty and entirely under the control of national governments. The same is true for its eventual successor, the European Stability Mechanism (ESM).

Both operate within a cooperative framework in which the Commission, the ECB, the IMF, and other institutions have their role and function—but, in essence, they are intergovernmental instruments. In that sense, they have not strengthened any federalist or supranational trend in European integration but, to the opposite, they have tipped the balance in favour of a federative approach.

Quite literally in financial terms, they have pooled national sovereignty of different nation-states—while at the same time avoiding by all means a meaningful shift of power towards the supranational level. The need for institutions, rules, procedures and the like was mainly answered at the national level and by intergovernmental means.

The governance debate was, from my point of view, much more important and fundamental to the future of Europe than the concrete

M. Heipertz, *Merkelism and the Fine Art of Flat Politics*, Palgrave Studies in European Union Politics,
https://doi.org/10.1007/978-3-031-87592-2_6

bailout programmes, their financing and the attached conditionalities. It seemed lamentable that institutions were set up only with the functional purpose of fulfilling financial requirements—no thoughts being given to the strategic choices which they nevertheless entailed about integration policy.

The governance debate was cornered between two overriding tactical and short-term considerations: First, the French demand of avoiding Treaty change. Second, the German demand for an arrangement that—at least from a German view of the world—would maximise the chance that loans would be paid back in full. Actors at the time seemed unaware that the consequences of an intergovernmental bailout mechanism would be path-dependent in institutional terms and, by its sheer existence, would preclude any alternative path for as long as the existing one somehow continued. Once embarked on this road, they would kick the can down that same road for as long as possible.

Strategic thinking about integration policy was probably most advanced in the ECB. This was on the one hand the body least powerful and most detached from decision-making in integration policy—a field far beyond the Bank's narrow monetary policy mandate. On the other hand, the ECB was also the body most affected and concerned, and it did have the luxury of many academically well-trained and practically experienced eurocrats able and eager to think conceptually about EU and euro area governance. Unlike the staff of national governments, ECB staff, similar to Commission staff, was used to working in a European supranational institution with a profoundly European look at politics. The identity of an ECB staff member is very different from one of a national civil servant. Hence, unsurprisingly, it was the ECB which on 10 June 2010 tabled a very comprehensive and far-reaching, pro-integrationist concept of governance reform for the Van Rompuy Task Force.

The ECB's note set out proposals for, first, strengthening surveillance over budgetary policies and more effective correction of excessive deficits and debts, second, an improved framework for competitiveness surveillance and the symmetric correction of economic imbalances and, third, the design of an appropriate and permanent framework for crisis management, safeguarding financial stability in the euro area while minimising moral hazard. The ECB boldly declared that its proposals required a quantum leap towards strengthening the institutional foundations of

EMU. It laid out the roadmap towards a 'deeper economic union'—bringing economic and fiscal policy on a level finally commensurate to the degree of integration already achieved in monetary affairs.

In terms of fiscal policy, the ECB essentially proposed to strengthen ex ante decision-making in the Eurogroup by underpinning it with an independent EU fiscal agency, setting policy parameters and validating national fiscal policy, based on reliable Eurostat data. Deviations would be sanctioned automatically and judicially, also through non-financial sanctions such as the suspension of voting rights, on-site monitoring, and special missions, forcing deviating countries to seek the fiscal agency's consent for budgetary measures.

Besides the agency, a second institution was to be set up for crisis management. It would give loans and purchase public debt of a Member State in distress, but under strong conditionality and against tradeable collateral which the Member State would have to provide, such as through state-owned property. Conditionality would be ensured through the installation of a so-called European Enforcement Officer in the national capital, depriving the recipient state of fiscal sovereignty. This idea was in fact very popular with civil servants in the German Ministry of Finance who, later in the process, would also demand a deviating recipient country to be placed under tutelage.

In terms of competitiveness, the ECB saw the need to urgently address the problem of significant divergences and intra-euro area macroeconomic imbalances. But it fell short of proposing an equally stringent and quasi depoliticised system as it had suggested for fiscal policy, and it understood imbalances entirely as a supply-side phenomenon, akin to the German view.

The ECB sought to partially replace 'soft' policy coordination by 'hard' elements like a corrective mechanism which would be mirrored on the SGP. It should feature an 'excessive vulnerability procedure' for so-called 'problem cases' that suffered from significant losses in competitiveness and ensuing trade deficits. The ECB suggested modelling this procedure on two competitiveness indexes, which it already regularly published, based on inflation and unit labour costs, as well as on deviations from 'stability-oriented wage developments'. Additional indicators could be cost and price developments, asset prices, credit booms etc. Persistent 'problem cases' with deliberate infringements of earlier recommendations should be subjected to sanctions like under the fiscal policy regime.

According to my diary, I was at first rather excited when reading the ECB's proposals—they entailed my wildest technocratic dreams come true. But then I had second thoughts: What about legitimacy? Was it at all conceivable that a national sovereign democratic state would capitulate before a European Enforcement Officer? And, if so, would the people accept that or rise in fury against both their government and that European proconsul? While harbouring great sympathy for the formation of a European Empire (see Beck and Grande 2005), I did not want to think of it as one which would be based exclusively on functional and bureaucratic effectiveness like China, void of democratic representation and participation by the people. Not for the first time, a peculiar thought crossed my mind: How would this go down with the Brits? Sure, they were not in the euro area—but would such thinking not encourage those in the UK who generally argued in disfavour of European integration?

Even for an ardent integrationist as myself, the ECB's concept entirely lacked core democratic elements of what I would have understood to mean 'Political Union', hence a real, representative European Parliament worthy of the name, to which both the fiscal agency and the crisis management body and, for that matter, the Commission itself, would be accountable as the executive branches of the state. In the terms of the academic literature on legitimacy, which I had in mind, the ECB's ideas were all about 'output legitimacy' and entirely blank of 'input legitimacy' (see Scharpf 2009).

In any case, the ECB proposals ran valiantly but bluntly against the united front of Member States' interests and had not the slightest chance of seeing the light of day. I was wondering whether my former colleagues in Frankfurt were aware that they had produced a piece of pure technocratic doctrine, like a teaching of moral theology from the Vatican, equally distant from the realities of (political) life but beautiful to look at as an abstract ideal and, maybe, a source of inspiration once sufficient remorse had sunk in with the sinners in national capitals.

On Monday 14 June 2010, Chancellor Angela Merkel received French President Nicolas Sarkozy in Berlin to discuss the governance reform of the euro area ahead of the next meeting of the Heads of State and Government in Brussels, scheduled for Thursday of the same week. The meeting had been postponed by one week, causing rumours about a rift between France and Germany.

Ahead of the meeting, Sarkozy had proposed once more the standard French theme of a *gouvernment économique* for the euro area, this time with a separate Secretariate General. But after one-and-a-half hours talking to Merkel, it became clear that there would be no new institutions. Both surprisingly agreed to suspend Member States' voting rights in the Council as a form of ultimate political sanctioning. Concerning budgetary policy, Sarkozy corrected earlier criticism of the German *Sparpaket* and announced instead that also France would seek to cut her expenditures. They also agreed in pushing for a banking levy and an FTT at the G-20 level. The European Council concluded on Thursday as follows:

> The EU has met the worldwide financial crisis with united resolve and has done what was necessary to safeguard the stability of the Economic and Monetary Union. In particular, in May agreement was reached on a support package for Greece as well as on a European financial stabilisation mechanism and facility, which was finalised in June. We have been laying the foundations for much stronger economic governance. We remain committed to taking all necessary action to put our economies back on the path of sustainable and job-creating growth. To that end, today:
> – we adopt "Europe 2020", our new strategy for jobs and smart, sustainable and inclusive growth. It constitutes a coherent framework for the Union to mobilise all of its instruments and policies and for the Member States to take enhanced coordinated action. It will promote the delivery of structural reforms. The emphasis must now be on implementation, and we will guide and monitor this process. We will discuss further, over the coming months, how specific policies can be mobilised to unlock the EU's growth potential, starting with innovation and energy policies;
> – we reaffirm our collective determination to ensure fiscal sustainability, including by accelerating plans for fiscal consolidation where warranted;
> – we confirm our commitment to ensuring financial stability by addressing the gaps in regulation and supervision of financial markets, both at the level of the EU and at the G20. We agree to rapidly advance on key legislative measures so that the new supervisory bodies can start work from the beginning of next year and set an ambitious position for the EU to take at the Toronto Summit;
> – we fully agree on the urgent need to reinforce the coordination of our economic policies. We agree on first orientations as regards the Stability and Growth Pact and budgetary surveillance as well as broader macroeconomic surveillance. We look forward to the final report of the Task Force in October.[1]

[1] https://www.consilium.europa.eu/media/21369/qc3010507enc.pdf.

On the evening of the same day, I listened to Egon Bahr in a think tank called the German Council on Foreign Relations. It was a fine mid-summer evening as we congregated in the splendid garden of the think tank's premises. Bahr had been the mastermind of Social Democratic foreign policy in the 1960s, and I heard him say about the EU: 'A lamentable structure, so lamentable that one would want to tear one's hair out.'

Bahr argued that European integration could only advance if Great Britain would leave the EU, and that Europe would have to emancipate itself from the US. With the single currency we had put our heart on the fence and now had to follow suit—the current situation being dismal and shameful. Germany was ready to forgo the nation state, while France still clung to it.

I said to him privately during the subsequent reception that he had given a pretty good account of why the European Council on the same day had delivered rather little. But I added that he should not underestimate the habit of Germany's government since Schröder to also cling to the nation state, despite its readiness under Merkel to accumulate financial obligations for the sake of Europe.

Proposals for Sovereign Debt Restructuring

It was obvious that the governance debate would only lead to some piecemeal strengthening of the SGP, to the extent that this was possible by changing secondary legislation, and nothing more. Any reform elements requiring Treaty change would remain inconclusive, at the request of France. At the same time, the German government still believed that the EFSF would be a transitory body, and it continuously tried to shift the focus towards a rules-based system for state insolvencies.

Berlin worked on the concept of a Sovereign Bond Restructuring Mechanism (SBRM), involving the Ministry of Finance, the Ministry of Justice and the Chancellery while keeping the Ministry for Economy and the Ministry for Economic Cooperation and Development informed.

The underlying idea of an SBRM was to prevent private creditors to be replaced by public creditors as risk-takers—as in fact had happened by accident through the Greek bailout and the subsequent setting up of the EFSF. Sovereign debt in private hands should remain in private hands, including the associated risk. Thereby, perverse incentives and moral hazard could be reined in that, otherwise, risked materialising ever more strongly.

The experts thought that once a logical and transparent system had been put in place, markets could gauge and price properly and would exert the necessary degree of discipline on profligate governments by themselves. It was their belief that market principles could be brought to bear on the sovereign debt situation and would in fact be far superior to the European approach of public bailouts under conditionality. By 'bailing in' private sector creditors rather than 'bailing out' public debtors, the idea was to reduce moral hazard and ensure appropriate risk premia. After all, the interest rate on any bond included a risk component and accrued as profit to the creditor—hence the creditor should then also bear the risk without being able to shift it onto the public purse. The conceptual model contained two phases:

In phase one, the debtor country would be given 'breathing space' by a measured prolongation of its debt, possibly in conjunction with moderate haircuts. The mix of haircuts and prolongation would be organised by a new institution dubbed 'Berlin Club' (as opposed to the traditional Paris Club dealing with debt issues of developing countries). The Berlin Club would safeguard the debt restructuring exercise with a guarantee for part of the debt stock.

Standardised collective action clauses (CACs) in all sovereign bonds would make the restructuring straightforward. The debtor country would commit in phase one to accept the conditionality of phase two in case the 'breathing space' did not suffice to regain market access and it would undergo an IMF programme of adjustment.

Phase two would come to bear in cases where the IMF programme had not led the debtor country to regain market access. Phase two would consist of a more wholesale debt restructuring in the event of insolvency, to be coordinated by the Berlin Club but also involving both the Paris Club and the London Club (dealing with private sector debt). The guarantee of the Berlin Club would be drawn in order to prevent default. The Berlin Club in turn would be able to seize collateral in exchange for paying out the guarantee. Throughout the process, the Berlin Club would act as a politically independent legal entity.

This way of thinking was particularly well developed in the Directorate-General VII (financial markets) at the Ministry of Finance and in the Economics Section of the Chancellery and stood in contrast to the predominant thinking of the so-called 'Europeans' in both Ministry and

Chancellery. Senior economic advisers in the Chancellery were determined to launch an initiative for an SBRM at the G-20 level during the second half of 2010. They explicitly saw the need as well as a good chance for their project in the case that the bailout approach would fail. The SBRM initiative built on an already mentioned, earlier debate at the IMF on a Sovereign Debt Restructuring Mechanism (SDRM). Anticipating difficulties at the G-20 level, the experts suggested transforming the EFSF into a European restructuring facility.

Pressure Mounting on Germany

The situation of financial markets meanwhile remained extremely tense and fragile. Preparing a G-20 summit for the end of the month, the so-called Financial Stability Board (FSB) among Central Bank Presidents and Finance State Secretaries convened in Toronto on 14 June 2010 under the chairmanship of Mario Draghi, then Governor of the Banca d'Italia. Participants feared that European banks could suffer shortages of liquidity and a déjà-vu of the Lehman crisis, given overall uncertainty and the drying-up of interbank markets. Some argued that the credibility of public support to the banking system was reaching its limits. (Ultimately, only the central bank can provide unlimited liquidity—as long as it does not care about price stability.) Draghi pointed to planned banking stress tests in the EU. These would be made public and flanked by so-called backstops, i.e. political declarations to deal with potential severe situations revealed by stress testing.

On the eve of the G-20 summit, Finance Minister Schäuble had to defend Germany's consolidation policy, chastised internationally as an ill-fated austerity obsession. The notorious hedge fund manager George Soros was one of the most vocal critics, notwithstanding a direct encounter of his with the Minister in Berlin. When picking up Soros at the main entrance of the Ministry, I was told rather bluntly that we did not understand how financial markets work. According to Soros, markets show a distorted picture of reality—e. g. 'Greece goes bankrupt'—and if we followed rather than led them, we allowed markets to determine reality rather than policy determining reality (for a market-sociological treatment of this issue, see Beckert and Arndt 2024).

Soros thought that stabilising the euro was necessary and in our own interest to avoid financial market upheaval. But, echoing a demand made by US Finance Secretary Timothy Geithner earlier that week, we should forget about austerity and do more for growth and domestic demand, including deficit spending. Also, US President Barack Obama had written to the G-20 leaders with a thinly veiled rebuff to Germany: 'I am concerned by weak private sector demand and continued heavy reliance on exports by some countries with already large external surpluses'.[2]

To alleviate the pressure, we placed an op-ed by Schäuble in the Financial Times newspaper according to which 'the German government knows it has a responsibility to promote growth in Europe and the world'. The op-end went on to say that 'we will rise to it not by piling up public debt but by fulfilling our traditional role as an anchor of stability' (Financial Times, 24.06.2010). In fact, we—including the Minister himself—were all too aware of the fact that our *Sparpaket*, the savings package, did not at all mean lower spending in nominal terms. Instead, we would simply allow GDP to grow minimally faster than primary expenditure in real terms, as discussed in the previous chapter. The 2010 budget, after all, was still deemed expansionary and those cuts that had been made represented less than 0.5% of GDP.

Our Financial Times op-ed stated in no uncertain terms that there were 'two different approaches to economic policy-making on each side of the Atlantic'. We argued that US policymakers liked to focus on short-term corrective measures, whereas we would take the longer view and were, therefore, more preoccupied with the implications of excessive deficits and the dangers of high inflation:

> So are German consumers. This aversion to deficits and inflationary fears, which have their roots in German history in the past century, may appear peculiar to our American friends, whose economic culture is, in part, shaped by deflationary episodes. Yet these fears are among the most potent factors of consumption and saving rates in our country. Seeking to engineer more domestic demand by raising government borrowing even further would, here at least, be counterproductive. On the contrary, restoring confidence in our ability to cut the deficit is a prerequisite for balanced and sustainable growth.

[2] https://www.reuters.com/article/us-g20-obama-letter-text-idUSTRE65H2NU20100618.

We went on to argue about demographic decline and the fact that our strategy not only spared but even increased public spending on R&D before culminating in our creed:

> We will abide by the rules of the "debt brake" and by its European equivalent, the Stability and Growth Pact, not for prestige reasons, not just because we are legally bound to, nor, as has been comically suggested, out of masochism, but because it is the best way to inspire confidence in our citizens and investors that the state can cope with the current situation.

At least one other government in Europe seemed to think alike: On 22 June, the British Chancellor of the Exchequer announced a consolidation package of similar straits. And even US President Obama, in his above-mentioned letter, hat stated that 'all G-20 countries should put in place credible and growth-friendly plans to restore sustainable public finances'. But our and the British efforts at consolidation were of course dwarfed in proportion by what we expected from Greece: cutting expenditure by 13 percentage points of GDP until 2014. You cannot have the cake and eat it, I thought. If you postpone consolidation forever, it will haunt you in a way that is anything else but 'growth-friendly'.

Six Pack Instead of Governance Reform

Meanwhile, as Van Rompuy's governance debate was stalling, the Commission set out to advance incrementally with the existing institutions and the existing book of rules. On 30 June 2010, Brussels published a Communication on 'Enhancing economic policy coordination for stability, growth and jobs—Tools for stronger EU economic governance'.[3] Therein, the Commission proposed a legislative programme which came to be dubbed the 'Six Pack' as it would consist of no less than six separate Regulations. Its triple aim was to increase budgetary discipline while at the same time reducing macroeconomic imbalances and enticing structural reform for increased competitiveness. Both the preventive as well as the corrective arms of the SGP were to be strengthened.

One of the innovations proposed was to sanction insufficient consolidation efforts during economic upturns. Another one envisaged to

[3] https://ec.europa.eu/economy_finance/articles/euro/documents/com_2010_367_en.pdf.

make debt adjustment paths more binding than before and to rebalance the focus of the SGP away from unilaterally controlling annual deficits towards continuously reducing excessive debt levels. At the same time, penalties for excessive deficits should be incurred much quicker than before, also through cutting EU transfers to deviating Member States. At the national level, debt brakes and fiscal watchdogs should be introduced. Coordination should be made smoother by introducing a 'European Semester' of reporting, assessment, and correction cycles of national fiscal and economic policies. New indicators were to be defined, including current account developments, labour costs, real estate price dynamics, private debt levels and the like. A macroeconomic imbalance caused by a particular Member State should be subject to peer review and, ultimately, also to sanctions as in the excessive deficit procedure.

Commissioner Rehn announced the legislative proposals for the end of September 2010, thereby effectively replacing the travails of the Van Rompuy Task Force. While discussions among Finance Ministers and at staff level continued pro forma in the latter—inter alia on Germany's demand for a state insolvency regime—they did not come to bear any more on the actual legislative work advanced in the EU.

Rehn declared that 'we do not have the luxury of time' (Börsen-Zeitung, 01.07.2010, own translation). Without explicitly mentioning Germany, Rehn also said that nobody wanted to diminish the export achievements of any country but, depending on the case at hand, there could also be recommendations for strengthening domestic demand.

The Six Pack was well received in the public domain, but most commentators were quick to understand that it shied away from proposing Treaty change. Sticking to an unchanged version of primary law, however, would make it impossible to substantially strengthen the regime of economic sanctions, let alone render them automatic. SGP sanctions would remain a political prerogative—and thereby not credible. I wrote down a very rough core assessment for political consumption: At best, the Commission initiative would help us selling the rescue policy domestically. At worst, it would further increase international pressure against our *Schwarze Null*.

As concerned our central demand in the Van Rompuy Task Force, a state insolvency regime, the situation was bleak: At the level of State Secretaries, the issue was discussed for the first time in July 2010 and had received no more than a lukewarm response. Most other Member States were focused on perpetuating the EFSF without foreseeing a mechanism for orderly state insolvency. Only the Netherlands, Finland and Denmark sided with us and argued that a state insolvency mechanism, from their point of view, was a precondition for having a permanent bailout fund. France was at least open to discuss haircuts of sovereign bonds held be the private sector—but argued that this issue should be postponed as long as markets remained highly nervous and would react negatively to such a debate.

As stated above, German thinking about state insolvency was aimed at preserving market access for the country in question while reducing the amount of foreign support to the utmost minimum and sharing the burden between private and public creditors in an orderly manner. In doing so, the serious moral hazard associated with bluntly bailing out a bankrupt state could be avoided. The restructuring exercise was still conceived of two phases: First, the country concerned would be given 'breathing space' and an adjustment programme by the Commission and the IMF, aimed at fully returning the country to capital markets over time. The ECB and its political independence should no longer be compromised as hitherto in the Troika. We also no longer proposed a Berlin Club, a name which had proven unhelpful in the discussion. Instead, we now looked at including the newly envisaged European Systemic Risk Board (ESRB) in this effort.

In essence, the required 'breathing space' would be achieved through debt restructuring, i.e. a combination of debt relief, prolongation, and haircuts, but also, if necessary, through guarantees. Short of a Berlin Club, it was unclear who should extend the guarantees, but, in any case, the collective action clauses (CACs) in all sovereign bonds would allow for majority decisions among the creditors, facilitating the concrete decision-making for the adjustment and probably also allowing to set up a combined guarantee, if necessary. We would also have been ready to consider an enhanced role of the EFSF for the issuance of a joint guarantee.

Our model then still foresaw phase two, should phase one not be successful: A lasting insolvency and hence inability of the country concerned to return to market funding. The guarantee would be drawn, and the country concerned would be placed under severe restrictions such as losing its vote in the Council and seeing its assets seized. Alas, nobody familiar with the thinking in Paris and Brussels saw high chances for our vision to become reality.

During the summer, the ECB turned surprisingly hostile to the German proposal of a debt restructuring mechanism. It argued that restructuring sovereign debt would undermine the rule of law and, beyond that, trust in the state generally. It would also pull the rug under financial market regulation by jeopardising sovereign bonds as benchmark assets. It would cause moral hazard and lead to more, not less, excessive debt. Also, it would encourage speculative attacks on European bonds and make the already volatile situation even more dangerous. Debt restructuring would occur not in an orderly but rather chaotic fashion. The preceding SDRM initiative, according to the ECB, had failed for good reasons and should not be resuscitated. Instead, the Euro area should strengthen the fiscal rulebook.

Internally, the experts at the Ministry refuted the arguments made by the ECB. After all, the work of the Paris Club and of the London Club and a long history of sovereign debt restructurings had proven their worth. The question was not whether debt restructuring occurred, but how and, more precisely, whether it could be done in an orderly fashion according to prior agreements, rules, and institutions. Contrary to the ECB's stance, trust could very well be built that way and market discipline would ensue. Clearly, the SGP had not brought about sufficient fiscal discipline in the past—so there lay little hope in fixing the problem by having even more and stricter rules.

However, reconfiguring the SGP rulebook was the only common ground for the further proceedings of the Van Rompuy Task Force. The Ministry realised that Germany was isolated on the issue of a state insolvency regime. Hopes for a Franco-German agreement on the matter turned out to be ill-founded. France and the other Member States were ready to consider a permanent crisis resolution mechanism—but its resemblance to the German proposal was only in name: Under that label, they envisaged a perpetuation of the EFSF.

Banking Stress Test

On 23 July 2010, the results of the banking stress test were made public. 91 European banks had undergone the exercise amidst extensive scuffling about methodology behind the scenes. The stress scenario imagined an economic downturn in conjunction with higher interest rates and risk premia on sovereign bonds of all European countries except Germany.

The main result was that seven banks (five from Spain and one each from Greece and Germany) would undercut the minimum 6% threshold for core capital, jointly lacking 3.5bn EUR in capital. The legal minimum of 4% was undercut by one Spanish bank. An additional 17 banks—again mainly from Spain—fell short of 7% core capital and another 15 banks—yet again mainly Spanish—did not reach 8%. The other 52 banks were deemed sound and safe.

We had been worried beforehand about the performance of the German *Landesbanken*. In fact, their situation was more dire than the stress test suggested—but they superficially benefitted for the purposes of the stress test from the recent past of state support, capital injections and spin-off of toxic assets onto public balances.

While the results were received with relief overall, they did show the weakness of the Spanish banking system. To me, this recalled an important theme: Starting with the original Greek bailout, the EFSF (and its ESM successor) reflected a continuous preference of rather bailing out states than banks. Subsequent cases other than Greece which we were about to face, especially Ireland and Spain, would lead to so-called 'banking programmes', but the actual bailout occurred through the national budgets, even if the recipient Member States then used important parts of the funds to capitalise their banks.

Such a course of action did not at all seem obvious to me at the time. Can you bail out states like banks? Given our varying experiences with the banking crisis of 2007 and 2008, I was under the impression that any national government has far greater control over their local banks than an intergovernmental group organisation can possibly have over a sovereign national state. The conditionality of national adjustment programmes has always been found wanting, falling prey to the ubiquitous issues of time-inconsistency and moral hazard. Contrast this with the potentially unlimited legal and supervisory control which a government can exert over a bank, including nationalisation as *ultima ratio*. But obviously, there was no legal way by which an intergovernmental body could wield power over national banks, at least at short notice. The theme of 'Banking Union' was still in the making.

Should Greek Debt Be Restructured?

Also in the summer of 2010, the IMF for the first time floated the idea of giving Greece more breathing space by relaxing the repayment of the bailout loans. The Fund had recognised that Greece would be unable to pay back its loans and proposed roughly doubling the repayment period. Of all institutions involved in the process, the IMF was the one least willing to thwart economic reality.

Officials at the Ministry were surprised at the IMF proposal and argued that the repayment burden was indeed considerable but had been clear from the start. The usual structure had been implemented: Roughly three years without debt service, followed by two years of redemption in eight instalments. The IMF had proposed to prolong the grace period to four years and a half and the repayment period even to ten.

Against this, the Ministry pointed to reputational risks for Greece, reducing her chance to return to market funding, as well as reduced incentives for discipline and reform. Beyond that, any prolongation would require renewed Parliamentary approval in Berlin. There was a risk that the Chancellor would lose face just months after the politically extremely costly and difficult proceedings which had enable the bailout to go ahead. The government would have to compensate KfW and stood an even greater risk of losing the pending case before the Constitutional Court. While privately agreeing to the economic arguments of the Fund, the Ministry flatly turned down the overtures from Washington and asked the Chancellery to do likewise.

From 26 July to 5 August 2010, the Troika visited Athens. Some close former colleagues of mine at the ECB were involved. Their mission was routinely foreseen to check programme implementation and to clear the second instalment of the loan package to be transferred to Greece. The Commission published the Troika's findings on 19 August. Commissioner Olli Rehn was quoted as saying:

> Greece has managed impressive budgetary consolidation during the first half of 2010 and has achieved swift progress with major structural reforms. Despite the significant progress made, challenges and risks remain. The main immediate challenge is to safeguard adequate liquidity and financial stability of the banking sector. At the same time, the structural reform

> agenda needs to be pressed ahead to unleash the huge potential for raising growth.[4]

We looked at the report in detail. Greek GDP was shrinking by 4 percentage points in 2010 and expected to contract further by about 2.6 percentage points in 2011. Unemployment was rising, the current account deficit was shrinking but stayed high. Inflation was much higher than expected at 5.5%—mainly due to higher levels of taxation. The budget deficit was slashed from 13.6% of GDP in 2009 to 8% in 2010 on the back of expenditure cuts by 17 percentage points—a staggering figure.

Meanwhile, structural reform legislation was sailing through Parliament as required, the only stumbling block being privatisations and the restructuring of state enterprises. The banking sector suffered from a lack of liquidity, and the government was therefore planning to support banking bonds by a state guarantee of up to 25bn EUR. Encouragingly, Greece had been able to place T-Bills for 3.5bn EUR with a duration of 26 weeks on the market. However, risk premia on Greek sovereign debt stayed very high which, according to the Commission, was a sign that markets were expecting debt restructuring at some point in the future.

In sum—the programme seemed on track and the second tranche would be paid out as planned. KfW had transferred 4.43bn EUR in the first instalment and was now instructed to send 1.5bn EUR in the second. By contrast, the government of Slovakia decided on 11 August 2010 not to participate in the Greek bailout, which caused considerable irritation in Berlin.

Behind the scenes, the Commission was now leaning towards the view of the IMF according to which the Greek programme should be restructured. This became clear a month later when the Commission estimated Greece's financing needs to be 86bn EUR in 2014 and 80bn in 2015—clearly too high for the taste of financial markets. To us, it seemed politically impossible to make even a prolongation acceptable to the Bundestag and the German public at large. Additionally, relaxing the programme a few months after starting it would, from our point of view, exacerbate moral hazard. All that mattered was the meticulous implementation of the policy measures prescribed by the programme—not their economic or societal effects.

[4] https://ec.europa.eu/commission/presscorner/detail/en/IP_10_1059.

Our own experts realised that the high volumes of required funding in 2014 and 2015 would be difficult to raise on the financial markets—but we preferred to cross that bridge only once we would get there. Rather a new programme then than a prolongation or any other form of restructuring now. This was the message we had prepared for Minister Schäuble to give to his Greek counterpart Papaconstantinou at a meeting on 22 September.

But the official publication of the so-called Maastricht data by Eurostat on 22 October painted a surprisingly bleak picture for the state of Greece's public finances and showed that the programme was maybe not yet off-track but certainly founded on false assumptions. Eurostat corrected the 2009 deficit ratio upward by 1.5 percentage points and the debt ratio even by 12.7 percentage points—partially related to the effects of off-market swap deals with the investment bank Goldman Sachs in 2005 and 2006. The debt ratio was now forecast to rise to 157% of GDP in 2013, more than 10 percentage points higher than foreseen in the programme. Obviously, Greece would also soon exceed the 8% deficit limit of the programme—which would thereby be openly seen to be off-track. The Ministry argued that we should demand even more expenditure reductions for the Greek 2011 budget which would be assessed by the next Troika mission in mid-November.

Brief Quiet Before the Next Storm

Before that, on 6 and 7 September, I was part of Minister Schäuble's delegation in Brussels for meetings of the Van Rompuy Task Force, Ecofin and Eurogroup.

The Task Force went badly—Germany was indeed isolated with her demand for an insolvency regime and, short of Treaty change, any serious strengthening of the SGP was also out of the question. We were not being entirely consistent in asking for a general scheme of debt restructuring while opposing the concrete IMF proposal to reschedule the Greek programme. But, obviously, we wanted private debt to be rescheduled while leaving our public credit untouched. In terms of tactics, in any case, we were making such important demands three months too late, after having given away our trump card of agreeing to the bail-out in the first place. The Ministry, instead of establishing a '*iunctim*', as this is called in diplomacy, had foolishly placed its hopes in a Franco-German initiative for the Task Force and now felt betrayed by Paris. Such moments made me think that the distribution of cleverness between Paris and Berlin was not exactly skewed to our favour.

Over the following weeks, at least the legislative proposals by the Commission on strengthening the SGP turned out relatively close to the German policy line, much more so than the parallel discussion in the Task Force, and the Ministry hence focused on accompanying the legislative work of the Commission on the emerging 'Six Pack' while grudgingly putting the state insolvency initiative on the backburner.

The Task Force petered out in October after half a dozen meetings, and all that was left of it was its concluding report[5] and rather unsubstantial mentioning in the Conclusions of the European Council of 28 and 29 October 2010.[6] The Task Force had not come anyway near the high hopes for institutional reform that, for a while, it had inspired within German government circles and, possibly, within the ECB. Nobody else seemed intrinsically interested in true governance reform.

An important matter for the Eurogroup discussion on 6 September was the final setting up of the EFSF. Its CEO, Klaus Regling, as well as the Commission and the ECB favoured a AAA rating not only for the bonds emitted by the EFSF, as proposed by Germany, but for the vehicle itself. We hesitated because this would either require more capital or lower the amount of capital available for prospective bailout operations. Schäuble made clear that it would have to be the latter because Germany was not going to increase her guarantee for the EFSF. Neither was Germany going to relax her insistence on pro rata liability.

Getting the EFSF ready for action became pressing because, in mid-September 2010, the fiscal emergency of Ireland was moving centre-stage.

[5] https://www.consilium.europa.eu/media/27405/117236.pdf.

[6] https://www.consilium.europa.eu/uedocs/cms_data/docs/pressdata/en/ec/117496.pdf.

CHAPTER 7

Ireland: Top Class Falling

A Banking Problem

Unlike Greece, Ireland had been a fiscal policy model pupil in the euro area, being praised for her solidity and sustainability by Commission and ECB alike. Ireland had generated budget surpluses on a regular basis until 2007, when the banking crisis struck. The spread of Irish 10-year sovereign debt over the German Bund rose to 344 basis points on 10 September. While Ireland's financing needs for 2010 were almost covered, the country would require some 8.7bn EUR in 2011 from financial markets.

But investors were becoming scared by unexpectedly high needs for capital in the Irish banking sector. According to the rating agency Standard & Poor's, the additional capital required in 2010 amounted already to 23bn EUR, the equivalent of more than 14% of Irish GDP. The Anglo Irish Bank alone allegedly required more than 20bn EUR, pushing the government deficit for 2010 to staggering 25.6% of GDP, according to the most recent estimate available (by Deutsche Bank).

In terms of liquidity, Irish banks had become very much dependent on the emergency tenders of the ECB. In August 2010, the ECB books showed 589bn EUR in outstanding loans to the banking sector, of which 100bn each were assigned to banks in Greece and Ireland—and rising.

M. Heipertz, *Merkelism and the Fine Art of Flat Politics*, Palgrave Studies in European Union Politics,
https://doi.org/10.1007/978-3-031-87592-2_7

This was causing serious concern and rift within the ECB, which decided to toughen its guideline on monetary instruments in October.[1]

The official Maastricht notification of Ireland's deficit was awaited with concern. The sovereign debt ratio was jumping from one of the lowest in the euro area—25% of GDP in 2007—to 92%, way above the Maastricht reference value. Only Greece and Italy recorded a higher debt ratio. Financial markets were rapidly losing confidence in Ireland's capacity to handle the crisis by renewed efforts in fiscal consolidation—these simply seemed impossible, both in economic and political terms. The Services of the Ministry had warned Schäuble as of mid-September 2010 that a discussion on a bailout for Ireland was becoming unavoidable.

On 27 September 2010, Schäuble once more fell ill and had to be hospitalised. In early October, the Finance Minister of Ireland, Brian Lenihan, suggested a restructuring of the debt of nationalised banks, a so-called 'haircut'. Compared to the size of the country, the Irish banking sector was grossly oversized and suffered from a high proportion of low-value real estate loans. It had been a political choice to largely increase the financial sector in Ireland, and the risks associated with that choice were now coming home. The public debt ratio rose from only 25% of GDP in 2007 to roughly 125% in 2013. Ireland was downgraded by the rating agencies and slid into political turmoil. Its spread over the bund rose to 435 base points on 12 October 2010.

From our point of view, there were—despite this bleak picture—some very strong features associated with Ireland which made the country very different from Greece. First, there was a strong and tested political consensus to keep the deficit under control, building on previous successful consolidation efforts in the 1980s (see Hauptmeier et al. 2007). Second, the Irish economy remained highly competitive, largely due to very low unit labour costs plus high productivity, and its current account was to remain broadly in balance, given sharply dropping imports.

As a result, our willingness to help Ireland was infinitely greater, compared to Greece. We were ready to stem a negative feedback loop between capital markets developments and the public finance situation of the country. We saw it in our interest to ensure the continued effectiveness of the Irish state.

[1] https://www.ecb.europa.eu/press/pr/date/2010/html/pr101009.en.html.

Ireland, having conducted a so-called Prudential Capital Assessment Review in September 2010, declared financing needs in the magnitude of some 45bn EUR. The government expected the one-off effects of stabilising the banking sector to amount to roughly 20% of GDP. It planned a haircut of subordinated bonds, particularly of the Anglo Irish Bank, in order to make the private sector participate in the overall cost. The stress testing of Anglo Irish had yielded a 3% risk that the base case of 7.3bn EUR in terms of required capital could grow by another 5bn EUR—and this risk was perceived as too high. The burst of the real estate bubble was now coming to bear on banks' balance sheets. Officials in the German Ministry of Finance were initially in favour of the planned haircut and in fact impressed by the audacity of the measure. This, finally, would be a real instance of debt restructuring.

The Irish government was planning a draft budget for 2011/12 in December 2010 with consolidation measures of roughly 2% of GDP or 3bn EUR. Public salaries had already been cut by 5 to 15%, but the government wanted to retain its highly competitive corporate tax rate at 12.5%. In fact, the issue of international tax competition was the one issue which made the Irish case somewhat less popular among German civil servants. With its aggressively attractive tax regime, Dublin had benefited from the relocation of over 400 companies in the banking and insurance industry, of which some 40 from Germany.

Prime Minister Brian Cowen had presided over the boom period as Finance Minister and was widely held responsible for the build-up of risk to the country. His term in office would end in 2012, but the envisaged consolidation measures would stretch to 2014 and were massively unpopular. The people were furious at the thought that bankers and supervisors were not held accountable for the mess they had created. The German embassy cabled to Berlin that the government was likely to fall soon. The planned haircuts on subordinated bond holders were hence also a way to assuage the public, demonstrating that investors did in fact share the burden.

Let's Take a Walk on the Beach

On 18 and 19 October 2010, there was a Franco-German-Russian summit in Deauville, Normandy, while, at the same time, Ecofin Ministers congregated in Brussels, inter alia for the concluding meeting of the Van Rompuy Task Force. The Deauville meeting with the Russians addressed geopolitical matters and issued a 'strategic vision of a common space founded on the values of democracy, the rule of law and in which there would be free movement of people, goods, services and capital'.[2] A parlance between Europe and Russia that has become almost unthinkable now.

Before the tripartite meeting with Russia, Chancellor Merkel and President Sarkozy met for bilateral talks on euro area issues. This exchange culminated in a famous one-to-one stroll along the beach of Deauville. Their high-power brokerage side-lined and effectively cut short the parallel institutional talks in the Van Rompuy Task Force, Ecofin and Eurogroup, thereby breaking the deadlock on the whole complex surrounding the SGP and the future of the EFSF.

The entire EU, in particular the Commission, were *désavoués*—but also the Ministries of Finance. We were reading the results from news agency clippings like everyone else, in the evening of Monday 18 October. This was not the Community method of doing European integration, nor was it intergovernmental. By contrast, it resembled a great power bargain in the style of the nineteenth century and was perceived as such.

The meeting produced a Franco-German declaration on economic governance[3] and an extended press briefing.[4] The declaration argued that SGP sanctions should be 'more automatic'—which, of course, was not the same as 'automatic' and, for my linguistic taste, amounted to a grammatical atrocity. Sanctions should be 'automatic' in the corrective arm of the SGP—yet, as before, subject to a Council vote by qualified majority. But this was precisely not the definition of 'automatic'. Importantly, France and Germany considered that:

> an amendment of the Treaties is needed and that the President of the European Council should be asked to present, in close contact with the Members of the European Council, concrete options allowing for the establishment of a robust crisis resolution framework before its meeting in March 2011.

[2] https://archiv.bundesregierung.de/resource/blob/656922/478604/81cb5f72d691edace00d9e33c67c5a27/2010-10-19-erklaerung-gipfeltreffen-deauville-eng-data.pdf.

[3] https://www.eu.dk/~/media/files/eu/franco_german_declaration.ashx?la=da.

[4] https://www.cvce.eu/en/obj/press_briefing_by_nicolas_sarkozy_and_angela_merkel_deauville_18_october_2010-en-7e4c59e1-9277-45ae-a53a-eb5820478cd5.html.

The amendment of the Treaties should produce the permanent framework and, strikingly, the suspension of voting rights 'in case of a serious violation of basic principles of EMU'.

The agreement on Treaty change looked like a breakthrough—if France had not been able to rely on other countries to withhold their unanimous support. Hence, for my taste, the 'stability coalition' of Germany, the Netherlands and Scandinavia got a very bad deal by Merkel, at close inspection:

We had effectively dropped our fallback option for truly automatic sanctions, which would have foreseen the Commission to initiate further steps under the EDP and reverting the vote in the Council, requiring a qualified majority to *stop* rather than to implement the EDP. This 'reverse majority' had been our last hope. It seemed well attainable in the Task Force and was also favoured by the Commission, which eyed it as an increase in its own power and was planning to propose the respective legislation.

But this last-ditch resort of reverse majority was now being dropped by Merkel in Deauville. I personally thought that the reverse majority required Treaty change, but the Commission and our own legal experts were confident to achieve it through secondary legislation alone.

In exchange for dropping our claim for reverse majority, we got some sort of intergovernmental conference with the still very faint possibility of Treaty change and the almost certain perpetuation of the EFSF. It was very likely that the conference would stage a replay of the inconclusive Van Rompuy Task Force while providing a fig-leave to perpetuate the bail-out architecture. Given that the EFSF would run out in 2013, a general election year in Germany, I thought this course to be quite risky in terms of domestic politics.

The Deauville deal was in fact so bad that I naively just hoped that Merkel got something in exchange for German national interests behind the scenes and entirely unrelated to EMU. I still had not grasped at the time that the national government of Germany was simply not in the business of pursuing the national interest of Germany.

The official comments of the summit by the Ministry of Finance were, of course, much more favourable. Parliamentary State Secretary Steffen Kampeter rejoiced about a 'great success' and a 'good day for stability culture in Europe'. France and Germany were the engine of Europe's capacity to act. My impression was that Kampeter genuinely believed in what he said. He was said to see himself as a possible replacement for Schäuble at the time.

Finance State Secretary Asmussen stated: 'We have always said that sanctions must become more automatic. Now they are becoming quasi-automatic' (FAZ 19.10.2010, own translation). Asmussen thereby consciously or unconsciously but in fact literally quoted one of his predecessors, Jürgen Stark, the chief negotiator on the SGP in 1995/96 who had also praised the initial Pact for its 'quasi-automatic sanctions' (see Heipertz and Verdun 2011).

The press, however, was in those days usually still well-informed and critical of the government. It saw the real nature of the deal through the mist of propaganda and carved out the strategic concessions made by Germany: 'Merkel gives in on the Euro Stability Pact. Under pressure from Sarkozy, the Chancellor drops her demand to automatically punish deficit sinners' (Süddeutsche Zeitung 19.10.2010, own translation).

To me, it seemed clear: What was missed in Maastricht 1995 could not be recovered in Deauville 2010 after having already conceded the logic of fiscal bailouts. Had we made strategic demands prior to the first Greek bailout, the situation would have been much different, regardless of the wisdom of our demands. I came to think that our affairs were being handled rather poorly.

German allies like Sweden were aghast, and even more so the ECB (FAZ 20.10.2010, Reuters 21.10.2010). Financial market commentators saw a logic at work which we shared, and which harboured our greatest fear: The weaker the SGP, the more important would be a permanent bailout fund (Financial Times 20.10.2010).

I personally saw the essence of the Franco-German agreement in both countries' resistance against further competences and power for the Commission through a strengthened SGP. There would be some sort of *directoire* and benevolent hegemonism—and Political Union would remain out of reach for the foreseeable future.

For that purpose, the Pact would only be marginally recalibrated. Germany could still try to reintroduce market pressure and discipline on fiscal policy through what it called a crisis resolution mechanism, despite being isolated on the issue. It would have to credibly block any prolongation of the EFSF to obtain that goal. Once the EFSF would be made permanent—ironically also under the label of crisis mechanism—Germany no longer would have any lever to push for strategic goals.

Alas, I sensed that our stance to hold out on the perpetuation of the EFSF was not credible at all and would crumble under market pressure, not least related to Ireland. Having said that, we had a general election coming up in 2013—how would the German electorate see a permanent EFSF short of any of the institutional underpinnings sought by Germany? Would the German electorate understand at all? Or would this strategic defeat fade away in public awareness? Would the people let us get away with it?

Following Deauville and the Ecofin, Members of the German Bundestag and Ministry officials struggled to digest the results and I eagerly listened to debates and explanatory meetings with senior staff from the Ministry and the Chancellery, whenever an opportunity arose.

It transpired from both the Deauville talks and the Van Rompuy Task Force that Europe was in fact divided between those who wanted to strengthen the SGP through automatic sanctions and those who resisted change. The former camp around Germany was much smaller and contained only very few countries. Vis-à-vis the Bundestag, both the Ministry and the Chancellery were busy pointing out that there were no contradictions between the Deauville declaration and the report of the Task Force.

As I had expected, the overall compromise entailed no real automaticity, given the fact that the Treaty did not allow for one. Within the EDP, the steps as of paragraph 8 of Article 104 of the TFEU were considered the 'hard' ones which could, ultimately and at the end of a long ladder of escalation, lead to financial sanctions. Typically, the decision-making in this segment of the Treaty was defined by the words "the Council *may* decide to...".[5]

All that Germany had gained in terms of quasi-automaticity (I preferred to call it 'pseudo-automaticity') would be a self-commitment of the Council, at best in secondary legislation, to indeed decide in favour of the next step of the EDP in each particular case, hence 'the Council *will* decide to...'.

Anybody with faint experience in European law and policy would soon realise that this political self-commitment was in fact not legally binding—sanctions under the SGP were and remained an issue of political discretion, and anything else remained unthinkable, at least outside

[5] https://eur-lex.europa.eu/LexUriServ/LexUriServ.do?uri=CELEX:12002E104:EN:HTML.

the mindframe of German lawyers. In any case, some of us started to voice more fundamental doubt about the wisdom of sanctions: After all, the current problems surrounding Ireland and, already visible, Spain had nothing to do with voluntary, reckless breaches of the reference values for debt and deficit ratios by those countries. The Irish crisis would not have been prevented by a stronger SGP.

Nevertheless, our experts still hoped to change primary law in favour of stricter sanctions, albeit not in the form of a fully-fledged Treaty reform which would have required a preceding Convention. Instead, the impending EU accession of Croatia, they argued, could be used to amend the Treaty incrementally through an Intergovernmental Conference (IGC). This required further investigation and risked running into objections by several Member States, above all the United Kingdom, despite the fact that an IGC had in principle been already conceded by Sarkozy.

The UK would also block any crisis resolution mechanism which would be legally binding for the entire EU. For the latter, one would hence need to take recourse either to an intergovernmental solution or to the hitherto quite untested mode of 'enhanced cooperation' entailed in the Treaty. With the exception of Germany, the Netherlands and Finland, all other countries in any case favoured a perpetuation of the EFSF rather than the introduction of a new mechanism of whatever form.

Besides these institutional questions, widely reported in the press, another subject of the Deauville talks was not discussed openly yet but, in fact, seemed even more interesting to us and was not contentious between France and Germany: Sarkozy and Merkel apparently had agreed to envisage a moderate restructuring of Greek public debt under the politically salient catchphrase 'private sector involvement' (PSI). This was the meaning of the cryptic phrase in the Franco-German declaration which stated that crisis resolution would require an 'adequate participation of private creditors'. It would take until summer 2011 before PSI was discussed in earnest—but the origins of restructuring Greek debt lay in Deauville. The statement had been formulated so cautiously as to let sleeping dogs lie and not make financial markets nervous.

In Berlin, we worried that the Deauville deal had estranged the Commission and, even more, the ECB, whose President Jean-Claude Trichet was visibly disconcerted and had asked for a footnote to be included in the text submitted by the Task Force to the European Council: 'The President of the ECB does not subscribe to all elements of this report'. Also, the members of the CDU and CSU caucus on the Bundestag were unhappy with the outcome. They lamented the insufficient hardening of the SGP, an issue which was of secondary importance to Trichet who was even more concerned about possible market deterioration due to the hints at possible haircuts and restructuring.

We made clear to our ECB contacts as well as to the Parliamentarians that we would also have favoured the Commission's initiative on the SGP but that Germany had been isolated on the issue of automaticity. Things had to move on, and the Franco-German deal at least had broken the deadlock and allowed us to envisage setting up a permanent crisis resolution mechanism as a next step. And, after all, sanctions would be tougher—albeit not automatic. Equally, we started to downplay our fixation on haircuts.

I observed on this occasion, as on numerous others, that nothing helps to accept defeat better than defending the result to third parties. After emphasising the good sides of the agreement for a while to different audiences, the Minister himself and his officials really looked at it much more positively than at first. The effect of autosuggestion is powerful in such situations. Robert Musil famously called it the 'normative power of the factual'.

Revisiting the Issue of Restructuring

The future mechanism for crisis resolution was now the most pressing issue. Key players of the European arena still had no common analytical ground—there were only, as we called it, 'building blocks' which lay around. Germany was ready to equip the new mechanism with fresh guarantees, possibly even capital, if it entailed some sort of insolvency regime or at least provisions on 'haircuts' for the bonds of affected countries.

We regarded 'private sector participation' as vital to reduce the moral hazard implicit in the EFSF scheme and to reduce the burden on taxpayers' money. As pragmatic way forward, we wanted uniform Collective Action Clauses (CACs) in all euro area bonds—rather than the cumbersome statutory approach which had failed already in the IMF discussions surrounding the Sovereign Debt Restructuring Mechanism (SDRM). CACs, as already mentioned, were far from being radically new—in fact, they were already included in all bonds issued under New York law as well as in EU bonds under foreign law. The missing element, from our point of view, was an orderly and transparent procedure for the conduct of negotiations between the debtor country and its private creditors. The overall aim of the mechanism would be to set the right incentives for sound fiscal policy—given the failure of the SGP to do so—and in fact to avoid state insolvency.

We planned to discuss these matters with France first and would then seek to buy in the Netherlands. The three of us would then lobby the Commission to come up with a proposal along the lines of our agreements. After Deauville, we wanted to take the lead together with France—and both Merkel and Schäuble publicly confirmed this. Schäuble, for example, proclaimed that France and Germany were the 'pacemakers' of Europe (FAZ, 02.11.2010).

Would the ECB support such an approach? Communication was the key problem—pointing to haircuts or even possible insolvency could easily derail market sentiment by backward induction. In any case, the Greek bailout was a separate issue and would, we initially thought, not be covered by any future new regime for bailouts and debt resolution. But, I feared, as pressure from Ireland and Spain mounted, we would probably be forced to agree quickly—and most likely forgo debt restructuring.

Behind the scenes, however, another problem was looming large for the ECB, and we were tacitly aware: Since the onset of the SMP-Programme, the ECB had been purchasing large volumes of sovereign bonds from Southern European countries. By end October 2010, these amounted to no less than 63.5bn EUR, and we assumed most of them to be Greek. Hence, the ECB could not be neutral and objective about restructuring Greek debt—the Bank would otherwise shoot itself in the foot.

Worse still, the ECB had become liable to blackmail. As it later turned out, holding the Greek SMP debt, the Bank was subject to threats by Athens to unilaterally impose haircuts. Such threats may later have led the ECB to approve continued emergency funding for Greek commercial banks despite the very real prospect of Greece leaving the euro area (Varoufakis 2017).

But this deplorable situation should not affect our desired restructuring mechanism. The introduction of CACs was forward-looking and would not pertain to the existing stock of debt, including the debt held by the ECB under the SMP. We wondered if the ECB could be worried about another consequence of CACs: Would they reduce the value of sovereign debt as collateral for central bank liquidity? On the other hand, the ECB had already proven its flexibility and pragmatism when it came to the adaption of its collateral regime to the needs of the moment. Hence, on balance, we did not think the ECB's resistance to our plan justified.

The ECB resisted, nevertheless. It argued that the mechanism would undermine the rule of law, that it would destroy precious confidence among investors, that it would cripple financial market regulation and that it would invite speculation. And, already looking at the prospect of an Irish bailout, the ECB made very clear that no haircuts should be imposed in the euro area whatsoever.

The Commission was also not supportive of our proposal and was working on its own approach. It wanted to avoid Treaty change and introduce the successor to the EFSF based on Article 352 (which we called the 'enabling clause', a drastic attribution by historical standards). The future regime should no longer be restrained by consensus decision-making and should extend credit lines even at a discount to the recipient country.

Brussels wanted to merge the EFSF, the EFSM and the balance of payments facility into one huge community instrument which should borrow on the market against an enlarged margin in the EU-budget and guaranteed by the EU Member States—an idea which we categorically resisted but which finally saw the light of day in 2021 with the so-called NextGenerationEU-Fund of 750bn EU set up under the pretext of the COVID-19 pandemic.[6]

The Commission was as hostile to private sector involvement as the ECB. Furthermore, the Commission saw no need for an additional granting of collateral by the recipient country—for example through national assets, as the Finns demanded. To our surprise, Brussels still appeared to believe in conditionality—since it was not its own funds that were put on the fence.

This made me think of a joke that I had first heard about European policy in the Western Balkans: You pretend to reform, and we pretend to believe you. Or, as German Finance Minister Schäuble put it: 'I have great respect for the determination of the Greek government. A few months ago, hardly anyone would have believed that the Greeks could implement such a drastic austerity programme. Now they are on the right track' (Spiegel, 08.11.2010, own translation).

Compared to this attitude, I personally had much greater sympathy for the Finnish proposal to collateralise EFSF bonds by the beneficiary

[6] https://op.europa.eu/en/publication-detail/-/publication/d3e77637-a963-11eb-9585-01aa75ed71a1/language-en.

Member State. Helsinki argued that collateral could, for example, be formed through the securitisation of loans from public banks or state assets. In fact, Article 5 of the EFSF Framework Agreement provided for credit enhancement already.[7] But this idea was falling on deaf ears in Brussels, Frankfurt, Berlin and, above all, Paris—although, to my mind, it would have been worth serious consideration.

Fully Back on Crisis Mode

Meanwhile, the yield of Irish 10-year government debt for the first time exceeded 8% on 8 November 2010, a spread of 563 basis points over the Bund. Portugal was not much lower at 6.87%. On the other hand, the Irish government assuaged us that they had succeeded in funding their financing needs for 2010, and Portugal had covered 93% of its needs for the same year. Ireland also announced yet another austerity package of 15bn EUR, to reduce the general government deficit from 32% of GDP in 2010 back to the reference value of 3% until 2014.

But we thought that Dublin was making overtly optimistic assumptions about economic growth in the face of such draconian measures: Without the new effort at consolidation, the IMF was expecting the Irish economy to grow by 2.3% in 2011—while the government targeted higher growth than that at 2.75%, including the latest measures. This seemed like wishful thinking to us, not least because the strenuous situation was taking its toll politically: On 2 November, a Member of Parliament of the governing party Fianna Fail resigned, and one day later, the High Court forced a by-election at short notice which put the government's ruling majority into question.

In this fragile situation, Italy started to twist our arm: Rome argued—with some justice—that our talking about private sector involvement was driving Southern yields upward. Some already called this the 'Merkel Crash' in bond markets (Spiegel 08.11.2010). To make matters worse, Italy made a hardly veiled threat that it would block EFSF support to Ireland if debt restructuring remained on the table—against the backdrop that several Member States and the Commission had started to argue strongly in favour of a 'pre-emptive strike' by the EFSF for Ireland and

[7] https://www.esm.europa.eu/system/files/document/20111019_efsf_framework_agreement_en.pdf.

Portugal at once. There were rumours that China was buying Irish and Portuguese bonds strategically.

On top of it all, the Greek programme showed serious signs of coming off-track: Monthly revenue data was far behind targets, and the deficit was not shrinking as fast as planned. Missing the deficit target would leave Greece (and us) with a very unpleasant choice between additional and so-called back-loaded cuts or fresh bailout money, accumulating to another programme—unless one was ready to revisit the matter of debt rescheduling. Being effectively shut out from financial markets for the foreseeable future, the Greek problem increasingly looked like a perpetual loop.

The situation for Ireland deteriorated in November 2010 day by day. The yield on ten-year public debt was approaching 9% by 12 November, and José Manuel Barroso, then Commission President and later to become chairman of Goldman Sachs International, assured the world stage from the G-20 summit in Seoul that Ireland would be saved if necessary. Irish Finance Minister Lenihan thanked for Barroso's solidarity but tried to convince the markets that Ireland would not require a bailout. The crisis was of particular concern for the British financial sector with an estimated exposure of around 150bn USD to Irish banks—closely followed yet again by German banks with an exposure to Ireland of about 138 bn USD.

After its meeting on 16 November 2010, the Eurogroup issued statements on Greece, Portugal, and Ireland—trying to calm the financial markets by declaratory politics. The Eurogroup declared on Greece:

> We welcome the strong commitment of the Greek government to undertake the required additional measures in the budget for 2011, in order to confirm the ambitious deficit target of € 17 billion next year. The government is currently specifying the details of such additional measures in the 2011 budget as well as in the revised Memorandum of Understanding. We stress in particular the need for further expenditure reductions, as well the acceleration and deepening of structural reforms in particular in the area of taxation, labour markets, business environment, health care and the efficiency of public administration. We remain confident that the significant progress made during the course of this year will continue, allowing the consolidation of the Greek budget to remain on track.[8]

[8] https://www.consilium.europa.eu/media/25732/117742.pdf.

On Portugal, the statement included similarly encouraging words:

> The Eurogroup, the European Commission and the ECB welcome the recent confirmation by the Portuguese government of its commitment to ensure a reduction of the public deficit to 4.6% of GDP in 2011, and the draft budget proposal recently released. The rigorous implementation of this deficit reduction plan will ensure the stabilisation of the public debt ratio as planned.[9]

Most critically, on Ireland they stated:

> We have full confidence that the four-year strategy to be announced by the end of the month will be thorough and detailed and will firmly anchor the 2014 target date for the correction of the excessive deficit. This strategy will also ensure that the public debt ratio will be put on a firm downward path. (…)
> However, market conditions have not normalised and pressures remain, giving rise to concerns that further reforms and stabilisation measures may be appropriate. We welcome the determination of the Irish government to engage in a short and focussed consultation with the Commission, the ECB and the IMF in order to determine the best way to provide any necessary support to address market risks, especially as regard the banking sector, in the context of the four-year budgetary plan and the upcoming budget. We confirm that we will take determined and coordinated action to safeguard the financial stability of the euro area, if needed, and that we have the means available to do so.[10]

Reading between the lines of the Eurogroup statement about Ireland, nobody could doubt that the next bailout case was edging closer. Germany was still arguing that, according to our domestic guarantee law for the EFSF, such support would be *ultima ratio*. But declaring something *ultima ratio* was a mere formality. Once politically agreed, it would be fulfilled by a consensus verdict of the euro area Member States, simply declaring that the emergency measures were necessary to safeguard the solvency of the country concerned and for the financial stability of the monetary union as a whole.

[9] https://www.consilium.europa.eu/media/25730/117744.pdf.

[10] https://www.consilium.europa.eu/media/25731/117743.pdf.

The Eurogroup would have to agree the adjustment programme for Ireland devised between the Troika of IMF, Commission and ECB. It was clear that neither the Irish government nor any other actor still desired to impose a haircut on existing bond holders. This change of mind provided short-lived relief in the Irish bond market.

The market was helped further by the bond purchases of the ECB under the SMP: The ECB bought bonds worth 700mn EUR during the first week of November 2010 and another 1.07bn EUR during the second week; most of them Irish. The yield of ten-year Irish bonds was temporarily falling towards 8%. The overall volume of SMP rose to 65bn EUR by that time, and about half of it was devoted to Greece (FAZ 16.11.2010).

When Ministers congregated on 16 and 17 November 2010, Germany went at great length to limit the damage caused by previous talk about private sector involvement. We acknowledged that only the future mechanism for crisis resolution would take recourse to debt rescheduling and that this would in no case pertain to the situation at hand. We then went as far as to explicitly exclude private sector involvement for the current problems of Greece, Ireland, and Portugal, and thereby pulled the rug under the domestic Irish efforts to make bondholders pay.

(Not) Discussing Macroeconomic Imbalances

At the same Eurogroup meeting, there was also a discussion about macroeconomic imbalances in the euro area. At present, the debate was directed concretely at Germany and Italy, according to a revolving sequence. This so-called 'peer review' was agreed by Ministers during the spring of 2010, and it was held in anticipation of the more formal imbalances procedure to be set up in the future. It was agreed to always discuss pairs of countries, one with a current account surplus, one with a deficit. In this case, France was commenting on Germany as a surplus country, and Austria was commenting on Italy as a deficit country. But before the commenting country would get its say, there would be official introductions by the Chair of the Eurogroup Working Group (EWG, i.e. the Finance State Secretaries), by the EU's Economic Policy Committee (EPC), by the Commission and by the ECB. Finally, the country under assessment would get a chance to reply.

Germany was seen as one of the most competitive economies of the euro area but suffering from weak domestic demand. Obviously, both issues were connected, given that Germany had achieved its competitiveness not without suppressing real wage growth, accumulating high savings and perfectionating her export-led growth model. It was palpable that the German current account showed one side of the medal, as far as imbalances in the euro area were concerned. The other side of the medal were countries with current account deficits, such as Italy.

As far as I could tell, the debate failed to pick up on the connection between current account imbalances and the fiscal crisis which we had now been witnessing for more than half a year. Many economists would argue that, in a monetary union and thereby under fixed exchange rates, the fiscal deficits had been incurred by countries funding their current account deficit. By analogy, fiscal austerity was their way of reducing the current account deficit. For that policy to work, it would require Germany to expand much more. But this was in contradiction to our policy strategy, the *Schwarze Null*. Things did simply not add up.

As easy as it was to connect fiscal and current account balances in the identities of public accounting—it was close to impossible to discuss these matters politically in conjunction. The debates on fiscal deficits, according to my impression, took well place by the same people and in the same room on the same day—but mentally and institutionally disconnected from the debate on macroeconomic imbalances. I sensed that this was one of the more serious shortcomings of economic policy coordination in the euro area—and, to make matters worse, one that would not be addressed by any of the reform measures under way.

The Eurogroup reports which contained the official policy recommendations to both Italy and Germany under the imbalances procedure differed from the assessments provided by France and Austria, respectively, and had clearly been streamlined under the supervision of Finance State Secretaries in the EWG. By consequence, they emphasised rigorous fiscal consolidation for both countries alike, Italy *and* Germany, besides measures of structural reform geared towards enhancing competitiveness, such as liberalising services, improving education, or facilitating research and development.

While the recommendations were welcomed by the German delegation—the report confirmed and justified the government's fiscal strategy—the Italian delegation argued that the high debt-to-GDP ratio should be measured against the comparatively large net wealth of private households in Italy (which indeed was among the highest in the EU) and should therefore not give rise to fiscal retrenchment. So, for all that it was worth, the new procedure of discussing macroeconomic imbalances in the euro area ended up reiterating the well-known exchange of different world-views about fiscal policy.

The Next Bailout

Much more relevant at the time however was Ireland and the uncertainty which persisted after the Eurogroup meeting. Participants struggled to convince the public that a bailout had not been requested or suggested in concrete terms. There were rumours, however, that the Irish government had sought to explore possibilities of a direct bank recapitalisation by the EFSF (FAZ 16.11.2010). This seemed plausible, given that the nationalised Anglo Irish Bank alone had consumed close to 30bn EUR in state capital—a sum coming close to 20% of Irish GDP.

But direct capital injections by the EFSF were impossible because the EFSF statutes only foresaw bailout loans to states. Hence, the Irish state would have to take the European money and convert it into bank capital in turn. This was the first instance in which I heard talk of a 'death spiral' between states and banks. In any case, staff from the Troika of IMF, the Commission, and the ECB arrived in Dublin on Thursday 18 November 2010 with the obvious task to assess the situation and craft a possible programme. Their arrival was widely reported and made minds converge once more on the rapidly increasing inevitability of the coming bailout.

On that same day, amidst heightened tension and struggles behind the scenes, there was a turnaround in the communication of the Irish government. For the first time, Dublin officially admitted that it would require assistance by its European partners to overcome the crisis. It fell to the Governor of the Irish central bank, Patrick Honohan, to declare that the government would ask for help: 'It's my expectation that will happen, yes … absolutely. It will be a large loan because the purpose of the amount to be advanced or to be made available to be borrowed is to show Ireland has sufficient firepower to deal with any concerns of the market'.[11]

Subsequently, the Irish Minister of Finance Brian Lenihan admitted in Parliament the possibility of a bailout package but tried to argue that it might remain a fallback option and would not necessarily need to be

[11] https://www.theguardian.com/business/2010/nov/18/ireland-bailout-central-bank-governor.

activated. Yet it also transpired that the conditions of the European emergency loan looked attractive at roughly 5%, compared to the market rate for Irish debt which was climbing back to around 9%. By Sunday, Lenihan confirmed that he would recommend the Cabinet to officially request EU assistance.

Almost instantly, the Eurogroup and Ecofin Finance Ministers issued a declaration, which had been agreed in a telephone conference just before:

> Ministers welcome the request of the Irish Government for financial assistance from the European Union and euro-area Member States. Ministers concur with the Commission and the ECB that providing assistance to Ireland is warranted to safeguard financial stability in the EU and in the euro area.
>
> In the context of a joint programme EU/IMF, the financial assistance package to the Irish state should be financed from the European financial stabilisation mechanism (EFSM) and the European financial stability facility (EFSF), possibly supplemented by bilateral loans to be negotiated by EU Member States. The United Kingdom and Sweden have already indicated today that they stand ready to consider a bilateral loan. (…)
>
> The programme will address the fiscal challenges of the Irish economy in a decisive manner. It will build on the fiscal adjustment and structural reforms that will be put forward by the Irish authorities in their Four Year Budgetary Strategy next week. This strategy will provide the details of the Government's commitment to achieve fiscal consolidation of EUR 6 bn in 2011 as part of a strategy leading to a 3% of GDP deficit by 2014, implying an overall consolidation of 15 bn in the 4 year strategy, which contains an annual review. (…)
>
> The programme will also include a fund for potential future capital needs of the banking sector. By building on the measures already taken by Ireland to address stress in its banking sector, a comprehensive range of measures – including deleveraging and restructuring of the banking sector – will contribute to ensuring that the banking system performs its role in the functioning of the economy. (…)[12]

It felt a bit like a déjà-vu when, later that day, I received a copy of a letter addressed by Lenihan to Messrs Jean-Claude Juncker, Eurogroup President, and Didier Reynders, European Union Presidency, dated 21 November 2010. The letter read as follows:

[12] https://www.consilium.europa.eu/media/25729/117898.pdf.

> Dear Sirs,
> On behalf of the Irish Authorities, I am writing to formally apply for financial assistance in the context of a joint EU-IMF programme. The external assistance sought is made under the terms of the European Financial Stabilisation Mechanism, the European Financial Stability Facility and the IMF assistance programme.
> I welcome the statement by the Eurogoup and ECOFIN Ministers which concurred with the EU Commission and the ECB that providing assistance to Ireland is warranted to safeguard financial stability in the EU and in the euro area.
> The Irish Authorities will cooperate fully in the preparation of the joint EU-IMF programme of assistance to the Irish State that will now be required to be developed.
> Yours faithfully, Brian Lenihan, Minister for Finance

By now, these proceedings almost seemed to be part of a ritual. This ritual also included a proverbial verdict: 'If the euro fails, Europe fails'. Originally coined by German Chancellor Angela Merkel, this summoning and rallying call was, on this occasion, provided by the President of Council, Herman Van Rompuy, shortly before Lenihan dispatched his letter (FAZ 17.11.2010).

A peculiarity of the Irish case was the pronounced exposure of British banks, besides German and other European ones. The British banking exposure to Irish public and private debt, according to the BIS, was estimated to be 149bn USD, compared to 139bn owed to German banks, 54bn to Belgian ones, and 50bn to French ones. This begged the question why only the euro area taxpayer should chip in to save the City across the Channel from write-downs.

In fact, Her Majesty's Treasury had already earlier signalled its willingness to participate in the upcoming bailout for Ireland. An official was quoted as follows: 'This is not Greece—we are close trading partners' (FAZ, 16.11.2010, own translation). But Prime Minister David Cameron had initially ruled out a bilateral loan, given that this would drive up the British deficit.

An obvious solution for including the UK in the Irish bailout was the Commission-based European Financial Stabilisation Mechanism (EFSM), rather than the EFSF that only contained euro area members. The EFSM had been set up in May 2010 with a far smaller budget and a much less ambitious remit than originally proposed by the Commission.[13] That notwithstanding, being backed by the EU budget, it would automatically imply the UK (prior to Brexit)—but it would do so only for the EFSM-funded part of the overall package. An additional bilateral loan would be required to bring the UK on par with its relative weight in respect of the EFSF loan as well. Later-on, also Sweden and Denmark signed up for such bilateral loans of non-euro area Member States to Ireland.

Before these events, the Irish government had been under considerable pressure to increase its competitive corporate tax rate. However, in the actual event, France and Germany had briefly dropped that demand to help the Irish government over the cliff. Lenihan explicitly thanked them. Moreover and as mentioned above, Ireland had a good track record of successful and ultimately even expansive fiscal consolidation exercises in the past. It would therefore be given more leeway within the conditionality of its programme.

A surprised German public was explained by Finance Minister Wolfgang Schäuble on 21 November why, after all, it was now seen as a good idea to bail out Ireland, next in line after Greece. In a TV interview after the evening news, Schäuble illustrated: 'This is about the stability of our common currency. (…) If we find the right answer for the Irish problems, then there is a good chance that there will be no further contagion'. He went on to say: 'In the future, we need a better solution so that this does not repeat itself'. It was unacceptable that 'some reap high interest rates, and in the end the taxpayer takes on the risk' (ZDF Berlin direkt, 21.11.2010, own translation).

Seen from Berlin for several days after the announcement, it was still not clear why precisely the Irish bailout had acquired such inevitability. The most fervent proponents appeared to have been Portugal and Spain, fearing contagion. But, by themselves, they would hardly have swung the mood of the Eurogroup heavyweights, above all France and Germany—nor that of the Irish government itself. The latter might have been persuaded by the above-mentioned interest rate differential between the bailout package and future market funding—yet that was far from evident.

According to most observers, the driving force behind the decision had been ECB President Jean-Claude Trichet. We speculated that the ECB had wanted to avoid a massive build-up of Irish sovereign debt on

[13] https://eur-lex.europa.eu/legal-content/EN/TXT/?qid=1484663483987&uri=CELEX:32010R0407.

its own balance, surpassing that of Greece and incurred only because of capital shortfalls in the Irish banking sector. The very clear rejection of private sector involvement or any form of haircut also bore the imprint of the ECB. Yet, for me and some of my colleagues at least, it was still surprising to see that alternatives were no longer being considered at all. Had anybody given thought to closing and liquidating some of the Irish banks—or were all of them automatically considered to be of systemic relevance?

Most worryingly, the Irish episode showed that Greece had not been the exception as which it had originally been framed. There could be other cases—and even those with an excellent track record of fiscal policy performance, with a highly competitive economy and with no history of fraudulent statistics. With Ireland, the Eurogroup's model pupil had fallen—this was bad news indeed. It could make the EFSF seem too small and be only the prelude for a much larger scheme.

In another respect, however, the Irish episode was similar to the Greek one: The request for international aid brought down the government. Just one day after the request for aid, Prime Minister Brian Cowen announced that Parliament would be dissolved after the austerity budget bill was passed. General elections would follow in spring 2011. Cowen's fall was brought about by the Greens, his small coalition partner, announcing that they would leave the government. Even prominent members of Cowen's own party, Fianna Fail, had called for the government to resign.

In Germany, too, the domestic response to the latest news on the European bailout front was anything but pleasant. Parliamentarians and important voices in the public asked pertinent questions: Why should the German taxpayer support a country which had a higher GDP per capita than Germany herself? The government took pains to convey that the bailout was in the interest of the financial stability of the euro area, as an Irish default would lead to uncontrolled contagion—both through other Member States and through the banking sector… Critics, however, pointed out that the bailout allowed the banks, which had made huge profits, to pass on their losses to the taxpayer. The government argued that the Irish state would benefit from the bailout loans, not the banks directly… But why had Ireland asked for help at all—after stubbornly refusing to take it in the weeks before? To contain contagion and to avail itself the credibility of a proper adjustment programme… And why were there no haircuts on bondholders—given that Germany had just proposed them as the right way forward? The current market situation would not allow... Was this not the beginning of the dreaded transfer union? No, this was a one-off measure designed precisely to prevent additional cases—and in the future, there would be a permanent mechanism for crisis resolution... Were we not subsidising Irish tax competition and thereby the race to the bottom in corporate taxation? Yes, but let us wait for the Troika proposal of the Irish programme—after all, competitiveness is what matters...

It struck me that both sides in this debate were right. This was not about the better argument—it was about the perception of necessity among those in power.

All efforts were now directed at defining the Irish programme. The government proposed a four-year austerity plan and included a reduction of the minimum wage, cuts to welfare and public salaries, and less exemptions from income taxability. Government spending was to be reduced by 10bn EUR through cuts in healthcare, education, agriculture, justice, and defence. Taxes were to be raised by 5bn EUR between 2011 and 2014—although no increase was planned for the competitive corporate income tax rate at 12.5%. By contrast, VAT was to rise from 21 to 23%. About 6bn EUR, equivalent to 40% of the overall adjustment, was to be frontloaded in 2011. The consolidation package of 15bn EUR was equivalent to 4% of GDP and came on top of the already decided five savings packages over the preceding two-and-a-half years, already totalling 15bn EUR. The assistance loans sought from its international partners should amount to 85bn EUR, according to Dublin.

On 28 November 2010, agreement was reached on the programme, and the Eurogroup declared:

> Ministers unanimously agreed today to grant financial assistance in response to the Irish authorities' request on 22 November 2010. Ministers concur with the Commission and the ECB that providing a loan to Ireland is warranted to safeguard financial stability in the euro area and the EU as a whole. Euro-area and EU financial support will be provided on the basis of a programme which has been negotiated with the Irish authorities by the Commission and the IMF, in liaison with the ECB. Ministers welcome the staff-level agreement on a three year joint EU/IMF financial assistance programme for Ireland. The Irish Government approved the programme on 28 November.

> Ministers unanimously endorse the measures announced today. Building on the strong fundamentals of the Irish economy, the programme rests on three pillars:
> – An immediate strengthening and comprehensive overhaul of the banking system
> – An ambitious fiscal adjustment to restore fiscal sustainability, including through the correction of the excessive deficit by 2015
> – Growth enhancing reforms, in particular on the labour market, to allow a return to a robust and sustainable growth, safeguarding the economic and social position of its citizens.
> The financial package of the programme will cover financing needs up to € 85 billion, including € 10 billion for immediate recapitalisation measures, € 25 billion on a contingency basis for banking system supports and € 50 billion covering budget financing needs. Half of the banking support measures (€17½ billion) will be financed by an Irish contribution through the Treasury cash buffer and investments of the National Pension Reserve Fund. The remainder of the overall package should be shared equally amongst: (i) the European Financial Stabilisation Mechanism (EFSM); (ii) the European Financial Stability Facility (EFSF) together with bilateral loans from the UK, Denmark and Sweden, and (iii) the IMF (€ 22½ billion each).[14]

As usual, a comprehensive set of information on the Irish programme was compiled in the IMF Staff Report, completed on 4 December 2010.[15] Also as usual, the binding list of measures, reforms and deadlines were compiled in the Memorandum of Understanding, published on 7 December 2010.[16]

Largely unnoticed by the public and in the shadow of the Ireland proceedings, Chancellor Merkel in direct exchanges with French President Sarkozy, Eurogroup President Juncker and Council President Van Rompuy had largely dropped the German demands for private sector participation and debt restructuring arrangements in the future crisis resolution mechanism. She conceded that such measures would not be taken automatically or by default, but only on a case-by-case basis and after

[14] https://www.consilium.europa.eu/media/25727/118051.pdf.

[15] https://www.imf.org/external/pubs/ft/scr/2010/cr10366.pdf.

[16] https://ec.europa.eu/economy_finance/articles/eu_economic_situation/pdf/2010-12-07-mou_en.pdf.

specific negotiations which would take market considerations into account (Financial Times Deutschland 29.11.2010).

To that effect, the Eurogroup on 28 November 2010 issued a second statement and declared about the future crisis resolution mechanism, which, as of now, was called the European Stability Mechanism (ESM):

> Rules will be adapted to provide for a case by case participation of private sector creditors, fully consistent with IMF policies. (...) In the unexpected event that a country would appear to be insolvent, the Member State has to negotiate a comprehensive restructuring plan with its private sector creditors, in line with IMF practices with a view to restoring debt sustainability.[17]

Equally marginalised was a decision by the Eurogroup to extend the repayment date for the Greek loans to seven and a half years instead of three, thereby bringing the deadline for Greece on a par with Ireland. Comparatively more attention was given by the German public to the fact that Germany's state guarantee for the EFSF would now effectively cover the first 10.1bn EUR to reflect the Irish bailout being drawn from the vehicle (plus Germany's contingent in the IMF loan). This was just the beginning of fiscal risk accumulating on the German balance...

...but this is where our story ends—for now.

[17] https://www.consilium.europa.eu/uedocs/cms_data/docs/pressdata/en/ecofin/118050.pdf.

CHAPTER 8

Conclusion: Ruling Europe by Muddling Through

Merkel's political style was 'flat' both in terms of process and outcome. Throughout this book, we have seen 'flat politics' as the result of 'muddling through': governance that eschews bold, hierarchical mandates in favour of incremental, network-based, and consensus-driven tactics under uncertainty. While this style enables flexibility and responsiveness, it also risks path-dependency and diluted accountability. The euro crisis case illustrates how 'flat politics' can both stabilise a short-term situation and undermine long-term institutional credibility. Recognising this dynamic is essential for future reforms of EU governance: bolstering democratic legitimacy and strategic capacity may require balancing 'flat' consensus and diluted responsibilities with clear and accountable leadership.

Comparing the Cases of Greece and Ireland

German Finance Minister Schäuble once famously stated in peculiar English: 'It will not happen that there will be a *Staatsbankrott*'.[1] Preventing state insolvency in the euro area by all means—that was the guiding principle of several years of muddling through the euro crisis.

[1] https://www.tagesschau.de/wirtschaft/kein-bankrott-athen100.html.

M. Heipertz, *Merkelism and the Fine Art of Flat Politics*, Palgrave Studies in European Union Politics,
https://doi.org/10.1007/978-3-031-87592-2_8

The means have changed over time. Starting with declaratory policy, Member States cobbled up a package of bilateral loans to Greece in May 2010. In the same instance, they disregarded a belated, half-hearted initiative by the financial sector, rejected a large community bailout fund proposed by the Commission and instead opted for an intergovernmental and temporary solution, the EFSF. That part of the story is covered by this book. Already before the first use of the EFSF—in the case of Ireland in November 2010—it became clear that the EFSF would be superseded by a permanent mechanism, the ESM. The ESM would still be intergovernmental but already based on joint capital.

The two case studies of this book, i.e. the first Greek and the Irish bailouts, have important features in common:

First, the financial markets lose their confidence in the respective country once a certain yield of sovereign debt is surpassed. There is a point of no return beyond which the only two alternatives emerge: insolvency or bailout. This dynamism quickly becomes a self-fulfilling prophecy, and the decision to exclude insolvency makes the bailout inevitable.

Second, policymakers hope and genuinely believe that announcing and preparing a bailout makes the latter superfluous. They think that there is something like an announcement effect, which can turn around the expectations of economic agents in a lasting manner. But the opposite is true: The availability of the bailout ushers in a mental convergence of markets, policymakers, and the public at large with the precise focal point of arriving at that bailout. This narrative neatly confirms the interpretation offered by Beckert and Arndt (2024) on 'imagined futures' and should be fertile ground for further research in behavioural finance.

Third, the bailout is done through fiscal *and* monetary policy. From the beginning, the ECB has played a crucial role through the SMP as well as through liquidity operations that support the financing of sovereign debt by banks. In that sense, the EU proves to exploit the maximum *marge de manoeuvre* that it enjoys and comes up with surprising, innovative solutions as detected by Sandbu (2017) and many other commentators. Over time, however, policymakers in creditor countries learn that they suffer high political costs for fiscal bailouts. Policymakers in debtor countries even more so, because of the corresponding adjustment/ austerity programmes so much criticised by Schmidt (2020) and a large group of other scholars. In fact, both the Greek and the Irish government fall, almost instantly upon turning to foreign assistance. Funding a bailout through monetary policy, by contrast, is politically far less visible and much less costly. No wonder, hence, that the use of EFSF and ESM has petered out over time and that the ECB is the only remaining actor to step in whenever required—this is 'monetary solidarity' of sorts (see Schelkle 2017).

Fourth, Germany insists on austerity as a way of enforcing the servicing and redemption of bailout loans by debtor countries. Competitiveness is the holy grail, regardless of another country's economic growth model (see Scharpf 2002). By consequence, Germany expects all other countries to basically outperform Germany as a supply-side, export-driven economy. One-size-fits-all monetary policy is supplemented by one-size-fits-all prescriptions for fiscal, economic, and structural policy alike. This logic drives over more nuanced assumptions underlying the approaches of the IMF, the Commission, and the tentative Eurogroup debates on macroeconomic imbalances (see Mody 2018).

Fifth, and by consequence of the above, Germany categorically rejects the notion of debt restructuring as far as the bailout loans are concerned. By contrast, it very much promotes that idea for outstanding government bonds, leading to a bizarre, further estrangement of the financial markets before that demand is eventually abandoned for the time period covered in this book (see Tooze 2018). Later-on, however, Germany at least enforces haircuts, in particular in Cyprus in the year 2013.

Sixth and last, Germany has a purely tactical and financial look at the situation, guided at least in part by the idea of ordo-liberalism (see Brunnermeier et al. 2017). Absent are considerations of underlying, institutional deficiencies in EMU and strategic thinking about European integration generally (see Tömmel and Verdun 2018). This would be at odds with the method of muddling through and is simply not part of Angela Merkel's political toolbox.

By consequence, Germany at no point in the process covered in this book makes strategic demands from its partners—in exchange for extending fiscal bailout and silently tolerating monetary bailout. The only half-baked exception from this rule is the above-mentioned project of debt restructuring and an accompanying strengthening of fiscal governance in the euro area—falling way short of a serious reform of the EU at large (see Schäuble 2024).

Equally instructive are important differences between the two case studies of this book:

First, there is no understanding in Berlin that adjustment/austerity has different effects in Ireland and Greece. For Greece, drastic austerity in fact reduces the chance that the loans are repaid, leading to successive programme iterations in future years. If the medicine doesn't work, more of it is delivered to the patient. This self-defeating loop is accepted already at the end of 2010, when it becomes clear that the original programme is getting off-track (see Blustein 2016).

Second, the underlying reason for the above is a profoundly different economic model (see Scharpf 2009). It would take a separate book to compare economic policies, cultures, and structures between Greece and Ireland, but certainly those two countries represent polar opposites on that spectrum. But, as the saying goes, to a man with a hammer, every problem is a nail. Once the way of doing bailouts is established and the according procedures and institutions are in place, the entire approach becomes path-dependent and universally applicable.

Third, Greece is the weakest link and hence the first element of the chain to give. It is considered and framed as a unique exception. This notion helps in the political struggle to achieve a majority in the Bundestag and to appease the people in Germany. Ireland, by contrast, falsifies that proposition. If Ireland can also fall, then nobody is safe. With Ireland, contagion becomes a reality. This immediately propels the magnitude of potential bailouts into a wholly different dimension. Ultimately, any provisions would need to cover for a much larger group of potential debtor states—quickly leading to requests for overall volumes beyond a trillion EUR.

The Berlin Experience

The initial question this book set out to answer is: How did the Merkel government react to the outbreak of the euro crisis?

As we stated before, this initial question subdivides into several subquestions, the first one being: What options did decision-makers in Berlin perceive? In principle, there were two immediate options—accepting state insolvency in the euro area or bailing out the country in question. An extension of the first option would be for Germany to exit from EMU. It is safe to say that both this extreme as well as the narrow version of the first option have never been seriously considered. In that sense, the bailout was indeed without alternative—not factually, but conceptually.

Second, what information was available to decision-makers in Berlin, and how did they make sense of the situation? It has hopefully become clear to the reader that, besides time pressure, the lack of information was the most important feature of muddling through—and in fact its main reason. As administrators, we were able to look at the arithmetic of sovereign debt coming due—defining the magnitude and timing of the bailout required. We were also able to gauge the first-round effects in the financial sector if the bailout would not come through. But that was it—these were the only main parameters available. Everything else should be described as 'known unknowns' and, especially, as 'unknown unknowns'—and the overall magnitude of these was perceived as so monumental that, indeed, the entire fate und future of Europe seemed to depend on it. 'If the euro fails, Europe fails'—this was more than a catchphrase—it was the perceived reality.

Third, what were the political constraints and influences, foreign and domestic? The introduction of the euro had already been massively unpopular in Germany during the 1990s. Greece's impending default vindicated the Eurosceptics. Members of Parliament of CDU and CSU faced massive resistance in their constituencies to the bailout legislation. Increasingly, it took substantial arm-twisting within the Parliamentary fraction to obtain the required majorities. Two elements were essential to the political communication: The loan-nature of the bailout—i.e. the false promise that the money would be returned in full and with interest—and the utmost sacrifices of corresponding austerity programmes. It is important to understand that the latter were required for the purpose of domestic German politics. Despite that, the domestic fallout was enormous—e. g. the loss of NRW in May 2010 and the later rise of the AfD.

Legal constraints and, in particular, those of constitutional law played a major role in the early stage of the crisis. Decision-makers were acutely aware of preceding verdicts of the German Constitutional Court, which had qualified Germany's membership to the single currency in no uncertain terms and seemed to contradict the intended bailout. But the legal risk did not materialise in the wake of the first Greek bailout, given that the constitutional judges shied away from assuming the essentially political responsibility of putting EMU in question and operated under political *tutelage*.

The legal risk subsequently evaporated altogether. Involving the Constitutional Court became not much more than a formality during subsequent stages of the crisis—with the only exception of questions that concerned the formal role and standing of Parliament in the proceedings. By ultimately confirming and vindicating the government's policy in the relevant cases brought before it, the Constitutional Court in fact helped to alleviate domestic pressure.

Foreign influence often went into the directly opposite direction, compared to domestic influence, so that the government was torn between domestic and foreign pressures (see Tömmel and Verdun 2018). With the exception of the former Deutschmark block, first and foremost the Netherlands and Austria, plus Finland and the Baltic countries, Germany was fairly isolated in the Eurogroup. France, Germany's primary foreign partner, was the champion of Southern Member States and usually presented their interests in a very effective way. Outside the euro area, the UK interest was mainly informed by the view of the City and financial markets in general, also coming to bear on Berlin in favour of bailouts, debt mutualisation, and monetisation.

From across the Atlantic, the US government held strong views about stabilising the euro area along similar lines and at times exerted decisive influence on Germany. Other outside forces, particularly the Commission, the ECB, the IMF and financial market representatives, all worked on lobbying the German government into bailouts and debt mutualisation as well as into acquiescing with monetary financing. Lastly, Anglo-Saxon economists almost without any exception as well as an important contingent of German economists took the same view and argued vocally in public, habitually magnified by the financial press.

By consequence, the Merkel government was oftentimes isolated and able to set the terms of the relevant decisions only to the extent that it actually dared making use of its veto power. The ultimate lever, German departure from the single currency, has never been used in the negotiations. German representatives in international fora are particularly uneasy with situations of international isolation and power struggles. It is therefore understandable why Merkel and, to a lesser extent, Schäuble often gave in under pressure in situations of high politics at the international level. Going it alone in the international and European spheres is nothing that German politicians can live up to easily. Being portrayed as Nazis in the Greek press, for example, does have an effect on them, and be it an unconscious one.

Fourth, which interests did the Merkel government pursue in the euro crisis? German political culture has largely lost the capacity to define strategic national interests. Much more common and, in fact, systematic is the frequent recourse to matters that are *raisons d'état*. European integration or 'European solidarity' are often to be found among them (see Schelkle 2017). Saving the euro was habitually equated with the national interest, not only for external communication purposes but, in fact, also in the beliefs of policymakers. Beyond that, the role and responsibilities of a quasi-hegemon was present on their minds. They did feel a responsibility for the euro area as a whole and not only for Germany—despite their more narrowly defined electoral mandate. This raises issues of democratic theory, even legitimacy, and was therefore not much discussed.

Only second order considerations took on a national twist, such as issues of liability or structural adjustment. Among those, the issue of moral hazard was identified as a core problem of the bailout approach—in fact, a problem to the euro area itself, not only to Germany as a creditor country. Only when faced with a conflict of interests between the survival of the euro area as a whole and particular Member States, especially Greece, was Germany able to differentiate and, to an increasing extent, prioritise the group interest.

How was decision-making in the Federal Ministry of Finance at times superseded by the Chancellery? During the early stage of the crisis covered in this book, there were hardly any differences between the Ministry and the Chancellery. A joint appraisal and extremely close cooperation occurred in particular at the senior administrative level. The only two major exceptions during that stage were the decisions not to demand an EMF but to set up the EFSF instead and, subsequently, the Deauville compromise. In those cases, Merkel called the shots and Schäuble had to adjust and follow—at breath taking speed. On later occasions, in particular Banking Union in 2012 and Grexit in 2015, there was even more need for hierarchical direction of the Ministry by the Chancellery.

The Euro Crisis Beyond 2010

Can we learn from the case studies on Greece and Ireland, during the early stage of that crisis, how later stages were being handled? In many ways, the period covered in this book describes a critical juncture. It was constitutive for the subsequent period until the year 2015 and, in some respects, until the time of writing and far into the future.

The most important path-dependency that emerged in 2010 was that euro area Member States plus the relevant institutions embarked upon a combination of fiscal and monetary bailout, rather than accepting state insolvency and the ensuing banking, financial, and economic effects. Fiscal bailouts occurred until 2015, the year in which the third Greek programme was enacted. Following Ireland, three more countries were issued with rescue packages by the EFSF and its successor, the ESM: Portugal, Spain, and Cyprus.

These subsequent country cases can largely be understood through the lens of this book: The argument of systemic importance was prevalent in all of them, and that was instrumental in obtaining political support for the programmes in Germany. A certain routine and sequence of events repeated themselves each time: Market deterioration beyond a point of no return, denial followed by acceptance, cognitive convergence towards a bailout plus programme, technical preparations by the Troika, announcement and declaration of systemic importance, legislative proceedings in Member States and enactment through the EFSF, later the ESM—not to forget the accompanying crisis or even fall of the government in question.

By the end of 2011, many European and Anglo-Saxon policymakers and market participants pressurised Germany to agree to a 'bazooka' or to erect a global 'firewall' against further contagion of the euro crisis. The question was whether to cap EFSF resources at the level already committed or to apply both EFSF 'old' and ESM 'fresh' money plus the 'firepower' of the IMF. The Eurogroup agreed on a combined ceiling of EFSF and ESM of 700bn EUR plus 150bn EUR in additional bilateral contributions by the IMF—impressing the markets with a total lending capacity well north of 1tn USD.[2]

Previously, Bundesbank President Jens Weidmann had to prevent the German government from agreeing to leveraging the Special Drawing Rights (SDRs) held by euro area Member States at the IMF or even their gold reserves—all in the attempt to boost the bailout resources of the EFSF. The ECB and other players had tabled that proposal to a G-20 meeting in Cannes on 4 November 2011.[3] Weidmann was not present in Cannes but intervened by phone and insisted, to the surprise of US President Barack Obama and other participants, on his independent authority

[2] https://www.consilium.europa.eu/uedocs/cms_data/docs/pressdata/en/ecofin/129381.pdf.

[3] http://www.g20.utoronto.ca/2011/2011-cannes-declaration-111104-en.html.

over SDRs and gold reserves, once the Bundesbank had gotten word of the plot.[4]

The frenzy about bazookas and 1tn USD firewalls had been set in motion earlier in 2011 by market participants fearing contagion of the crisis not only to Spain but even to Italy. In Italy, a power struggle between Prime Minister Silvio Berlusconi and Finance Minister Giulio Tremonti had shaken market confidence. The 'Tremonti-Crash' in fact secured his stay in power, given the fact that markets had more trust in him than in Berlusconi. It neatly helped Tremonti to subdue a broiling scandal surrounding his apartment and one of his advisers.[5] In Berlin, we groaned at the prospect of Italy's possible default, only to sigh with relief when we got the impression that the whole affair smelled more like a cover-up.

Nevertheless, the firewall-debate had been for real, and it had ensured that EFSF and ESM ran in parallel for a while. The ESM benefitted from paid-in capital and embodied the permanence and regularisation of the bailout approach, originally labelled as temporary and exceptional in 2010. Each legal step into that direction was accompanied by lawsuits before the German Constitutional Court—in a way quite similar to that described in this book. The Court habitually validated the course taken by the government, but it repeatedly strengthened the formal rights of Parliamentary oversight—also in a way that can be gauged from events in 2010.

Another process that repeated itself time and again was the role of autosuggestion in political arguments. Switching from resistance and denial in the face of unwanted turns of events into embracing them, applying rehearsed policy with incremental changes, and defending that as a sheer necessity in public, government agents and politicians alike became used to the rescue routine and sincerely believed their own propaganda.

However, there were also important differences between 2010 and subsequent events. It will take another book to look at these different developments in turn. For example, later programmes differed markedly in design and orientation. There were clear examples of policy learning as suggested by the method of successive limited comparisons, not least on

[4] https://www.reuters.com/article/idINIndia-60370520111107.

[5] https://www.nytimes.com/2011/07/12/business/global/italy-evolves-into-eus-next-weak-link.html.

the issue of bail-in and haircuts. Also, existing programmes experienced significant change and overhaul at certain points in time. Fully fledged debt restructuring became a concrete issue and was finally implemented amidst tremendous agitation. The approach of the institutions changed over time, and that of Germany even more.

Such telling examples of policy learning also had to do with changes in the senior administrative leadership of the Finance Ministry. And the fact that Germany became bolder in her demands was not least a consequence of certain Christian Democrats becoming increasingly impatient—explicitly not Angela Merkel, but to a noticeable extent certainly Wolfgang Schäuble and a growing group of dissenters in the CDU and CSU. Not only were they personally frustrated, particularly by Greece, but they also realised that domestic resistance in Germany was growing, leading in 2012 to a Eurosceptic party that even took up the TINA narrative in its name: *Alternative für Deutschland* (AfD).

Most importantly, the monetisation of state finance through the ECB grew in importance and established itself eventually as the preferred and only form of stabilisation policy, leading to a successive conclusion of the EFSF and ESM programmes. The story of fiscal bailouts started and ended with Greece: In 2015, the euro crisis reached its dramatic climax when Schäuble was seen as pushing in concrete terms for Grexit, only to be reined in by Merkel.

The link between states and banks, which had shown up most visibly already in the Ireland episode, became a central focus during later stages of the crisis not covered in this book. This connection was seen as a vicious circle that had to be overcome by 'Banking Union'. However, there was a striking divergence in strategic interests associated with Banking Union, most notably between France and Germany. Negotiations remained deadlocked for many months before culminating at the European Council of 29 June 2012.

As with the Deauville summit described in this book, German Chancellor Merkel was widely seen as having given in to the French-led South on this occasion, abandoning central positions held by the Ministry of Finance. According to the summit statement, the ECB would henceforth be involved in setting up the SSM, and the ESM would be made available to recapitalise banks (rather than sovereigns only).[6]

[6] https://www.consilium.europa.eu/media/21548/20141020-banking_union_-_relevant_ec_conclusions.pdf.

Following this Council decision, the concrete negotiations on the SRF and the SSM proved highly intricate and protracted. They rendered the resulting institutional architecture of Banking Union extremely complex and not beyond doubt as to its effectiveness if they had been put to the test.

In reminiscence to the story described in this book, Franco-German compromises often gloss over fundamental differences in economic culture and worldview. At the root of the dysfunctional institutional architecture of EMU, there seems to be something like a general misunderstanding between the two most important European countries. The intergovernmental approach to resolving the crisis was ultimately bogged down by the intricacies of irreconcilable and diverging national interests.

By consequence, the balkanisation of European financial affairs resurfaced time and again, leading to the repeated resurgence of spread dynamics—until the ECB finally stepped in once and for all. All attempts at grand institutional design faltered. Prior to Draghi's 'whatever it takes', the euro was losing its institutional credibility fast.

In 2011, the author had the opportunity to discuss the euro crisis with a Senior Manager of Saudi Arabia's Public Investment Fund, one of the largest sovereign wealth funds of the world. I asked him frankly how he ascertained the risk associated with euro assets. He replied, equally frankly: 'We have liquidated all positions in the euro area'. Overcoming my surprise, I asked him what he would say if he had to advise the German government on the situation. He laughed and said: 'Liquidate, my friend'.

One year later, we did look at this option, if only in hypothetical terms. The anecdote illustrates that the euro crisis in essence was a crisis of credibility, feeding on a continued lack of institutional effectiveness and problem-solving capacity. It also explains why the ECB eventually lost patience with fiscal policymakers and took matters into its own hands. Overruling the Bundesbank, the ECB managed what the Eurogroup persistently had failed to achieve—a lasting turnaround in market sentiment.

Draghi substituted the lacking institutional credibility of the euro by the expectational effect of the impressively 'deep pockets' of the central bank. The euro crisis was not overcome but transformed. This transformation led to a hitherto unthinkable expansion of the supply of money which, according to several schools of economic thought, at some point translates into inflation. Following further monetary expansion in 2015 (dubbed "quantitative easing"), inflation indeed emerged more visibly in the euro area after 2021, exceeding a rate of 10% in some countries by 2022 and prompting the ECB to raise interest rates aggressively.

In parallel to the continued build-up of central banks' balance sheets in the euro area, the German public became increasingly aware of the so-called Target balance of the Bundesbank vis-à-vis the ESCB and the ECB. Target is the payment settlement system between central banks in the euro area. Critics argue that the Target balance shows continuously increasing capital flight within the euro area, predominantly from Italy to Germany (Sinn 2020). They fear that Germany would have to write down her Target assets in the event of a euro break-up.

The Target-debate added to a general fatigue regarding euro stabilisation policy in Germany. The domestic political limits of fiscal bailouts were not only reached in creditor countries but also in recipient countries. Cyprus in 2013 was the last additional country adding to the list of recipients. Slovenia, which had also contemplated applying for a bailout, reconsidered its options upon events unfolding in the Cypriot drama. Germany, ahead of a general election and very much in contrast to the Irish episode, had insisted on a substantial bail-in and haircuts of bank depositors.

The great showdown of the fiscal leg in stabilisation policy occurred in Greece in the year 2015. A second programme also having failed, Greek debt had to be rolled over once more, towards a third programme. This occurred amidst substantial domestic turmoil and power falling to the radical-Left Syriza party in the context of a referendum against the bailout altogether.

Short of a roll over, Greece 'roll-over' found itself in default and solely dependent on the ECB's emergency liquidity assistance (ELA) to continue keeping Greek banks afloat. The Hellenic Republic exempted the European Investment Bank (EIB) from the default, honouring its obligations towards Luxembourg, but threatening to impose a very serios write-down of Greek debt held everywhere else, including, above all, at the ECB. This threat could potentially backfire in the proceedings before the German Constitutional Court against the Bundesbank's participation in the monetisation of stabilisation policy. It therefore had the potential to blackmail the ECB into accepting the continued provision of ELA-funds and was used as that by the Greek government (Varoufakis 2017).

Germany proposed a temporary Grexit and achieved an according constellation of national interests at the level of Finance Ministers in the Eurogroup, for the first time using her veto power to the utmost.

However, the Eurogroup constellation was overturned by Angela Merkel at the level of Heads of State, ultimately leading to the third Greek programme.[7]

Behind the scenes, strategic considerations and US influence had aligned with French interests to retain Greece in the euro area—not dissimilar from events five years before, described in this book. The third Greek programme also implied ultimate acceptance of euro area moral hazard by Germany, giving in amidst political unrest within CDU and CSU.

Of the two only viable institutional long-term options—further integration versus disintegration—none was politically tenable, none was conceptualised, and none was seriously discussed in private or in public. This clearly shows the shortfalls of tactically muddling through compared to strategic planning and choice. It may well be the difference between politics and statecraft, and only a serious crisis situation reveals the political quality of the person in charge.

After simmering on and muddling through, gradually, the onset of monetisation transformed the crisis over time. The fiscal rescue programmes were repaid successively and ahead of schedule, and the newly set up ESM became almost idle.

A new topic gained in importance: Investment policy became the core element of Jean-Claude Juncker's campaign platform during the elections for the European Parliament in 2014. Germany prevented the reassignment of ESM funds for the purpose of a new European investment vehicle, leading instead to the so-called Juncker-Plan and the European Fund for Strategic Investments (EFSI) and its successor, the so-called InvestEU-Programme, both essentially based on existing and enlarged operations of the EIB, repackaged, and dressed for the purposes of political communication.

With the EU Solidarity Fund (EUSF), Member States have further embraced joint liability after Brexit and COVID-19-19. Germany has lost the power to prevent an ever closer debt union and has instead accepted it as inevitable. Inflation and the political economy of fiscal dominance over the central bank hover looming over the euro area, albeit with surprisingly little domestic impact so far in the former Deutschmark zone. So, the

[7] https://www.consilium.europa.eu/media/20353/20150712-eurosummit-statement-greece.pdf.

institutional and strategic issues can be dodged as before and muddling through continues.

This leads us, based on the narrative of this book, to three general conclusions about the euro and European integration going forward.

Lessons for the Euro and European Integration Going Forward

What can be said about EMU, the euro, and the EU, based on the narrative of this book? Do the case studies enhance our understanding of European integration in monetary and economic affairs?

Clearly, the rules-based framework centred on the SGP and the combination of 'hard' and 'soft' forms of EMU governance have not been able to prevent the crisis. It was perfectly possible to flout the rules (Greece), but even when respecting them (Ireland), insolvency could occur. Repeated efforts at reforming the governance system since 2004 have not made any difference in that respect. Despite the no-bail out clause, financial markets also exerted insufficient fiscal discipline.

Central institutional elements of the financial and economic architecture were missing. By consequence, there was, at the outset, a dramatic shortfall in problem-solving capacity. The approach to the original banking and financial crisis was a national one—given that national fiscal policy acted as the backstop. The initial approach to the ensuing Greek insolvency was predominantly also national but complemented by an IMF-component for sheer lack of problem-solving capacity at the national and European levels.

Only subsequently, with the setting up of the EFSF and the ESM, and by acquiring experience in the ECB and in the Commission, did the EU start to gain the capacity to prepare and implement bailouts and adjustment programmes. The 'epistemic community' of Finance State Secretaries in the EWG became increasingly familiar with the business of stabilising the euro area and supervising the relevant processes and projects—very much according to the paradigm of 'muddling through' proposed by Lindblom. Also, staff in national Ministries of Finance was slowly built up and acquainted itself with the required know-how, but to a far lesser extent than in the Troika institutions. Even national Parliaments, to the extent that they mattered, particularly in Germany, devoted resources and invested in the acquisition of knowledge and talent for the purposes of following and processing the euro crisis.

Do we gain better insight into the institutional situation of the EU and the euro area—and can we make suggestions for certain improvements of deficiencies that have become clear?

A massive field of competence build-up occurred in the field of financial markets, above all banking supervision and banking resolution. An entire set of new institutions or agencies was set up, mainly under the umbrella of the ECB or in conjunction with the ESCB: The European Banking Agency (EBA), the European Securities and Markets Authority (ESMA), the European Insurance and Occupational Pensions Authority (EIOPA), the SSM, and the already mentioned ESRB, SSM, SRB, and SRF—bearing strong reminiscence to the 'agency approach' to European integration. The bulk of this development occurred in the period not covered by this book.

Unlike the EFSF and the ESM as the core institutions for fiscal bailouts, these agencies show less of an intergovernmental trait and can better be seen as institutions in line with a supranational or Community approach. Their setting up gave rise to hard political wrestling among European partners.

For example, EBA was moved from London to the continent in the wake of Brexit. Merkel was seen as giving away Frankfurt's pole position in attracting EBA, as Germany was applying in parallel for the European Medicines Agency (EMA), which also had to be relocated from London. Merkel refused to prioritise between these two applications and, by consequence, lost both to France and the Netherlands, respectively.

These examples show that there was institutional progress in some areas. By contrast, the shortfalls in fiscal and economic governance or even in Political Union have not been addressed at all. Several attempts at strategic and institutional reform have failed—in ways rather similar to the episode described in this book, related to the Van Rompuy Task Force.

It seemed impossible to depart from muddling through—but the reasons for that are far from clear. There was strategic thinking, at least in some quarters. Far-reaching deliberations about the institutional future of European integration was most advanced in the ECB. As concerns the Ministry and ministerial exchanges with European partners, above all France, the author registered heightened interest in institutional thought during the year 2012, when the crisis came to its ultimate climax.

Indeed, there was a moment in Europe for thinking the impossible and considering the extremes—such as disintegration and German departure from the single currency versus full integration towards a Political Union.

The minds of policymakers and civil servants alike were no longer engaged in muddling through only, but instead had started to think about the root causes of the crisis and how to fix them.

Looking seriously at the prospect of disintegration seemed to help focusing on institutional reform instead. The ECB was behind the scenes the most influential and convincing supranational institution in that deliberation. Paradoxically, it was also the ECB that equally put an end to that exercise by going 'all in' with monetisation (Chang and Leblond 2014) and Draghi announcing in the summer of 2012 his famous 'whatever it takes'. His move relieved national governments from the burden of both fiscal stabilisation and strategic deliberation—one could safely go on as before and muddle through.

It is, however, important to keep in mind that the root cause of the euro crisis was precisely the lack of a Fiscal and Political Union. Without a serious federal budget and without means of fiscal equalisation, without jointly issued debt and without joint taxes, without a democratically accountable federal government and federal tasks such as defence and foreign security, without a certain degree of federal control and jurisdiction over national fiscal policy—without a federal European polity of purpose—I hold the long-term prospects of the single currency to be dire. Relying on monetisation only for keeping afloat the unfit vessel will not do: Inflation is not a good recipe of statecraft. There seems to be a natural end to muddling through.

Polycrisis

Based on the narrative of this book, can we infer insights into other crises and how they were addressed, under Merkel and in general? In other words: What can maybe be said quite generally about the government of a contemporary Western country in crisis reaction mode, even pertaining to recent phenomena such as the COVID-19 pandemic or the Ukraine war?

Edgar Morin's (1999) term 'polycrisis' captures the notion of a multitude of episodes in which governments, societies and economies come under considerable stress for various reasons. These episodes at times seem disconnected, others are clearly interdependent. Sometimes they occur in a sequence, at other times they arise coincidentally.

A traditional pastry in Germany is the *Baumkuchen*, a pyramid cake with many layers that resemble the rings of a cut tree. Looking at the polycrisis that affects Germany and Europe is like slicing through the layers of this *Baumkuchen*, each layer depicting other strata of the polycrisis.

From a German governmental perspective, the most relevant layers under the reign of Angela Merkel started with the banking and financial crisis of 2007/8 and translated into an economic crisis, including strong reverberations on the labour market. The next layer of crisis was the bailout episodes Greece and Ireland, covered in this book, and followed by Portugal, Spain, and Cyprus. Other layers are far beyond the scope of this book, but its narrative does shed some light on them, as will be seen in the following examples.

In 2012, the nuclear disaster of Fukushima in Japan exacerbated the collapse of confidence in nuclear energy in Germany. Merkel enacted a drastic change in energy policy and the first exit from nuclear energy in the Western world. At the same time, the German economy became ever more reliant on cheap gas and oil from Russia. A decade later, the Ukraine war turned Germany's energetic dependence on Russia into an energy crisis of historic proportions.

The energetic reliance on Russia was convenient and provided the illusion that Germany could exit from nuclear ***and*** carbon sources of energy in parallel by going for a combination of heavily subsidised renewable energy sector and gas. The crisis situation as of 2022 is a direct result of muddling through without any (geo-)strategic consideration whatsoever in the years before. It is marked by both a preceding serious deviation of policy from reality and by a radical change of reality itself.

As far as the deviation from reality is concerned, the building-up and eruption of the crisis resembles that of the euro crisis covered in this book: The denial of reality is followed by a sudden and drastic adjustment of policy parameters, stemmed with a tremendous fiscal effort—in this case the purchase of highly expensive liquified natural gas from overseas and the build-up of the required infrastructure at record speed. Policy reacts by muddling through, trying hard to find the next best exit to the most urgent problem—not affording itself the presumed luxury of strategic foresight, which, in fact would rather have been a necessity.

Geopolitical tensions rose throughout the Merkel era between the US-led Western world and the rising regional powers China, Russia and, to a lesser degree, Turkey. These tensions proved fertile ground for a multitude of security and military incidents, ranging from war in Georgia to the capture of Crimea or repeated armed conflict between Armenia and Azerbaijan as well as major Western interventions and military engagement in Northern Africa, the Near East and Afghanistan.

German domestic policy considerations covered in this book explain, to some degree, the calamitous run-down of her military capabilities under Merkel—defying the geopolitical situation. Despite becoming increasingly incapable of military force projection, Germany involved herself heavily in Afghanistan and was part of the West's resounding crash there in 2021. When hostilities intensified between Russia and Ukraine in 2022, Germany was caught entirely off guard.

Again, we see a combination of policy deviating far from reality for a long period—thanks primarily to misguided muddling through—and a sudden change of reality itself. Military planners and experts in foreign and security policy strongly criticised the shredding of German capabilities. This pertained also to Merkel's momentous decision to abolish military conscription in 2011. This measure was hugely contested within the CDU and CSU but presumably in line with the political preferences of a majority of the people. It was also in line with incrementalism as the formal abolition (or so-called suspension) of military conscription only came as the end-point of long, gradual, and agonising decay. In overcoming internal party-political resistance, particularly among the Bundestag fraction of CDU and CSU, the incident, while being less dramatic than the bailout decisions, still mirrors some of their features.

Similar to the bailout decisions of 2010, on military and energy policy, there was also considerable foreign pressure by the US administration on the German government to change course. But on military and energy policy, Trump's demarche vis-à-vis Berlin was maybe even counterproductive. Being massively unpopular in Germany, Trump may have hardened the German domestic policy stance in favour of Russian gas and in favour of the continued degrading of the Bundeswehr. Yet the military turnaround in 2022, the so-called *Zeitenwende*, is, again, underpinned by an enormous fiscal effort. Similar to the story of this book, the deep fiscal pockets and credit-worthiness of Germany allow, up to now, to make good on previous mistakes.

In 2015, Germany attracted more than a million illegal migrants from the Near East, Africa, and Central Asia. This influx was somewhat slowed down but continues until the time of writing, being superseded by refugees from the war between Russia and Ukraine. In the acute crisis situation of 2015, Merkel decided against border protection and legal frameworks, taking only short-term domestic emotional preferences into account.

Her decision was not in line with the basic orientation of the membership of the CDU and the CSU—in strong resemblance to the bailout decision of 2010. Even more so than in 2010, Parliament was bypassed: To the criticism of constitutional lawyers, arguing that essential decisions (*wesentliche Entscheidungen*) of the government require legislative, i.e. parliamentary, backing, the Bundestag did not take a vote on migration policy. Party-internal resistance was stifled, although migration policy did give rise to the temporary formation of a conservative caucus called *WerteUnion* and led to substantial voter defection to the AfD.

The political effects of the migration crisis worked along the same lines and enhanced those of the euro crisis, covered in this book. There was a shredding of conservative positions in the CDU and CSU, enabling the AfD to establish itself in the political spectrum of Germany. For a while, CDU and CSU were able to attract more voters of centre-left orientation than they lost on the right—but this effect was not permanent. Voter absenteeism rose in an almost unbroken trend as underprivileged parts of the people experienced a gap in representation (Elsässer, Hense and Schäfer 2018).

A similar, if not more pronounced, effect could be observed on the other side of the Channel, where the Brexit movement was able to gain momentum, not least because of the way the EU and Germany grappled with the various crises. As a Treasury official in London once confided to the author: 'You have done more to keep Greece in the euro area than to keep the UK in the EU'.

Brexit was a strategic disaster for Germany, not only in terms of trade but also regarding the fact that Britain and Germany used to have strongly aligned budgetary, economic, and financial policy preferences. Together, they required only one other EU Member State to form a blocking minority in the EU Council. After Brexit, it has become far easier for Southern EU Member States to form majorities against Germany—not only in the EU Council but also in other EU bodies such as the EIB.

In 2020, yet another crisis layer materialised through the COVID-19-19 pandemic. This episode provides the starkest example of 'ruling by muddling through' if we assume complete absence of information about the lethality of the SARS-CoV-2 virus at the outbreak of the pandemic. Similar to the onset of the euro crisis, there was a phase of denial when, for example, carnival was still celebrated in the Rhineland and public health officials and politicians declared that face masks were useless.

The turn-around in March 2020 with the full-blown lockdown was abrupt but seemed justified, if not late. The harshness of the COVID-19 policy then quickly became path-dependent, similar to the bailout policy in 2010. But, far stronger than in the euro crisis, there was a dogmatic monopolisation of the public discourse in Germany—disregarding more liberal examples like Sweden and morally defaming dissenting expert and opinion contributions. The media as well as state broadcasting showed remarkable uniformity and the overall degree of conformism in German society was disconcerting. Importantly, the real or perceived requirements of disease control led to severe infringements of the freedom of assembly and demonstration, besides curtailing civil liberty in many other ways.

The COVID-19 crisis gave rise to muddling through in its purest form: Policy measures were added in a rapid succession of incremental hardening, and, with the suppression of dissenting voices, agreement as the only test of a 'good' policy was obtained each time in the swiftest manner. Such agreement was routinely enacted through a body that formally even had no constitutional basis in Germany, a conference between the Chancellor and the Prime Ministers of the *Länder*.

Ruling by Muddling Through

What was the nature of government prevalent in Germany and in the EU at the time of the euro crisis? After 'steering' in the 1980s (Mayntz 1987, Mayntz and Scharpf 1995) and the 'governance turn' in the 1990s (Kohler-Koch and Rittberger 2006), did the age of 'polycrisis' (Morin 1999) give rise to a different type of political rule? After 'problem-solving capacity', 'modes of governance' and the 'regulatory state'—do we need a new conceptual approach to understand policy-making in Germany and Europe?

We argue that the euro crisis—as one layer of crisis among many—is part of a change in the nature of government from 'multi-level governance' towards 'muddling through'. The institutions of multi-level governance remain in place but are overwhelmed by complex situations beyond their control. Muddling through, as argued by Lindblom, is the preferred way of dealing with complexity. State level and European actors engage in a frantic process of trial and error. *Fahren auf Sicht* (driving at sight) is a rather fitting and well-known self-description of political life in Germany during crisis management.[8]

In the 'fog of crisis'—to borrow from the 'fog of war'—incrementalism may be the only way to reach concrete decisions. As such, it is not problematic per se. A problem arises, however, if the nature of the crisis is such that its root causes lie in important structural, institutional, and architectural deficiencies. We have argued that this is the case for EMU. An incrementalist approach to policy-making should not overlook the opportunities that the crisis brings for fixing such fundamental, underlying problems.

In essence, Lindblom's juxtaposition of the 'branch method' versus the 'root method' suggests a false dichotomy. Statecraft is not about either one or the other method—instead, the stateswoman or statesman is required to think profoundly about the strategic vision that should be guiding his or her incremental, tactical steps. Otherwise, muddling through without strategic vision is equivalent to a slippery slope. As Lindblom himself admits, muddling through entails the very serious danger described as 'Beagle Fallacy': A beagle hound has a very good sense of smell but rather limited eyesight.

Muddling through incrementally produces new institutions which complement the original set-up of multi-level governance. The most important of these are intergovernmental, but also the Community level is gradually strengthened. Muddling through also entails the at times very sudden and drastic departure from central positions in political and legal terms—such as the no-bailout clause.

Institution-building and profound policy change show that political choices at critical junctures create path-dependency. A crisis situation is, almost by definition, a critical juncture. Policies made during crisis often are locked in, not least institutionally. The cases described in this book bear plenty of examples.

Incremental steps can lead to profound change—sometimes compared to 'salami tactics'. Muddling through the crisis as described in this book leads to policy changes which are drastic and sudden, in this case in particular by comparison with long-held convictions of the ruling political parties CDU and CSU.

[8] https://www.faz.net/agenturmeldungen/dpa/merkel-ueber-athen-krise-man-muss-auf-sicht-fahren-13677480.html.

But under the urgency of crisis, the entire German political centre-right is subdued into submission and hierarchically forced to accept the outcomes of policy and to support them in Parliament and in public discourse. By consequence, there is no more bottom-up decision-making or Lindblom's favoured 'polyarchy' but pure and simple top-down direction with strong tendencies towards oligarchy. Deviations are sanctioned, increasingly under moral terms and increasingly also in the wider sphere of public discourse. At the time of writing, it is far from clear whether the political centre-right will ever recover and what this may entail for the prospect of democracy in Germany. After all, democracies can die (Levitsky and Ziblatt 2019).

There is nothing essentially democratic about muddling through. It may well contain or lead to authoritarian straits of rule. Muddling through is not to be confused with weak power—in fact, it is rather the opposite. As we have seen in the case studies of this book, the Chancellor of Germany not only remains the most central figure within the political system, but Merkel in practice even enjoys a considerable increase in power by enacting her approach of muddling through.

Those who worry about the vitality of representative and Parliamentary democracy may wonder whether the period under consideration has caused lasting damage.

Most notably, not only the state-funded media but also the free press have toed the government's line. Still, the most widely read dissenting newspaper during the euro crisis was the *Frankfurter Allgemeine Zeitung*, which continuously criticises the government's bailout policy—to the point where Finance Minister Schäuble refuses to be interviewed by this paper at all.

But this critical role of one of Germany's major newspapers disappears during the later stages of muddling through polycrisis. Media uniformity mirrors and intensifies a streamlining of society at large. Muddling through as described in this book stifles the public forum and transforms the body politic—the Leviathan—into a swarm. This process is significantly enhanced through so-called 'social media' and the role of cultural and academic elements of society. Interaction between the political level, mainstream media, culture, academia, and the digitally consenting, highly vocal majority of the people turns into a self-enhancing feedback loop. Hostility towards dissenters grows. In today's Germany, they lose their jobs and reputation, and one after the other of them fall silent—or, more recently—become targets for inspection by the domestic secret service, the *Verfassungsschutz*.

Authoritarian rule is a possible outcome of muddling through. But not a necessary one.

Bibliography

Alexander, Robin: Die Getriebenen. Merkel und die Flüchtlingspolitik. Report aus dem Innern der Macht. München: Siedler, 2017.

Beck, Ulrich and Edgar Grande: Empire Europa. Politische Herrschaft jenseits von Bundesstaat und Staatenbund, Zeitschrift für Politik 4/2005, S. 397–420

Beckert, Jens and Lukas Arndt: The Greek Tragedy Narratives and Imagined Futures in the Greek Sovereign Debt Crisis, MPIfG Discussion Paper 4/2024. https://pure.mpg.de/rest/items/item_3592041_1/component/file_3592429/content

Bertelsmann Stiftung (ed.): Managing the Crisis. A comparative analysis of economic governance in 14 countries. Gütersloh: Bertelsmann Stiftung, 2010, http://www.eeg.ru/files/managcris_de.pdf.

Blustein, Paul: Laid Low. Inside the Crisis that overwhelmed Europe and the IMF. Waterloo: The Centre for International Governance Innovation, 2016.

Brunnermeier, Markus K, Harold James and Jean-Pierre Landau: The Euro and the Battle of Ideas. Princeton: Princeton University Press, 2017.

Chang, Michele and Patrick Leblond: All in: Market expectations of eurozone integrity in the sovereign debt crisis, Review of International Political Economy, *22*(3), 626–655, 2014, https://doi.org/10.1080/09692290.2014.941905.

Crecine, John P. and Aaron Wildavsky: The Political Economy of the Budgetary Process. Chicago: Markham Publishing Company, 1972.

Crouch, Colin: Post-Democracy. Hoboken, New Jersey: Wiley&Sons, 2004.

Elsässer Lea, Svenja Hense and Armin Schäfer: Government of the People, by the Elite, for the Rich: Unequal Responsiveness in an Unlikely Case, MPIfG

M. Heipertz, *Merkelism and the Fine Art of Flat Politics*, Palgrave Studies in European Union Politics,
https://doi.org/10.1007/978-3-031-87592-2

Discussion Paper 5/2018, https://pure.mpg.de/rest/items/item_2598861_4/component/file_2599529/content.

Enderlein, Henrik: Nationale Wirtschaftspolitik in der europäischen Währungsunion. Frankfurt a. M.: Campus, 2004.

Hauptmeier, Sebastian, Martin Heipertz and Ludger Schuknecht: Expenditure Reform in Industrialised Countries. A Case-Study Approach, Fiscal Studies 3/2007, https://papers.ssrn.com/sol3/papers.cfm?abstract_id=1061835.

Heipertz, Martin: How strong was the Bundesbank? A Case Study of Policy-Making of German and European Monetary Union. Brüssel: CEPS, 2001, https://www.ceps.eu/ceps-publications/how-strong-was-bundesbank-case-study-policy-making-german-and-european-monetary-union.

Heipertz, Martin: Der Europäische Stabilitäts- und Wachstumspakt: Institutionendesign im Selbstbindungsdilemma. Köln: Universität, 2005, https://kups.ub.uni-koeln.de/1446/1/Dissertation_Heipertz_KUPS.pdf.

Heipertz, Martin and Amy Verdun: Ruling Europe. The Politics of the Stability and Growth Pact. Cambridge: Cambridge University Press, 2010.

Henning, C. Randall: Tangled Governance. International Regime Complexity, the Troika, and the Euro Crisis. Oxford: Oxford University Press, 2017.

Hübner, Marina: Wenn der Markt regiert. Die Politische Ökonomie der Europäischen Kapitalmarktunion. Frankfurt a. M.: Campus, 2019.

Howarth, David and Amy Verdun: Economic and Monetary Union at Twenty. A Stocktaking of a tumultuous second Decade. Milton Park: Routledge, 2021.

Jones, Erik, R. Daniel Kelemen, and Sophie Meunier: Failing Forward? The Euro Crisis and the Incomplete Nature of European Integration, Comparative Political Studies, Vol. 49(7) 1010–1034, 2016.

Jones, Erik, R. Daniel Kelemen, and Sophie Meunier: Failing Forward? Crises and patterns of European integration, Journal of European Public Policy, Vol. 28 (10), 1519–1536, 2021.

Kindleberger, Charles P.: The World in Depression, 1929–1939. History of the World Economy in the Twentieth Century. Berkeley/Los Angeles: University of California Press, 1973.

Kohler-Koch, Beate and Berthold Rittberger: The 'Governance Turn' in EU Studies, Journal of Common Market Studies, Annual Review, 27–49, 2006.

Levitsky, Steven and Daniel Ziblatt: How Democracies Die. Harlow: Penguin, 2019.

Lindblom, Charles E.: The Science of 'Muddling Through', Public Administration Review 1959, S. 237–248, https://www.jstor.org/stable/973677?origin=crossref.

Macho, Thomas: Schuld und Schulden – Wie moralisch ist die Ökonomie? Aus Politik und Zeitgeschichte, 2016 https://www.bpb.de/shop/zeitschriften/apuz/218005/schuld-und-schulden/.

Mayntz, Renate: Politische Steuerung und gesellschaftliche Steuerungsprobleme – Anmerkungen zu einem theoretischen Paradigma, Jahrbuch zur Staats- und Verwaltungswissenschaft, 1987, S. 89–110.

Mayntz, Renate and Fritz W. Scharpf (ed.): Gesellschaftliche Selbstregelung und politische Steuerung. Frankfurt a. M.: Campus, 1995.

Mérand, Frédéric: The Political Commissioner: A European Ethnography. Oxford: Oxford University Press, 2021.

Mody, Ashoka: EuroTragedy. A Drama in Nine Acts. Oxford: Oxford University Press, 2018.

Morin, Edgar and Anne Brigitte Kern: Homeland Earth. A Manifesto for the New Millenium. Advances in Systems Theory, Complexity, and the Human Sciences. Cresskill, N. J.: Hampton Press, 1999.

Richter, Heinz A.: Geschichte Griechenlands im 20. Jahrhundert, Band 2, 1939–2004. Ruhpolding: Rutzen, 2015.

Sandbu, Martin: Europe's Orphan. The Future of the Euro and the Politics of Debt. Princeton: Princeton University Press, 2017.

Sargent, Thomas J. and Neil Wallace: Some Unpleasant Monetarist Arithmetic, Federal Reserve Bank of Minneapolis Quarterly Review 3/1981, S. 1–17.

Scharpf, Fritz W.: The European social model, Journal of Common Market Studies 4/2002, S. 645–670.

Scharpf, Fritz W.: Legitimacy in the multilevel European polity, European Political Science Review 2/2009, S. 173–204.

Schäuble, Wolfgang: Erinnerungen. Mein Leben in der Politik. Stuttgart: Klett-Cotta, 2024.

Schelkle, Waltraud: The Political Economy of Monetary Solidarity. Understanding the Euro Experiment. Oxford: Oxford University Press, 2017.

Schmidt, Vivien A.: Europe's Crisis of Legitimacy. Governing by Rules and Ruling by Numbers in the Euro area. Oxford: Oxford University Press, 2020.

Schuknecht, Ludger: Public Spending and the Role of the State: History, Performance, Risk and Remedies. Cambridge: Cambridge University Press, 2021.

Schuknecht, Ludger and Vincent Siegerink: The political economy of the G20 agenda on financial regulation, European Journal of Political Economy 2020, https://doi.org/10.1016/j.ejpoleco.2020.101941.

Simon, Herbert A.: Administrative Behavior: A Study of Decision-Making Processes in Administrative Organizations. New York: Macmillan, 1947.

Sinn, Hans-Werner: The Economics of Target Balances. London: Palgrave Macmillan, 2020.

Tömmel, Ingeborg and Amy Verdun: Political Leadership in the European Union. Milton Park: Routledge, 2018.

Tooze, Adam: Crashed. How a decade of financial crises changed the world. New York: Viking, 2018.

Varoufakis, Yanis: Adults in the Room. My battle with Europe's deep establishment. London: The Bodley Head, 2017.

Wessels, Wolfgang: The European Council. London: Palgrave Macmillan, 2016.

Wessels, Wolfgang: EU Leadership in Crisis? Fusion Theory and the European Council's Role in Managing the Euro Crisis. In: Leadership in the European Union. Assessing the EU's Role in the World, edited by Ingeborg Tömmel, London: Palgrave Macmillan, 2017.

Wessels, Wolfgang: Ever Closer Union and Fusion Theory: The Dynamics of EU Governance. In: EU Governance in Times of Crisis, edited by Jürgen Neyer and Christiane Dietze, pp. 23–41, Berlin: Springer, 2018.

Wessels, Wolfgang and Julia Lang: The Role of the European Council in the Euro Crisis: The Rise of a New Superpower? Journal of European Integration, vol. 37, no. 7, pp. 863–879, 2015.

Wessels, Wolfgang and Carolin Rummel: The EU's Resilience during the Euro Crisis and Beyond: The Role of the European Council as a Core Institution. Journal of Common Market Studies, vol. 54, no. 1, pp. 46–63, 2016.

Wildavsky, Aaron: The Politics of the Budgetary Process. Boston: Little, Brown and Company, 1964.

Zohlnhöfer, Reimut: Between a Rock and a Hard Place: The Grand Coalition's Response to the Economic Crisis, German Politics 2/2011, S. 227–242, https://doi.org/10.1080/09644008.2011.582100.

Index

M. Heipertz, *Merkelism and the Fine Art of Flat Politics*, Palgrave Studies in European Union Politics,
https://doi.org/10.1007/978-3-031-87592-2

F

G

H

I

GPSR Compliance

The European Union's (EU) General Product Safety Regulation (GPSR) is a set of rules that requires consumer products to be safe and our obligations to ensure this.

If you have any concerns about our products, you can contact us on ProductSafety@springernature.com

In case Publisher is established outside the EU, the EU authorized representative is:

Springer Nature Customer Service Center GmbH
Europaplatz 3
69115 Heidelberg, Germany

Batch number: 09159682

Printed by Printforce, the Netherlands